Yours very sincerely
T. W. Webb

CELESTIAL OBJECTS

FOR COMMON TELESCOPES

BY

THE REV. T. W. WEBB

EDITED AND REVISED BY

MARGARET W. MAYALL

DIRECTOR, AMERICAN ASSOCIATION
OF VARIABLE STAR OBSERVERS

IN TWO VOLUMES

VOL. I

DOVER PUBLICATIONS, INC.
NEW YORK   NEW YORK

This new Dover edition, first published in 1962, is a revised and enlarged republication of the sixth edition of *Celestial Objects for Common Telescopes* (by the Rev. T. W. Webb and revised by the Rev. T. E. Espin), published by Longmans, Green and Co. in 1917.

Dover Publications, Inc.
180 Varick Street
New York 14, N.Y.

PREFACE TO DOVER EDITION

In 1859, the Rev. Thomas William Webb published the first edition of his *Celestial Objects for Common Telescopes*, a book destined to become the classic handbook for the amateur astronomer for many years. Now, more than 100 years later, it is being reprinted so that the amateur astronomer of today may have it to use and enjoy. For many years it has been exceedingly difficult to obtain in the out-of-print market.

Volume I, Part I, "The Instrument and the Observer," and Part II, "The Solar System," is reprinted *in toto* from the sixth edition, revised by the Rev. T. E. Espin in 1917. No attempt has been made to bring it up to date; the student of astronomy must realize that the information contained in the book is of historical value in that it represents the solar system as it was known in the Rev. Webb's time, with some revisions by the Rev. Espin in 1917. However, the descriptions of planetary and lunar features are still among the most delightful and meaningful available to us, and will always be appreciated by observers.

Two new tables of solar system information are included in this edition as Appendices II and III of Volume I. Appendix II gives information concerning the planets, asteroids and sun, and Appendix III deals with the satellites of planets.

Volume II, which is composed of Part III, "The Starry Heavens," contains the finest and largest collection available of objects which can be seen with moderate-sized telescopes. Nearly 4,000 objects are listed. The descriptions include many interesting notes by various observers, especially on the colors of double stars and the sizes of the instruments used.

The constellations are arranged in alphabetical order, and for each there is a list of double stars, stars with interesting spectra, variables, clusters and nebulae.

Positions throughout the main body of Volume II are for the Epoch 1920. A new Index has been especially prepared for this edition and gives positions of all objects mentioned in the text for the Epoch 2000. In most instances, either the 1920 position or the 2000 position is accurate enough for the purpose of easy location of an object. If the position of an object for any particular year between 1920 and 2000 is desired, it may be interpolated from the two given positions. In addition, the new Precession Table, Appendix III of Volume II, will also be valuable in this respect. The editor is grateful to Mr. Giovanni B. Lacchini for permission to reproduce this table.

Appendix IV lists the constellations in current use, with the genitive case and the adopted three-letter abbreviations for each.

A number of changes have been made throughout the volumes in order to correct errors discovered in the course of preparing the new Index.

A new selection of illustrations has been compiled for this edition. In addition to the many recent photographic studies of celestial objects, the reader will find a new map of Mars by Professor Gerard de Vaucouleurs, replacing the chart by Antoniadi in the Sixth Edition. Goodacre's excellent Index Map of the Moon has been retained in this new edition and is separated into four quadrants for easy reference.

We are grateful to the Lick Observatory, Mt. Wilson and Palomar Observatories, Harvard College Observatory, Mr. Walter Semerau, Professor de Vaucouleurs, the members of the Observing Group of the Amateur Astronomers Association of New York, National Research Council of Canada and the American Association of Variable Star Observers for supplying the new selection of illustrations.

As far as possible, double stars have been checked in *Aitken's Double Star Catalogue.* Spectra have been listed from the *Henry Draper Catalogue,* and data on variable stars have been taken from the *Second General Catalogue of Variable Stars* by Kukarkin and Parenago. Clusters and nebulae were researched in *Dreyer's New General Catalogue* and *Messier's Catalogue.* Many bright objects were checked in the *Yale Catalogue of Bright Stars.*

Boston, Mass., 1962   M. W. M.

PREFACE TO SIXTH EDITION.

In this sixth edition the general plan remains the same as in the previous edition. Additional notes have been added in Vol. I. where necessary, and Mr. W. F. Denning and the Rev. Theodore E. R. Phillips have kindly looked through the pages, and have mainly drawn these notes up. Such notes are indicated where necessary by the letters D and P at the end. It has been found quite impracticable to give the many observations of minute details of the Sun and Planets, nor indeed is it now necessary as these are published as 'Memoirs of the British Astronomical Association' from the work of the observing sections. Where, therefore, further information is required by the amateur, these should be consulted, since the work is done most thoroughly, and the memoirs are inexpensive. As the map of Mars was quite out of date, with the kind permission of the council of the B. A. A., a chart by Antoniadi has been reproduced. Mr. Walter Goodacre has kindly revised the chapter devoted to the moon, and has added a series of valuable notes which are published as an appendix. The map of the moon in the previous edition was also quite out of date, and the new one is by Mr. Goodacre, who has so thoroughly made himself the authority on this subject. Mr. Franks has kindly written a note on the micrometer, since much valuable work may be done by the amateur, even with a moderate aperture, in the measurement of double stars. The note on photography confines itself to bare details of method, and the note on the spectroscope remains the same, since the visual method has been entirely superseded by the photographic. The

blocks used in illustration of Vol. I. have been kindly
lent by the Council of the R. A. S.   In Vol. II. the illustrations of Nebulæ and Clusters are from plates kindly
supplied by the Director of the Lick Observatory.   The
Editor of the *English Mechanic* has kindly lent the blocks
for the test fields ε Lyræ and Σ 2773.

Vol. II. has been rewritten, and every effort has been
made to bring it up to date.   Publications on double stars
are now numerous, but not easy of access to the amateur,
and it was thought well to complete the list as far as
Mag. 6·5, and to give as far as possible later measures
where there is motion.   In the case of some of the rapid
Binaries nothing could be done beyond giving a general
idea of direction and distance.   For some later unpublished
measures I am indebted to the kindness of the Astronomer
Royal, also to Mr. Franks and Rev. Th. E. R. Phillips.
Mr. Innes, at my request, undertook to bring the list of
Double Stars in the Southern Hemisphere up to date, the
boundary being fixed beyond S. Decl. 31°.   Mr. T. Lewis,
who is so eminently the authority in England on double
stars, has kindly furnished me with many valuable hints.
As the previous index omitting the star places was found
inconvenient, a new index giving the places as well as the
page is now given, on the lines kindly suggested to me by
Dr. W. H. Maw, for the double stars.   This has been
extended to the Nebulæ, red stars, and spectroscopic
objects, and it is hoped that it will meet the requirements
of those who work with Equatorials.   The star places are
for 1920, and have been simply corrected for precession,
and no greater accuracy has been aimed at than in the
previous editions.   Mr. W. Milburn has rendered valuable
aid in arranging the stars for the new index, and in reading
through the proof sheets of each volume.

CONTENTS.

Many things, deemed invisible to secondary instruments, are plain enough to one who ' knows how to see them' SMYTH.

When an object is once discovered by a superior power, an inferior one will suffice to see it afterwards SIR W. HERSCHEL.

Inertia mors est philosophiæ—vivamus nos et exerceamur
KEPLER.

Pulchra sunt omnia faciente Te, et ecce Tu inenarrabiliter pulchrior, qui fecisti omnia S. AUGUSTINE.

Sic enim magnalia sapientiæ suæ decoravit Is, qui est ante sæculum et usque in sæculum ; nihil redundat, nihil deficit, nec locus est censuræ cujusquam. Quam desiderabilia opera ejus ! * * * * * et quis saturabitur videns gloriam eorum ? KEPLER.

PLATES

INTRODUCTION.

THE intention of the following treatise is to furnish the possessors of ordinary telescopes with plain directions for their use, and a list of objects for their advantageous employment.

None but an eye-witness of the wonder and glory of the heavens can thoroughly understand how much they lose by description, or how inadequate an idea of them can be gathered in the usual mode, from books and lectures. It is but the narrative of the traveller instead of the direct impression of the scene. To do justice to this noble science,—to appreciate as we ought the magnificent testimony which it bears to the eternal Power and Godhead of Him 'Who by His excellent wisdom made the heavens,' we must study it, as much as may be, not with the eyes of others, but with our own.

This, however, is no easy matter: nor is the want of a telescope the only difficulty. Instruments quite sufficient for the student's purpose are far less expensive than formerly; a trifling outlay will often procure them, of excellent quality, at second-hand; and many are only waiting to be called into action. But a serious obstacle remains to the inexperienced possessor. How is he to use his telescope in a really improving way? What is he to look for? And how is he to look for it? For want of an answer many a good instrument is employed in a desultory and uninstructive manner, or consigned to dust and inactivity.

Materials for his guidance exist, indeed, in profusion, but some of them are difficult of access; some, not easy of interpretation; some, fragmentary and incomplete: and the student would find it a discouraging task to reduce them into a serviceable form. This, then, is what has been attempted for him in the following pages, by one who, during many years, would have rejoiced to avail himself of some such assistance, if he had known where to meet with it, and who does not know where it is to be met with, in a convenient shape, to the present day.[1]

Nothing would have been easier than, on so fertile a subject, to have expanded this treatise to a much larger bulk: but it would thus, in some measure, have defeated its own object. In order therefore to reduce the size of the volume, without omitting such details as may seem to be required by the present state of Astronomy, the reader will have to excuse a condensed mode of expression, the result of necessity rather than of choice.

Limited in extent, imperfect in execution, and in parts only suggestive in character, this little book may perhaps serve as a foundation on which students of astronomy may raise the superstructure of their own experience ; and in that case the author's intention will be fulfilled. He will be especially gratified, if his endeavour to remove some difficulties may tend to increase the number of those who 'consider the heavens.' For he is convinced that in such a personal examination of their wonders will be found an interesting and delightful pursuit, diversifying agreeably

---

[1] The original edition was published in 1859.

and instructively the leisure hour, and capable of a truly valuable application, as leading to the most impressive thoughts of the littleness of man, and of the unspeakable greatness and glory of the CREATOR. To such a study, the impressive words of the late Sir R. H. Inglis may be most suitably applied : ' Every advance in our knowledge of the natural world will, if rightly directed by the spirit of true humility, and with a prayer for GOD's blessing, advance us in our knowledge of Himself, and will prepare us to receive His revelation of His Will with profounder reverence.'[1]

[1] Report of British Association, 1847.

ADVERTISEMENT to the FIFTH EDITION.

———◆———

BEFORE commencing the work of editing a new edition of 'Celestial Objects,' by the courtesy of the editor of the *English Mechanic*, a request for suggestions from amateurs was made in the columns of that paper. The Astronomical and Physical Society of Toronto appointed a Special Committee to draw up a note of any improvements that might be made. From these sources much valuable information was derived, and in the following pages the suggestions have been adopted as far as possible. The enormous increase in the number of telescopes and observers has led to the publication, in the last twelve years, of innumerable observations in every branch of Practical Astronomy, and has made it impossible for any observer to follow up all the various branches of Planetary and Stellar Astronomy. It seemed best, therefore, to seek the help of specialists, and in the following pages the additional matter has been contributed by Miss Brown for the Sun, Mr. T. G. Elger for the Moon, Mr. A. Stanley Williams for Mercury, Venus, Mars, Rev. W. R. Waugh for Jupiter, Rev. A. Freeman for Saturn, Mr. W. F. Denning for Comets. Mr. Denning has also kindly contributed a chapter or

Meteorites. For this kind help and assistance my sincere thanks are due.

The original text has been left unaltered as far as possible, and the new matter added in footnotes. Since Parts I. and II. are used mainly for reference, they have been placed in a volume by themselves, while Part III., which would naturally be in constant use in the Observatory, forms a volume by itself. For Volume II. I am entirely responsible, and it has been re-written. The catalogue of Struve has been used as a basis, instead of the 'Celestial Cycle,' as the latter work has been republished by Mr. Chambers, and has thus become generally available. In selecting new objects it was thought best to go down to a certain limiting magnitude. After careful consideration, and consultation with those eminently fitted to give an opinion, it was determined to insert all double stars where the primary was above mag. 6·5, and the distances less than 20″. The double stars in the old edition have been retained, with the exception of one or two very wide pairs from Struve's Appendix. It is thus hoped that the requirements of telescopes of all sizes will have been met.

The objects have been arranged in order of R.A. in each constellation, saving thereby the fifty pages of Appendix II. in the fourth edition. The R.A. has been given to a decimal of a minute at the earnest request of various observers, but with no idea of attempting greater accuracy than in former editions. Professors Burnham, Hall, Perrotin, Schiaparelli, Messrs. Maw and Tarrant have kindly furnished me with their double-star measures, and where any motion was mentioned in the last edition the later measures from their lists have been added. While, however, of some stars there are many measures, others have rarely been observed since Dembowski's remeasurement of the double stars of Struve. Mr. Tarrant is at present engaged in the systematic work of remeasuring all Struve's stars, and this will be a valuable addition to our knowledge of Celestial Motions. Some measures are my own, but want of experience and suitable apparatus have caused them to be few and incomplete. The latest orbits of Binaries have been furnished me by Mr. Gore.

Under the heading of 'Stars with Remarkable Spectra' will be found the most interesting stars of the III, IV, and V types, and all the variable stars at present known. These have been taken from the new edition of Birmingham's 'Red Stars,' and from material kindly placed at my disposal by Professor Pickering. This list has been made as complete as possible, since so many of III and IV type stars are variable, and work on stellar variation offers one of the most promising fields to the amateur. The periods, etc., of the variable stars are taken from Chandler's or Gore's catalogue.

Some additional matter will be found under Nebulæ and Clusters; but, as a rule, it was felt that the fourth edition was fairly complete in this respect, and that the former objects are more suited for the photographic plate than the eye. Some slight additions have been made to the Southern Objects, but the completion of this part must be left till a large telescope has been erected in the south. Besides the help already acknowledged, my thanks are due to Mr. Mee, Mr. Knott, Captain Noble, Mr. Wesley, for valuable assistance, and to Mr. Ranyard for the engravings of 'The Hercules Cluster,' etc. Mr. Sadler has added various notes throughout the work.

In response to a generally expressed wish, two notes

have been inserted at the end of Part I. on Celestial Photography and on the Spectroscope as applied to the Telescope. The only omission of any importance is the list of transits of strange bodies over the Sun's disc, the general consensus of opinion being against their retention.

T. W. WEBB.—A REMINISCENCE.

THOMAS WILLIAM WEBB was born Dec. 14, 1807, and was the only son of a clergyman, the Rev. John Webb. His mother died when he was still a child, and he was educated by his father. From very early years he showed a remarkable taste for experimental science. In 1826 he entered at Magdalen Hall, Oxford, and in 1829 he took a second class in Mathematics. In the same year he was ordained in Hereford Cathedral, and in 1843 he married Henrietta Montague, daughter of Mr. Arthur Wyatt of Troy House, Monmouth. In 1852 he was appointed to the living of Hardwick. In 1882 he was made one of the Prebendaries of Hereford Cathedral. On Sept. 7, 1884, Mrs. Webb died from apoplexy, a terrible blow to him, but borne with that patient resignation and perfect faith which·was one of the marked features in his character. From this time his health gradually failed, and he died May 19, 1885.[1]

His first telescope was a fluid achromatic, which was replaced by a refractor of $3\frac{7}{10}$ in., of 5-ft. focal length, by Tully; in 1859 he obtained a $5\frac{1}{2}$-in., of 7-ft. focal length, by Alvan Clark. In 1864 he was using an 8-in. silver on

[1] These particulars are taken from M.N. of the R.A.S., vol. xlvi. ; see also a memoir in Mee's 'Observational Astronomy.'

glass reflector of 6-ft. focus by With, and was engaged in trying this side by side with the Alvan Clark Refractor. From 1866 to his last observation (1885, March 19) he used a $9\frac{1}{3}$-in. silver on glass reflector, by With. This was mounted equatorially on a Berthon stand with rough circles, and in spite of several attempted improvements, the positions obtained with it were never satisfactory. The telescope was placed in a little observatory made of wood and canvas, and stood a few yards SE. of the vicarage front door. Mr. Webb left behind him four large notebooks filled with observations, solar, lunar, planetary, and stellar. The observations are interspread with numerous exquisite drawings. The manuscript observations are a model of neatness, patience, and care. The stellar and nebula observations amount to 3463. Each page has a red line ruled for a margin, and each observation is prefixed with a number, entered in the margin. The rough notes were made at the telescope, prefaced by the state of the air, the powers used, etc., and written out in full next day. The earliest recorded manuscript observation is one on Jupiter, Dec. 2, 1834. From 1847 to 1856 Mr. Webb was engaged in observing the objects in the Bedford Cycle with the $3\frac{7}{10}$, and in 1859 he published the first edition of 'Celestial Objects.' In later years, besides work in connection with the four editions of his book, he gave considerable time to the observation of Red Stars for the first edition of Birmingham's Red Star Catalogue. Mr. Webb discovered a considerable number of new ones, and amongst them he detected, on Christmas Day, 1869, the variable S Orionis, which was also the last star he observed, 1885, March 19. His sight, although latterly slightly astigmatic, was remarkably good, especially for planetary detail. A curious instance of difference of

vision was well illustrated one superb evening, when Mr.
Webb and the writer were observing Saturn with the $9\frac{1}{3}$-in.
reflector at Hardwick.   Mr. Webb saw distinctly the
division in the outer ring which the writer could not see a
trace of, while the writer picked up a faint point of light,
which afterwards turned out to be Enceladus, which Mr.
Webb could not see.

Mr. Webb was a father to all amateur astronomers, and
the post brought an appalling amount of correspondence
from them to Hardwick.   All were carefully, kindly, and
encouragingly answered in letters charming alike for their
elegant writing, and the extraordinary amount of learning,
and originality, and witticism.   Mr. Webb's versatility
was one of the features that struck every one who knew
him intimately.   Not only did he conduct researches into
each branch of Astronomy with untiring patience, but he
painted and sketched admirably, as did also Mrs. Webb.
Like Mr. Birmingham, he was fond of music, and the
talents he displayed in completing his father's work, 'The
Civil War in Herefordshire,' showed an antiquarian of no
mean order.   Everything, too, in Nature had a charm for
him, and the amount of knowledge and powers of observation in this respect were well known to any one who had
the privilege of a country walk with him.   Setting out
early in the afternoon, with a knapsack laden with all
kinds of little comforts for the sick, he would walk with
vigorous stride up the hills to see some distant parishioner,
and converse all the way, handling the most difficult topics
with keen logical ability, at the same time with most un-
assuming humility, and deference to the thoughts of others.
And then, when the cottage was reached, there was no
mistaking the warmth of welcome and the smile of pleasure
with which he was received.   And there he would sit, the

children gathering round him, and talk to his people of
their everyday life, and local matters, making himself one
of themselves, and imparting the sunshine of his life to
theirs.

So passed his life at Hardwick—a life of continuous
work, seeking neither offices in societies nor Church pre-
ferment, but working for work's sake, and that from the
highest motives, as is well shown by an extract from his
observation-book, with which these few lines may well
conclude. It well summarizes his motives, and shows his
guiding principle in life.   It runs :—

'Gratias D. O. M. refero, qui servo suo indignissimo
per tot annos benignissime concesserit, ut opera Ejus
mirifica cum tanta voluptate contemplatus essem. Quamo-
brem verba illustrissimi Kepleri mihimet assumo, dicendo,
"Quis saturabitur videns gloriam eorum ?   O Qui lumine
naturæ desiderium in nobis promoves luminis gratiæ, ut
per id transferas nos in lumen gloriæ, gratias ago Tibi,
Creator, Domine, quia delectasti me in factura Tua, et in
operibus manuum Tuarum exultavi."   Amen.'

PART I.

O multiscium et quovis sceptro pretiosius Perspicillum! an, qui te dextra tenet, ille non rex, non dominus constituatur operum Dei ? Vere tu
> Quod supra caput est, magnos cum motibus orbes
> Subjicis ingenio.—KEPLER.

THE TELESCOPE.

ALTHOUGH the professed design of this volume is to provide a list of objects for common telescopes, it may not be out of place to premise a few remarks upon the instruments so designated.

By 'common telescopes' are here intended such as are most frequently met with in private hands; achromatics with apertures of 3 to 5 inches; or reflectors of somewhat larger diameter, but, in consequence of the loss of light in reflection, not greater brightness.[2] The original observations

---

[1] 'Aperture' always means the clear space which receives the light of the object; the diameter of the object-glass in achromatics, or the large speculum in reflectors, exclusive of its setting.

[2] Maskelyne estimated the apertures of metallic reflectors and achromatics of equal brightness as 8 to 5. Dawes gives this value for Gregorians, but like Herschel II. rates Newtonians as 7 to 5. Arago strangely asserted that no light was lost in achromatics; but the effects of absorption and reflection are so considerable, that with very large apertures the advantage of the achromatic disappears. The silver-on-glass specula, invented by Foucault and Steinheil, but perfected in England, take their place between the metal Newtonian

in the following pages were chiefly made with such an instrument—an achromatic by the younger Tulley, $5\frac{1}{2}$ feet in focal length,[1] with an aperture of $3\frac{7}{10}$ inches, and of fair defining quality; smaller instruments of course will do less, especially with faint objects, but are often very perfect and distinct: and even diminutive glasses, if good, are not to be despised; they will show *something* never seen without them. I have a little hand telescope, $22\frac{1}{4}$ inches long when fully drawn out, with an object-glass of about 14 inches focus, and $1\frac{1}{3}$-inch aperture: this, with an astronomical eye-piece, will show the *existence* of the solar spots, the mountains in the Moon, Jupiter's satellites, and Saturn's ring. Achromatics of larger dimensions have become much less expensive than formerly, and silvered specula of very considerable size are now comparatively common; even for these it is hoped that this treatise, embodying some of the results of the finest instruments, may not be found an inadequate companion as far as it goes.

In judging of a telescope, we must not be led by appearances. Inferior articles may be showily got up, and the outside must go for nothing. Nor is the clearness of the glass, or the polish of the mirror, any sign of excellence: these may exist with bad 'figure' (*i.e.* irregular curvature), or bad combination of curves, and the inevitable consequence, bad performance. We need not regard bubbles, sand-holes,

---

and the achromatic, approaching more nearly to the latter, especially when the plane mirror is replaced by a prism (which, however, does not always conduce to critical definition). Buffham assigns equal light to silvered Newtonians of 9, $6\frac{1}{2}$, and $4\frac{1}{2}$, and achromatics of 8, $5\frac{3}{4}$, and 4 inches respectively. Sa finds $6\frac{1}{2}$-in. silv. refl. equal to 6-in. achr.

[1] The focal length is measured from the object glass, or speculum, to the spot where the rays cross and form a picture of the sun or any celestial body.

scratches, in object-glass or speculum; they merely obstruct a very little light. Actual performance is the only adequate test. The image should be neat and well-defined with the highest power, and should come in and out of focus sharply; that is, become indistinct by a very slight motion on either side of it. A proper test-object must be chosen; the Moon is too easy: Venus too severe except for first-rate glasses; large stars have too much glare; Jupiter or Saturn are far better; a close double star is best of all for an experienced eye; but for general purposes a moderate-sized star will suffice; its image, in focus, with the highest power, should be a very small disc, almost a point, accurately round, without 'wings,' or rays, or mistiness, or false images, or appendages, except one or two narrow rings of light, regularly circular, and concentric with the image:[1] and in an uniformly dark field; a slight displacement of the focus either way should enlarge the disc into a luminous circle. If this circle is irregular in outline, or much brighter or fainter towards the centre,[2] or much better defined on one side of the focus than the other, the telescope may be serviceable, but is not of high excellence. The chances are many, however, against any given night being fine enough for such a purpose, and a

[1] The real diameter of a star in the telescope would be inconceivably small. The apparent or 'spurious' disc, and rings, results from the undulatory nature of light. They seem, however, to be somewhat affected by atmospheric causes. Herschel II. speaks of nights of extraordinary distinctness, in which '*the rings are but traces of rings*, all their light being absorbed into the discs.' I have entered 1852, March 23, as 'a very fine night, though the rings and appendages around the brighter stars were rather troublesome;' 1852, April 1, 'an exceedingly fine night at first, with scarcely a trace of rings or appendages.' See also the star 70 Ophiuchi, in the following catalogue.

[2] The small mirror in a reflector causes a central darkness out of the focus, which should be nearly the same on either side of it.

fair judgment may be made by day from the figures on a watch-face, or a minute white circle on a black ground, or the image of the sun on a thermometer bulb, placed as far off as possible. An achromatic, notwithstanding the derivation of its name, will show colour under high powers where there is much contrast of light and darkness. This 'outstanding' or uncorrected colour results from the want of a perfect balance between the optical properties of the two kinds of glass of which the object-glass is constructed : it cannot be entirely remedied, but it ought not to be obtrusive. In the best instruments it forms a fringe of violet or blue round luminous objects in focus under high powers, especially Venus in a dark sky. A red or yellow border would be bad ; but before condemning an instrument from such a cause, several eye-pieces should be tried, as the fault might lie there, and be easily and cheaply remedied. Reflectors are delightfully exempt from this defect ; and as now made with specula of silvered glass, well deserve, from their comparative cheapness, combined with admirable defining power, to regain much of the preference which has of late years been accorded to achromatics. The horizontal view of objects at all altitudes in a Newtonian reflector with rotating tube [1] is extremely pleasant, when a little experience has been gained in finding and following : the same advantage, however, attends the use of a diagonal eye-piece with the achromatic, but with loss of light. The chief disadvantage of reflectors is the greater aperture, and consequently greater atmospheric disturbance, corresponding with the same amount of light : and the occasional renewal of the film causes a little expense or trouble.

The eye-piece, or ocular, is only a kind of microscope,

---

[1] In Calver's larger reflectors the end of the tube carrying the flat alone rotates.—(Es.)

magnifying the image formed in the focus of the object-glass or speculum. The size of this image being in proportion to its distance from the glass or mirror which forms it, the power of the same eye-piece in different telescopes varies as the focal length. Hence the disadvantage of a short telescope; to get high powers, we must employ minute and deeply-curved lenses, which are much less pleasant in use; with a telescope twice as long, half the curvature in the eye-piece produces an equal power. The magnified focal image, as in the camera, is always inverted, and so in the astronomical eye-piece it remains.[1] For terrestrial purposes it is erected by two additional lenses; but a loss of light is thus incurred, and as the inversion of celestial objects is unimportant, erecting eye-pieces (always the longest of a set) should never be employed for astronomy; the eye soon becomes accustomed to the inverted picture, and the hand to the reversed motion in following the object. The lateral vision in the Newtonian reflector interposes another difficulty, easily mastered, however, by practice, and by attention to the direction of motion through the field. A multitude of eye-pieces is needless, but three at least are desirable; one with low power and large field, for extended groups of stars, nebulæ, and comets, supplying also, if necessary, the place of a 'finder' for deeper magnifiers; a stronger one for general purposes, especially the moon and planets; and a third, as powerful as the telescope will bear, for minuter objects, especially double stars. A greater number of eye-pieces admits, however, of what is often important—an adaptation

[1] It is erect in the Galilean eye-piece and the Gregorian reflector. But the use of the former is almost confined to opera-glasses, as its field with high powers is exceedingly small; and the latter, an inferior construction, is now little employed. The field of the Newtonian is also not inverted when the eye-piece is to the south, but the stars travel from left to right.—(Es.)

of the power to the brightness of the object. Ordinary astronomical eye-pieces are shorter in proportion to their power. It is a better plan to change them by means of a short tube, or 'adapter,' than by a screw; in which case they are more liable to be dropped and injured. The power may be much increased by unscrewing and taking away the 'field-lens'—that farthest from the eye; but the centre of the field only will be distinct. The highest powers of large telescopes are sometimes made thus, with single lenses for the advantage of light; but the lens is then turned the other way, convex towards the eye, as it gives sharper vision.[1] Sir W. Herschel used the double convex form, as having shallower curves. The common kind, with two lenses, having the flat side of each next the eye, is called the Huygenian or negative eye-piece: the positive or Ramsden eye-piece has a flatter field, but is not, like the other, achromatic. The interposition of a combination called a Barlow lens[2] raises the power with little loss of light; and as one may be made to suit all the eye-pieces, it doubles the set at a small expense. Browning's achromatic eye-piece, and Horne and Thornthwaite's aplanatic, and the Kellner construction (for large fields) are all excellent in their way.[3]

[1] The single lens is much preferable when really high powers are used, though the available part of the field is very small.—(D.)

[2] A most serviceable eye-piece is made by a Barlow lens fixed in a tube with a second tube sliding in it carrying a Ramsden eye-piece. As the power varies with the distance between the Barlow and the eye-piece, it is possible to increase the power by slowly drawing out the eye-piece and its tube. A simple double concave lens may be used in this way with a reflector.—(Es.)

[3] There are, of course, many other eye-pieces of peculiar construction now on the market. Es. finds that the Ramsden eye-piece with a Barlow gives the sharpest definition with the reflector. Denning always employs the Barlow lens and has invariably found it an effective addition to the ordinary eye-piece.—(Es.)

The brightness of the field varies inversely as the square of the power: and hence minute stars are commonly more visible with deep eye-pieces; the reverse, however, for some unknown reason, sometimes occurs.

If the power of our oculars has not been engraved upon them,[1] we may get a fair approximation to it by viewing an equally divided scale at a distance (for low powers, a brick wall will answer) with one eye through the telescope, and with the other alongside of it, and noting how many unmagnified divisions are covered by a single magnified image. Or, better still, we may have recourse to the Berthon Power-gauge, a little apparatus the simple, efficient, and inexpensive character of which entitles it to very warm commendation.[2]

The test of excellence in separating power has been fixed by Dawes at the quotient, expressed in seconds, of 4·56 divided by aperture in inches. Thus a 10-inch object-glass or speculum ought to separate double stars at 0″·456 of distance between their centres. This value practically concurs with those given by Dallmeyer and Alvan Clark. Reflectors somewhat surpass achromatics in this respect, as theoretically they ought to do : but they are apt to be more troubled by rings and flare, and scattered light. The best telescopes of either kind will bear a power of 100 per inch of aperture on stars : for planets, or the moon, half that power will usually more than suffice.

An object-glass of inferior definition may sometimes be

[1] These figures are not, however, always to be depended upon, and must be wrong if the eye-piece was made for an instrument of a different focal length. The celebrated Short exaggerated the powers of his reflectors : and those of the great achromatics of Dorpat and Berlin were found by Struve and Encke to be overrated.

[2] See *English Mechanic*, March 5, 19, April 9, 1880, respecting an excellent method of employing it.

improved by stopping out defects, or contracting the aperture. Streaks or specks of unequal density are very injurious : they may be detected by turning the telescope to a bright light, taking out the eye-piece, and placing the eye in the focus ; every irregularity will then be visible in the illumination which overspreads the object-glass ; and, if of small extent, may be stopped out by a bit of sticking-plaster. If the performance is not thus improved, try a contracted aperture : make a cap of pasteboard fitting over the object-glass like the usual brass cap, but with a circular opening a little less than the clear aperture ;—if the indistinctness is thus diminished, but not removed, try several discs of pasteboard placed successively within this cap, with progressively contracted openings, till distinct vision is obtained ; there we must stop, or valuable light will be lost. An excentric opening in the pasteboard disc may sometimes be serviceable, being turned round the axis so as to expose different parts of the glass or mirror, till the best effect is produced : in other cases, a central pasteboard disc, supported by narrow arms from the sides, and leaving an open ring of light all round, may be tried. But for comets or nebulæ, it will be best to restore the original aperture, as with faint and ill-defined objects light is more essential than distinctness. The centring of a reflector is more liable to derangement than that of an achromatic ; it is, however, easily rectified by the cautious use of the screws which are provided for the purpose. When in correct adjustment, the eye-piece being removed, a dark spot will be seen in the centre of the small mirror, which is the image of that mirror reflected by the large speculum : in proportion as it deviates from a central position, the adjustment is incomplete, and the performance defective.

The definition of reflectors may often be greatly improved by the use of a tube perforated with large and numerous

openings :[1] it is also desirable, where practicable, to inter-
pose between the observer and the instrument, in cold
weather, a movable screen of felt or some non-conducting
material.[2]

A good stand is essential : if unsteady, it will spoil the
most distinct performance; if awkward, it will annoy the
observer ; if limited in range, it may disappoint him at some
interesting juncture. It may be well left to a respectable
optician; but where expense is a serious consideration, a
little mechanical ingenuity and knowledge of such contri-
vances will devise one which will answer sufficiently. The
old arrangement, with a vertical and horizontal, or 'altitude
and azimuth' motion, is simple and manageable : the equatorial form, which makes the telescope revolve on an axis
parallel to that of the earth, has great advantages, in following the object by a single motion, and where the expense
of divided circles and spirit-levels is admissible, in finding
planets and bright stars by day, and identifying minute
objects by night : but, to do its work, it must be placed
accurately in the meridian, and out of that position has little
superiority. The reflector, too, must rotate in a cradle, or the
ocular will assume very awkward inclinations.[3] In any case,

[1] The large reflectors at the Mt. Wilson Observatory (60-inch),
and the Crossley 36-inch at the Lick Observatory, have lattice-work
tubes.—(Es.)

[2] Phillips is strongly of opinion that if the instrument is to be
used in the open air a wooden tube is far preferable to one of iron.
On still frosty nights especially, an iron tube often needs to be
protected from radiation by some sort of covering on its upper side,
or the air currents set up within are very troublesome. Such currents
inside the tube seem to be but little experienced when the instrument
is sheltered by a dome, especially if the floor be of cement, and not
wood.

[3] This may be avoided by using the old English form of equatorial,
which is much to be preferred to the German one.—(Es.)

if the stand is to be movable, let it be strong enough for steadiness without being too heavy for portability.[1]

A sidereal clock is often considered a necessary adjunct to an equatorial mounting, in order to find objects invisible to the naked eye. But it may be dispensed with by the following method of 'differentiation' in all cases, excepting during the brief season of twilight, when neither sun nor stars can be employed. Write down the difference of Right Ascension (taking particular notice whether additive or subtractive) between the required and some known object—the sun by day, a neighbouring bright star by night. Seek the known object by the finder, and place it in the centre of your largest field: clamp the R. A. circle: set the telescope to the declination of the object sought, and clamp it there: unclamp in R. A. and move the telescope E. or W. as the case requires, to the value of the ascertained difference in R. A., and the object will be found in the field, somewhat W. of the centre, by a distance dependent on the duration of the process.

An observatory is by no means essential, but it would be difficult to over-estimate its advantage in point of comfort as well as economy of time. It used to be an expensive luxury; but a very simple and cheap 'telescope-house,' combining shelter with open-air freedom, to the great merit of which I can bear full testimony, has been devised by the Rev. E. L. Berthon, and is described in the *English*

---

[1] A very cheap equatorial stand is described in *Astron. Register*, No. 14, vol. ii. Franks observes that a common equatorial mounting may be made very efficient at a trifling expense by the addition of plain metal circles, on which slips of paper graduated with pen and ink are fastened by glue dissolved in strong acetic acid, and afterwards sized and varnished. A good pillar-stand may be made by letting a 4-inch iron pipe deep into the ground, in which a small table with a long foot revolves.

Mechanic, Oct. 13 and 20, 1871. The Rev. W. Conybeare
Bruce has also handled the subject very ably in the same
publication, Feb. 6 and 27, and April 2, 1880.

We will close this section with the encouraging words
of the Council of the Royal Astronomical Society, in their
Report for 1828: 'Every one who possesses an instrument,
whose claims rise even not above a humble mediocrity, has
it in his power to chalk out for himself a useful and honour-
able line of occupation for leisure hours, in which his labour
shall be really valuable, if duly registered; . . . those who
possess *good* instruments, have a field absolutely boundless
for their exertions.'[1]

———◦◇◦———

THE MODE OF OBSERVATION.

An ordinary telescope may be easily prepared for use: to
fix it on its stand; to point it by means of the finder; to
adjust the focus to the eye (remembering that different eyes
require different adjustments), are processes scarcely requiring instruction. But many mistakes may be made in detail ;
and in this, as in everything else, there are various methods
of doing the thing the wrong way. The present section will
therefore consist of negative rather than positive directions,
pointing out rather what should be avoided than what should
be done.

1. Do not begin by fixing the telescope in a warm room
and opening the window. A boarded floor is bad, as every
movement of the observer is liable to produce a tremor; but

[1] To this may justly be added that even with the naked eye a
person with good vision and by persevering effort may obtain many
really useful and entertaining observations.—(D.)

the mixture of warm and cool currents at the window is worse; it is an artificial production of the fluttering and wavering which, as naturally existing in the atmosphere, are such an annoyance to astronomers. If a window must be used, let it be opened as long beforehand as may be, and let the object-glass be pushed as far as possible outside; there should be no fire in the room; and any other windows, as well as the door, should be shut before beginning to observe : the nuisance may thus be sometimes abated; but the right place is unquestionably out of doors.

2. Do not wipe an object-glass or metallic speculum more than can possibly be helped. Hard as the materials are, scratching is a very easy process; and the ultimate result of ordinary wiping may be seen in an old spectacle-glass held in the sunshine. The most valuable part of a good telescope deserves much more careful treatment; and, if protected from dust and damp, it will very seldom require to be touched. Nothing but great carelessness would expose it to dust : and the dewing of the surface may be almost always avoided. The object-glass or speculum, if kept in a cold place, should not be uncovered, if possible, in a warmer air till it has gained something of its temperature; and it must be invariably closed up in the air in which it has been used before it is removed indoors; or, in either case, it may be dewed like a glass of cold water brought into a heated room. The object-glass, however, being much exposed to radiation, requires additional protection; and this may be easily contrived. A tube of tin, pasteboard, or very thin wood, such as is used for hat-boxes, or, best of all, calico stiffened with shell-lac and varnished, fitting on to the place whence the brass cap has been removed, and three or four times longer than wide, will, in general, keep the object-glass bright. This 'dew-cap' must fit tight enough to stand firm, or it will

bend down and intercept the light; but not so tight as to cause trouble in removing it to put on the brass cap in the open air. It is better to blacken its interior—indeed, necessary, if of tin; this may be done with lamp-black mixed with size or varnish, so as neither to show a gloss nor rub off; or a piece of black cloth or velvet may be glued or pasted inside it. A lining of blotting-paper is serviceable in heavy dew. A dew-cap on the finder will often save much trouble. Should it be necessary to leave the telescope for some time in the cold, a clean handkerchief thrown over the end of the dew-cap will be a complete safeguard. Should an object-glass or speculum become damped after all, do not close it up in that state; if the cloud of dew is very slight, it may quite disappear in a warm room, especially if exposed to a fire; if dense, however, it may leave a stain which ought to be quickly removed, as well as any little specks of dirt or dullness which will form, one knows not how. To do this, dust the dried surface first with a soft camel's hair pencil or varnishing brush, which will remove loose particles; then use, very cautiously, a very soft and even piece of chamois leather, which has not been employed for any other purpose, and must be always kept in a wide-mouthed stoppered bottle or wrapped up from dust; or a very soft silk handkerchief (which Lassell uses for glass) preserved with similar care. But the wiping must be as gentle as possible; rubbing is inadmissible in any case. Proctor advises sweeping from a small space near the edge as a centre. Any refractory stains may be breathed upon, or touched with pure alcohol, and wiped till dry : but if the glass has become discoloured, we must put up with the defect; and care should be taken not to mistake specks in the substance of the glass for foreign matters lodged on its surface. A slight tarnish may frequently be removed from a metallic speculum by lemon-juice, or a solution of citric acid, or spirit of hartshorn, carefully wiped off in a short time : if this does not restore its brightness, it is better to leave it alone : a slight loss of light is not so great an injury as would result from strong friction. The taking out or replacing of an object-glass or mirror is a delicate operation, and hurry or carelessness may easily make it a very dangerous one; speculum metal is nearly as brittle as glass : but this material is rapidly going out of use, from the superiority of the silver-on-glass mirrors, which are now becoming appreciated as they deserve. The management of these need not be described here, as special instructions should always accompany them, such as will be found in Calver's ' Hints for Reflecting Telescopes.'

Dimness of vision often results from damp on the eye-lens. This will rapidly disappear, without wiping, in a warmer temperature. If the finder does not act well, this may be suspected to be the cause. For these and many other reasons, a small lamp, the light of which can be concealed at pleasure, is a convenient adjunct to the telescope : any glass surface held at a safe height over it will speedily be cleared of moisture. A ground or papered glass front to a lamp is advantageous for reading.

Eye-piece lenses require occasional wiping ; the leather may be pressed to their edges with a bit of soft wood. A piece of blotting-paper rolled to a point, and aided by breathing, answers perfectly. Their flat faces are easily scratched if laid downwards on a table. The screws demand very gentle usage : a previous turn backwards, before screwing in, causes the thread to fall with a snap into its place.

Brass-work should not be rubbed with polishing powder, which might injure the lacquering.

3. If the telescope does not seem altogether right, notwithstanding all the pains you can take in bringing it to

focus, do not meddle with screws or adjustments, unless you thoroughly understand the construction, or can obtain good directions. In most cases a screw-driver is a dangerous tool in inexperienced hands.

4. Do not use any part of a telescope or stand roughly, or expose it to any blow or strain. It is a delicate instrument, and well deserves careful preservation.

5. Do not spare trouble in adjusting the focus. It is well known that different eyes require a change, sometimes a great one : and the same observer's focus in not invariable, being affected by the temperature of the tube and the state of the eye, the adjustment of which, as Dawes has pointed out, shortens with intense gazing, and is apt to vary with the relative brightnesses of objects, besides being, to a certain extent, under the observer's control.

6. Do not over-press magnifying power. Schröter long ago warned observers against this natural practice, which is likely to lead beginners into mistakes. A certain proportion of *light* to *size* in the image is essential to distinctness; and though by using a deeper eye-piece we can readily enlarge

[1] Experiments have been made by Denning with 65 eye-pieces and employed on his 10-inch 'With' and $12\frac{1}{2}$-inch Calver reflectors. The following powers are most serviceable with the $12\frac{1}{2}$-inch—

Mercury	250	290	312
Venus	250	315	440
Mars	290	350	440
Jupiter	200	290	350
Saturn	312	350	440
Moon	300	440	710
Comet seeking . .	25	30	40

These are for good nights. Powers of 710, 912, 1210, and 1544 were used on Jupiter on one exceptional occasion (Nov. 6, 1905), but though the markings were well seen even with 1544, no advantage was gained over a power of about 300. Single lenses are far preferable for light and definition in the centre of the field.

the size, we cannot increase the light so long as the aperture is unchanged ; while by higher magnifying we make the inevitable imperfection of the telescope and the atmosphere more visible. Hence the picture becomes dim and indistinct beyond a certain amount of power, varying with the brightness of the object, the goodness of the telescope, and the steadiness of the air. Comets and nebulæ, generally speaking, will bear but little magnifying. For the moon and planets, the power should be high enough (if the weather is suitable) to take off the glare, low enough to preserve sufficient brightness and sharpness : the latter condition being preserved, minute details are likely to come out better with an increase of power. Stars bear much more magnifying, from their intrinsic brilliancy ; and they are enlarged very slightly in proportion : their images ought never, with any power, to exceed the dimensions of minute discs,—*spurious discs*, as they are termed, arising from the undulatory nature of light, and usually smallest in the best telescopes. A very high power has, however, so many disadvantages, in the difficulty of finding and keeping the object, the contraction of the field, the rapid motion of the image (in reality, the magnified motion of the earth), and the exaggeration of every defect in the telescope, the stand, and the atmosphere, that the student will soon learn to reserve it for special objects and the finest weather, when it will sometimes tell admirably. A very low power is apt to surround bright objects with irradiation, or glare. Experience in all these matters is the surest guide.

It may be very useful to know the diameter of the field of each of our eye-pieces. This may be obtained from the time which an object in or very near the equator takes in passing *centrally* through it : any star having but little declination will answer (γ *Virginis* and δ *Orionis* may be

especially mentioned), or the moon or a planet in a corresponding position.   Several trials may be made, and the
mean result in minutes and seconds of time multiplied by
15 will give the diameter of the field in minutes and seconds
of arc, or space, at the equator.

7. Do not be dissatisfied with first impressions.   When
people have been told that a telescope magnifies 200 or 300
times, they are often disappointed at not seeing the object
apparently larger.   In viewing Jupiter in opposition with a
power of only 100, they will not believe that he appears
between two and three times as large as the moon to the
naked eye; yet such is demonstrably the case.   There may
be various causes for this illusion;—want of practice,—of
sky-room, so to speak,—of a standard of comparison.[1]   A
similar disappointment is frequently felt in the first impression of very large buildings; St. Peter's at Rome is a well-
known instance.   If an obstinate doubt remains, it may be
dissipated for ever when a large planet is near enough to
the moon to admit of both being viewed at once—the planet
through the telescope, the moon with the naked eye.

8. Do not lose time in looking for objects under unfavourable circumstances.   A very brilliant night is often
worthless for planets or double stars, from its blurred or
tremulous definition; it will serve, however, for grand
general views of bright groups or rich fields, or for irresolv-
able nebulæ, which have no outlines to be deranged : a hazy
or foggy night will blot out nebulæ and minute stars, but
sometimes defines bright objects admirably; never condemn
such a night untried.   Twilight and moonlight[2] are often

---

[1] If the moon be viewed through a tube without lenses, such as a
roll of paper giving an apparent field comparable with that of a
telescope, the sense of great size at once disappears.—(P.)

[2] Secchi has found the detail of the Great Nebula in Orion much
more visible in moonlight, which is also known not to obliterate even

advantageous, from the diminution of irradiation. Look for
nothing near the horizon; unless, indeed, it never rises
much above it; nor over, or to the leeward of a chimney *in*
use, unless you wish to study the effect of a current of heated
air.   If you catch a really favourable night, with sharp
and steady vision, make the most of it; you will not find
too many of them.   Smyth, who thinks our climate has
been unfairly depreciated, says : ' Where a person will look
out for opportunities in the mornings as well as evenings,
and especially between midnight and daybreak, he will find
that nearly half the nights in the year may be observed in,
and of these sixty or seventy may be expected to be splendid.'   But ordinary students must of course take their
chance, with their fewer opportunities.   With due precautions as to dress, nothing need be feared from ' night-air : '
that prejudice is fully confuted by the well-known longevity
of astronomers, even of such as have habitually protracted
their watchings

" Till the dappled dawn doth rise." [1]

9. In examining faint objects, do not prepare the eye for
seeing nothing, by dazzling it immediately beforehand with
a lamp, or white paper.   Give it a little previous rest in the
dark, if you wish it to do its best.[2]

10. When a very minute star or faint nebula is not to
be seen at once, do not give it up without trying *oblique* or
averted vision,[3] turning the eye towards the edge of the field,

such objects as the satellites of Mars and Uranus, or some of the
minuter *comites* of double stars.

[1] It may be of service to note that if the feet and hands are kept
warm, there is never any feeling of unbearable cold.—(Es.)

[2] An electric pocket lamp is the best light in an observatory, and
it is better to use a red light than a white one.—(Es.)

[3] Probably this is the explanation of a fact noted by Barnard and

but keeping the attention fixed on the centre, where the object ought to appear; this device, with which astronomers are familiar, is often successful; its principle depends probably on the greater sensitiveness of the sides of the retina.[1]

11. Do not avoid the trouble of recording regularly all you see, under the impression that it is of no use. If it has no other good effect, it tends to form a valuable habit of accuracy; and you might find it of unexpected importance. And, like old Schröter, *trust nothing to memory.* If there has been haste—and sometimes if there has not—it is surprising what unforeseen doubts may arise the next day: make at least rough notes at the time, and reduce them speedily into form, before you forget their meaning.[2]

12. Do not be discouraged, by ignorance of drawing, from attempting to represent what you see. Everybody ought to be able to draw; it is the education of the eye, and greatly increases its capacity and correctness; but even a rough sketch may have its use; taken on the spot, and compared with the original, it will not be all untrue; it may secure something worth preserving, and lead to further improvement.[3]

others that a faint object like a nebula is more easily caught when the telescope is moved rapidly across the field of view.—(Es.)

[1] Herschel II., when about to verify his father's observations on the satellites of Uranus, prepared his eye with excellent effect, by keeping it in utter darkness for a quarter of an hour.

[2] It is a good plan to have a small note-book for rough notes at the telescope, and then enter the observations in a large book next day. Such seems to have been Webb's plan. Also observations of Planets, Nebulæ, variable stars, etc., should be entered in separate books.—(Es.)

[3] In planetary observation daytime or twilight views are sometimes very effective. Mercury and Venus are often splendidly defined an hour before sunrise or the same interval before sunset. The best telescopic pictures of detail on Mercury, Venus, Mars, and Jupiter

In conclusion, may I be permitted to remind the young observer not to lose sight of the immediate relation between the wonderful and beautiful scenes which will be opened to his gaze, and the great Author of their existence? In looking upon a splendid painting, we naturally refer its excellence to the talent of the artist; in admiring an ingenious piece of mechanism, we cannot think of it as separate from the resources and skill of its designer; still less should we disconnect these magnificent and perfect creations, so far transcending every imaginable work of art, from the remembrance of the Wisdom which devised them, and the Power which called them into being. Such is eminently the right use of the Telescope—as an instrument, not of mere amusement or curiosity, but of a more extensive knowledge of the works of the Almighty. So new an aspect as has thus been given to the material universe—so amazing a disclosure as has thus been permitted to man, of the vastness of his Maker's dominion—can hardly be ascribed to blind accident or human contrivance: in thus employing Galileo's invention, we may well feel his grateful acknowledgment, that it was the result of the 'previous illumination of the Divine favour'[1] to have been not only beautiful, but true.

have been obtained by Denning with the sun above the horizon. But the solar orb must be low, his light moderated, and the telescope protected from his rays, or currents, ruinous to its performance, will be set up in the interior of the tube. In daylight or twilight planetary markings often appear to stand out with livid distinctness, whereas after dark some of the more delicate lineaments and spots are effaced in the glare, especially when large apertures are employed.

[1] Divina prius illuminante gratia.

I.

NOTE ON THE POSITION MICROMETER.

As, nowadays, so many amateurs engage in the fascinating pursuit of measuring double stars, a few words on that most useful tool of the astronomer—the micrometer—may not be out of place. And, as the bifilar position micrometer is the form in almost universal use by double-star observers, the following remarks apply to that exclusively. Briefly, then, its construction is this. A rectangular brass box contains two sliding forks, actuated by fine screws, and capable of passing each other for some distance. At the extremity of each fork is stretched a spider line—the pair being exactly parallel when viewed in the eye-piece on the outside of box. These spider lines are not precisely in the same plane, because of passing each other, but they are so near as to be practically in focus together. Each screw works against a spiral spring, to take up lost motion ; and is provided externally with a milled nut for turning it, and a graduated head or disc with 100 divisions. These heads are fixed friction-tight, so they can be set to zero whilst firmly grasping the milled nut with the other hand. At right angles to this pair of movable wires or webs is placed another pair, close together and parallel to each other, but fixed. These are the *position* wires—the movable ones being for measuring *distances*. In the eyepiece will also be seen, parallel to the fixed wires, but near the edge of field, a notched plate or comb, corresponding to the thread of the screws (100 to the inch) which actuate the sliding forks. Every fifth and tenth notch is cut deeper than the rest, to facilitate counting the whole revolutions of the screw. The parts of a revolution are read on the divided head ; and, as the screw is 100 threads to the inch, each one of these parts is equivalent to the $\frac{1}{10,000}$ of an inch. The aforesaid rectangular box, with its fittings, is attached to a position-circle of 360°, with a toothed edge and pinion geared to it, by which it is rotated. By means of the 'vernier' (there are usually two, on opposite sides), the circle can be read to minutes of arc, but the usual practice is to read it to tenths of a degree. A modern improvement, almost essential with large and heavy equatorials, is to have the rectangular box itself work in slides across the position circle, and movable backwards and forwards by a 'bisecting screw.' To move such ponderous masses as these great telescopes by means of slow motion rods would inevitably cause vibration with high powers—so the final bisections are made by moving the eye end alone. Another useful device is to have the eye-piece fitted also on a sliding plate ; so avoiding the awkwardness of bisecting wide pairs with the wires near edge of field.

To use a micrometer, however, one must have a *driving clock*; and these used to be expensive luxuries. But there are now cheap and simple mechanisms obtainable which come within the reach of the amateur. I have even seen the movement of an 8-day clock used with good effect in driving an equatorial. Whatever the style of construction, it does not really matter about its keeping strict sidereal time for an hour or so—if its motion is smooth and regular—as it is only necessary to have double stars bisected for a matter of a few seconds at a time.

The other essential in using a micrometer is the *illumination* of the spider lines by night. The old-fashioned oil lamps are abominations scarcely to be tolerated by the present generation, when electric lamps are everywhere so common. The portable dry cells are so cheap and easily obtainable, even in remote country districts, that there is little excuse for not using the most convenient light that ever existed for the telescope. And, if one prefers to be independent even of the village store, there is a modified form of Leclanché cell on the market, which will run these miniature lamps for intermittent use over a period of twelve months without recharging. Now, as to the way of applying illumination to the micrometer, there are two radically different systems in use. The older plan was to apply the lamp to a perforation in the side of the telescope tube ; causing it to impinge on a dead gilt ring placed at an angle of 45°, and thence reflected to the eyepiece. Between the lamp and the outside of tube was a screen of red glass, and a regulating sector or iris diaphragm, whereby the intensity of the light could be diminished at will. The result was a field feebly illuminated with a red glow, on which the webs were seen as *black* lines. For many objects this is still the best plan, as it gives sharper definition, and decreases the apparent thickness of the webs by irradiation. The more modern way is to have the webs *bright* on a dark field background. Of course much fainter stars can be so measured, but there is the drawback that the apparent thickness of the webs is thus increased by irradiation. A simple way of applying this 'end-on' illumination was brought out by Hilger, who placed a glass ring just behind the webs and outside the field of view. A V-shaped notch was cut in this, to receive one of the tiny red incandescent lamps; the result being bright webs on a dark field.

This plan was successfully used on the guiding telescope of the late Dr. Roberts' photo-equatorial— where it was necessary to be able to bisect pretty faint stars; for very often in the neighbourhood of nebulæ there are no bright stars available for guiding. In case of difficulty in procuring red bulb lamps, a very good substitute is to dip the ordinary white glass ones in solution of carmine (to be obtained of photographic dealers). It seems scarcely needful to say that *red* illumination for micrometers is found, from long experience, to be the most satisfactory; further, it is the only colour permissible where photography is to be attempted.

A few words in conclusion as to the practical application of the micrometer to the measurement of double stars. The first thing to do is to determine the value of *one revolution* of the screw, for on this depends the accuracy of all distance measures. A sufficiently bright, slow-moving star, not too near the Pole (on account of perceptible curvature of path) must be selected. Such an one is β Ursæ Minoris, which can readily be seen in daylight; it should also be near the meridian, to avoid varying refraction. Separate the movable webs or wires until they are, say, 20 whole revolutions apart, and make the star run along one of the position wires. Then place star outside field and stop the driving clock. Now note the time very accurately when the star transits each wire, taking the beat of the seconds pendulum of the sidereal clock. This must be repeated at least six times (the more the better), and the arithmetical *mean* of the intervals taken. Multiply this by the cosine of the declination, and the product by 15, to convert time into arc. Then divide by 20, which will give the value of *one* revolution of the screw. As a further check, it is best to carefully measure some wide pairs whose distance apart has been accurately determined by experienced observers—such as Bessel's stars in the *Pleiades,* or some of Struve's Appendix I. pairs, avoiding any that have been shown to possess 'proper motion.' When the value of one revolution is satisfactorily determined, a table should be prepared, giving the equivalent in seconds (and fractions) of arc for every division on micrometer head, from 1 to 100. In an extra column enter fractions of one division, from 0·1 to 0·9; also whole revolutions, from 1 to, say, 15 or 16. The observer is now ready to commence measuring; and, after inserting the micrometer, focussing on the star (focussing on the wires being done previously), and adjusting the illumination to the proper amount, he has to determine the zero on the position circle before beginning the night's work. Here let me offer a time-saving wrinkle. Usually the micrometer is kept in a neat mahogany box, and has to be screwed into its adapter each time of using. Instead of this make a plain deal box, long enough to hold the micrometer and adapter complete, firmly screwed together. Having set the position circle to read 90° and 270° on the verniers, insert adapter in the rack tube, and when in focus, mark near top of tube, a spot which will come just within the outer end of rack-tube. Take out adapter, drill a small hole at the mark, tap and solder a stout brass pin into it projecting about ¼ inch. Replace, and mark very carefully by a scratch the point at which this pin touches the rack-tube, when a star runs along one of the position wires. Take out again, and file a **V**-notch on end of rack-tube where the scratch is, to engage the pin. Clean off burr, and replace as before, when the adapter and micrometer should go straight to zero, and in focus at same time. I find that the zero is always within about $\frac{1}{10}$ of a degree by adopting this plan, and the slight outstanding correction is rapidly read off and easily applied. As regards the illumination of field, it is an improvement to use a disc of finely ground glass, in addition to the red screen, as it diffuses the light more evenly. For bright wire illumination, the simplest way of regulating the intensity is by means of a resistance coil, one terminal being attached to the sliding bridge.

Having selected the double star to be measured, let the brighter component run along one of the position wires (seeing that the verniers read 90° and 270° before inserting) and read off zero correction, whether + or −. This will be applied to all the angles measured on the same night. Now rotate circle until one of the position wires threads both components ; read off and enter angle. Do this three or four times, taking care to give a sharp turn to the pinion head between each measure, alternately in opposite directions. Next for distances. With components parallel to a position wire, place preceding star on the *zero* movable wire (which it is much better never to disturb, when once set) and which will be the one on the left-hand. Move the right-hand screw away from zero, and therefore against the spiral spring, until both stars are bisected. Read off division, and fraction, if any, on head ; if over a whole revolution has been made, it will be seen by the comb-plate. Turn back screw and repeat the process—these will be both *direct* readings. Now turn back movable wire until it is a greater distance on the other side of zero, place the other star on zero wire, and bring up movable wire to bisect both again—the motion being still against the spring, as before. Read off, and repeat. These will be *indirect* readings. The object of this procedure is to eliminate the zero error of the stationary wire. As an example, I quote at random, from my observing book, a set of measures of Σ3009 :—

Seconds of arc.

$$\text{Direct} \begin{cases} 0 + 27\tfrac{1}{2} = 6\cdot97 \\ 0 + 28\phantom{\tfrac{1}{2}} = 7\cdot11 \end{cases}$$
$$\text{Indirect} \begin{cases} 1 - 73\phantom{\tfrac{1}{2}} = 6\cdot85 \\ 1 - 73\tfrac{1}{2} = 6\cdot73 \end{cases}$$
$$\text{Mean} \quad \overline{6\cdot92}$$

(The equivalents in arc are, of course, deduced from the table.)

Unless the stationary head is fitted with a locking bolt, there is a risk of touching the wrong screw in the semi-darkness. I tie up the fixed head firmly with a bit of rag and string, leaving just enough of the circle visible to see the index ; then it is next to impossible to touch the wrong screw, whatever the angle may be. The measures taken at the telescope may be put down in any rough note-book ; entering name of object, co-ordinates, magnitudes and colours ; power used ; sidereal time of observation—in addition to the measures. Next morning these will be properly entered in the permanent observing book ; casting up totals, taking means, converting measures into arc, etc. The 'epoch' is then added, from the table in the *Nautical Almanac*, headed 'Day of the Year.' Lastly, these measures must be repeated on several nights, and the mean of these adopted as the final value.

W. S. F.

II.

Note on Celestial Photography.

Celestial photography has been so largely undertaken since the earlier editions that a few hints may be useful to the amateur. The moon may be photographed in the focus of any telescope. It must be remembered, however, that in the refractor the visual and photographic images are not identical. In large telescopes a correcting lens is applied, but the actinic focus of a lens may be readily obtained by focusing the image through a violet screen of glass or gelatine which alone transmits the chemical rays. For photographing the stars, commercial lenses have been used with success by Gill, Pickering, Es, Wolf, etc. It will be obvious that the space-penetrating power will depend upon the aperture of the lens, its focal length, the sensitiveness of the plate, the duration of exposure. For this work lenses with large angular apertures are preferable, and short focal length, as the shorter the focus the smaller the images. At the present moment, single long-focussed lenses of 13-inch aperture are in use at several observatories, and are employed in making a chart of the heavens.[1] From the great focal length of the lens, however, the field is naturally small, and the whole sky has been covered meanwhile by the energetic Director of the Harvard Observatory. Admirable work has thus been done by Wolf with a lens of somewhat over 5-inch aperture, and by Barnard and others,[2] the camera being strapped to an ordinary equatorial telescope.[3] These photos have greatly increased our knowledge of the heavens, for beside detecting new nebulæ, and remarkable groupings and configurations, they have shown that the milky way consists of stars intermingled with nebulous matter, and suggest the possibility that the background of the milky way, and perhaps of the whole heavens is one vast nebula. Photography gives us a ready way of detecting variation in the light of the stars. Should any star vary, plates taken at intervals will show it, and though the actual magnitude on either plate will be affected by the colour of the star, red stars decreasing, bluish stars increasing in size, yet the plates, when compared together, will at once show if there is variation, both alike having the same colour equation.[4] Probably the best way of determining differences

---

[1] This was determined upon in 1887, and soon afterwards commenced, and is yet uncompleted. The catalogues of stars from the plates are well advanced, however; Oxford and Greenwich have completed their work. The leading observatories in the world, with the exception of North America, are engaged in it. Valuable results as regards P.M. have been obtained at Oxford by Turner and Bellamy, and Nova Geminorum, No. 1, was detected in the course of their work.

[2] And more recently by Longbottom and D'Esterre.

[3] The wonderful chart of the sky, made under the direction of Professor Pickering with a 1-inch Cooke Lens, shows stars below 11 mag. The Franklin-Adams charts are now published, and were made with a 10-inch lens. Barnard has also published his marvellous photos of the Galaxy made with a 6-inch lens. A splendid series of photos of Halley's comet was obtained by Ellerman at Hawaii in 1910, with lenses of 6-inch and 2¼-inch. Barnard has also used a lantern lens with great success.

[4] The majority of new variable stars that have been announced in recent years have been detected in this way. In some cases the

of magnitude, is by allowing the stars to trail for a minute or more at the end of the exposure, thus leaving for the brighter stars lines instead of round images, which are frequently over-exposed. As regards developers, there are so many that it is difficult to choose. It must be remembered that the object is to obtain the faintest detail. Therefore, the plates should be of the most rapid kind,[1] and the developer of the strongest. Most photographers have in stock a one-fluid developer, made of hydrokinone and caustic potash. This is excellent, but care should be taken to see that the plate is completely flooded by the developer. During development the solution should be kept in motion. This may be done by a clockwork rocker. The plate should be carefully shielded from the light and left in the solution for fifteen or twenty minutes at least, as the faintest detail must be got out. As soon as the surface begins to turn dark development must be stopped. It should then be washed, and immersed in the usual fixing solution of hyposulphite of soda. Plates exposed to the action of caustic potash are liable to frill. Should there be any signs of frilling the plate should be immersed in a strong bath of alum and water. Finally, it should be well washed in running water, and then placed aside to dry. As in celestial photography, the exposure must be long compared with daylight work, every precaution should be taken to insure success. The dishes should be clearly marked, so that even in a dim light there should be no confusion. Both dishes and bottles and hands should be kept scrupulously clean. The lens should be well protected so as not to become dewed over, and an examination of it should be made between the exposures to see that no dew has been deposited. A slight film of dew will ruin a whole night's work. Plates should be invariably handled by the edges, and the film should never be touched with the finger. Plates may frequently be intensified with advantage. If the angular aperture of the lens is large, moonlight will rapidly fog the plate, and no lengthy exposure should be tried when there is any moon. Even on a dark night plates exposed for an hour often show a distinct boundary between the part exposed to the sky and that shielded by the edge of the carrier. If the focal length of the photo and visual telescope are nearly the same, the star must be followed with a high power, as a small error in the driving-clock will cause the stars to shift on the

---

photographs show greater variation than the visual measures, showing that the star becomes more red as it declines in light.

[1] And recent experience has shown that they should be new.

plate. When the plate is examined under a magnifier the stars should appear as round dots, the size varying with the magnitude. With nebulæ, the shorter the focal length the smaller and brighter the image, consequently a small lens of short focus will show greater extension than a large one of long focus. In photographing comets, the nucleus should be carefully followed with the guide telescope, as comets generally have a rapid motion of their own. Wolf and Charlois and others have detected a large number of asteroids by photography. If an ecliptic star is accurately followed the asteroids in the region will come out as lines on account of their motion during the exposure.

The various results of focal length, aperture, and exposure may be shown from the following table, condensed from one given in the *Harvard College Observatory Annals*, vol. xviii. No. 7.

Aperture. Inches.		Focal length. Inches.		Exposure. Minutes.		Limiting Magnitude.
2·1		—	...	15	...	11·1
4		—	...	25	...	11·5
8 (Bache)	...	44	...	25	...	13·5
8 (Bache)	...	44	...	61	...	14·7
13 (Henry)	...	134	...	180	...	14·7
8 (Bache)	...	44	...	82	...	15·1
13 (Henry)	...	134	...	240	...	15·5
20 (Robert's reflector)		98	...	120	...	15·5

This table shows the great advantage of large aperture and short focal length.

A simple and effective camera to screw into the eye-end of the telescope has been brought out by Messrs. Horne and Thornthwaite. It is fitted with shutter and double dark slide, and two photos can be taken on the same plate.

III.

NOTE ON THE SPECTROSCOPE APPLIED TO THE TELESCOPE.

The Sun. To see the prominences the slit should be nearly closed and placed tangentially to the edge of the sun's image. The instrument should then be focussed on one of the hydrogen lines. Now open the slit very gradually and the prominence will be seen on the line. Clapham has seen the prominences with a 5-prism direct vision on 3½-inch refractor; J. Evershed,[1] jun., has done excellent work with 2½-inch achromatic and six small prisms, the observations being made on the C line, which Mr. Evershed finds preferable to F. Sidgreaves sees the prominences easily with a single dense glass prism of 60° on 5½-inch refractor.[2]

The Moon and Planets, as might be expected, give a solar spectrum with some slight differences. In Mars there have been supposed to be evidences of aqueous vapour, which, however, Keeler and Campbell deny; as also in the case of the brighter asteroids. The spectrum of Uranus is crossed by absorption bands of great intensity, which may be easily observed without any slit, and Huggins, by photography, found also solar lines, showing reflected sunlight.

The Stars. Here we dispense with a slit, and substitute a cylindrical lens. An elaborate instrument, however, is unnecessary. Huggins long since showed that the stellar spectra may be well seen by holding a small direct vision prism between the eye-piece and the eye. A better plan is to mount the prisms, not less than five—those of the rainband spectroscope answer admirably—in a sliding adapter before the eye-piece.[3] Some star with banded spectrum, such as α Orionis and α Herculis, should be focussed to a line, and then the spectroscope and eye-piece moved slowly outwards till the bands are distinctly seen. By separating the distance between the prisms and the eye-piece increased dispersion will be obtained. The observer should practise on stars with banded spectra, like α Orionis and α Herculis, till he has thoroughly mastered the instrument. Stellar spectra were divided by Secchi into four types, and the later researches of Pickering have shown that this is the best division.[4] Vogel, however, adopts only three. Classification may be made as follows:—

Type I.[5]—(a) The hydrogen lines and some other lines are dark, as in Sirius and Vega.

---

[1] Now the director of the Kodaikánal Observatory.

[2] The Thorp-Beck photo-replicas of gratings are said to answer admirably. The grating is photographed on a prism, thus obtaining direct vision.

[3] This form of spectroscope is now on the market, and is made by Horne and Thornthwaite. A further improvement has been made by Hilger using Jena glass, and doing away with two prisms.

[4] Pickering has added Types V and VI.

[5] The Harvard classification now generally used is by letter, thus:—

(b) Lines are wanting, and the spectrum is perfectly continuous.

(c) The hydrogen lines are bright, as in γ Cassiopeiæ.

Type II.—The stars show a strong resemblance to the solar type; as in Aldebaran, Arcturus, etc.

Type III.—The spectrum is columnar, the bands being sharply defined on the more refrangible side and fading away on the less. In some cases, as, for instance, in α Orionis, the bands are resolved into innumerable fine lines. Most of the long-period variable stars belong to this type, but have in addition bright lines of hydrogen, etc., like Mira.

Type IV.—The stars have large absorption bands, due to carbon; the bands are sharply defined on the less refrangible side. 19 Piscium is the brightest of this class. The greater part are irregularly variable to the extent of one magnitude, and some are long-period variable stars, as U Cygni; V Cygni; T Cancri.

Type V.—These stars consist of bright lines and bands.

Type VI. is visually similar to Type IV.

The spectrum of Novæ is a complex one, having bright lines flanked with dark ones.[1] Motion in the line of sight displaces the lines of the

---

Type I.—A, Hydrogen lines; B, Helium (Orion) stars.

    II.—F, G, K.

    III.—Ma, Mb, variables Mc, Md, where there are bright hydrogen lines.

    IV.—N (some have bright lines).

    V.—O, Wolf Rayet stars.

    — —P, Gaseous nebulæ.

    VI.—R, Found among some stars of Type IV.

The letter Q is used for Novæ, and one distinguishing characteristic is that the line Hε is always bright in them.

[1] The sequence of phenomena observed in Novæ is generally as follows:—

(1) Sudden rise of the star; spectrum continuous with dark lines of hydrogen, colour white or yellowish-white.

(2) The hydrogen lines become double, having bright and dark components, the latter on the more refrangible side.

(3) Oscillations in light sometimes rapid, and great enlargement in breadth of lines which, in the case of hydrogen, contain several reversals. The continuous spectrum fades.

(4) Appearance of the nebula lines, star yellow.

spectrum. If the body is moving towards the observer the wave length is shortened, and the line moved towards the violet, if it is moving away the wave length is increased and the line moved towards the red. This is analogous in sound to a train passing rapidly when the locomotive is whistling. It will be noticed that the note is sharpened as it approaches and flattened as it recedes. Much valuable information has been obtained as to motion of the stars in the line of sight by this method. The doubling of the lines shows that the star consists of two bodies in rapid revolution. The first star of this class discovered was ζ Ursæ, the observers at Harvard finding that the K line in the stellar photographs was doubled every fifty-two days. β Aurigæ in the same way shows a period of revolution of four days. Professor Vogel has detected orbital motion in Spica. Thus a new field is opened out,[1] and when the telescope will no longer separate stars on account of their proximity, the spectroscope comes in and shows us Binaries where the period is no longer of years but of days, we may perhaps go further, and say of hours, since photographs show that the displacement of the lines in Algol agrees with the period of variation, and some of the Algol stars have periods of less than a day. For photographing the spectra of stars a prism before the O.G. is often used. This turns the star's image into a line, and by slightly altering the rate of the driving-clock, the line is expanded on the photographic plate into a band.

Nebulæ. The visual spectra of nebulæ usually consists of three prominent lines grouped in the bluish-green. One is the F line; the line that is the brightest has been referred to magnesium by Lockyer, but this is denied by Huggins and Keeler. The third line Lockyer finds due to iron. Other lines have been seen from time to time.[2]

---

(5) Hydrogen lines have brightened up steadily according to their refrangibility. At this stage α hydrogen is the most intense, and the star is red.

(6) The star continues to fade, and the hydrogen lines are fading, commencing with α hydrogen; the star is orange.

(7) The nebula lines are now more prominent than the hydrogen, the star becoming bluish-white.

(8) The star is now a planetary nebula.

(9) The nebula lines fade and the spectrum becomes continuous and similar to Type V.

[1] The number of Sp. Binaries is rapidly increasing.

[2] These bodies are usually called gaseous nebulæ, and are situated

Comets. When the comet is a great distance from the sun, the spectrum shows three bands due to hydro-carbon. At Perihelion many other lines appear, notably those of sodium and iron.

---

for the most part in or near the Milky Way. The remaining ones are often called "white nebulæ," and give a continuous spectrum. The great Andromeda Nebula yields solar lines, and in the case of some spiral nebulæ there are both bright and dark lines. The central star of a gaseous planetary nebula is often two or three magnitudes brighter on the photographic plate than visually, and the spectrum seems to be that of Type V. Miss Cannon, from the examination of the photos of 140 gaseous nebulæ, finds that they may be divided into three distinct classes.

PART II.

O domus luminosa et speciosa, dilexi decorem tuum, et locum habitationis gloriæ Domini mei, fabricatoris et possessoris tui!—ST. AUGUSTINE.

THE SUN.[1]

THE solar phenomena are specially wonderful. The unrivalled pre-eminence of that glorious sphere, the dependence of our whole system upon the mysterious processes developed at its surface, the rapid and extensive disturbances of which it is the scene, as well as (in fine weather) the daily visibility of the object, all combine to invite research. But the student had better not begin here: more than one astronomer has suffered from that piercing blaze: Galileo probably thus blinded himself wholly, and Herschel I. in part. With due precaution, there is no danger; but the eye and hand had better first acquire experience elsewhere. Much depends on the dark glass of the solar cap which is to be screwed on the eye-piece; red is often used, but is not always dark enough, and transmits too much heat; green

---

[1] The new matter in the last edition was furnished by Miss Brown for the Sun, Mr. Elger for the Moon, Mr. A. S. Williams for Mercury and Venus and Mars, Rev. W. R. Waugh for Jupiter, Rev. A. Freeman for Saturn, Mr. Denning for Comets and Meteors. In the present edition by Mr. Denning, the Rev. Theodore E. R. Phillips, and myself.

is cooler, but seldom sufficiently thick. The Germans have
employed deep yellow. Herschel I. adopted, with great
success, a trough containing a filtered mixture of ink and
water. Cooper, at Markree Castle, Ireland, used a 'drum'
of alum water and dark spectacles, and could thus endure
the whole aperture, $13\frac{3}{10}$ inches, of his 25-foot achromatic.[1]
With large apertures, a plane surface of unsilvered glass
placed diagonally, as originally suggested by Herschel II.,
so as to reflect only a small fraction of the light and heat,
is found of eminent service. Merz, of Munich, has so
reduced the light by polarisation at four such surfaces,
that a dark glass, the tint of which is of course better dispensed with, becomes unnecessary; and the same end is
attained in a very ingenious double-prism eye-piece devised
by Prof. Pickering : neither apparatus, however, is free from
accidental colour.[2] An eye-piece constructed by Andrews
with two lenses of complementary tints, burnished in loosely
to avoid fracture from expansion, has succeeded with a small
aperture. In screen-glasses combinations of colour are
good. Red succeeds perfectly with green, or with green
and blue. Herschel II. used green and cobalt blue.[3]
A Barlow lens, carefully silvered, is said to act admirably,
though a light screen might still be necessary. If there
is to be only one solar cap, deep bluish-grey, or neutral
tint, will be quite satisfactory; if several, it would be worth

[1] Not, however, an example to be imitated. Dawes thought that
with a focus of 30 inches, 2 inches of aperture were enough for perfect
security. A $4\frac{1}{2}$-inch silvered mirror is not safe for screen-glasses.

[2] An unsilvered glass mirror has been found an excellent instrument for solar observation.—(P.)

[3] The value of complementary, or at any rate dissimilar, tints in
protecting the eye was known before the telescope. Fabricius observed a solar eclipse in 1590 'per duplex diversi coloris vitrum;'
and Apian speaks of them 50 years earlier.

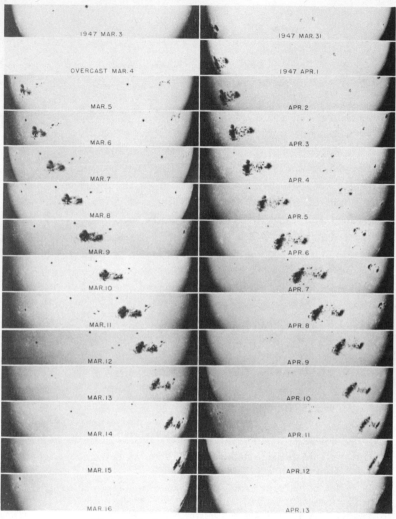

(Photographs from the Mount Wilson and Palomar Observatories)

A day-by-day record (27 photographs) of the great sunspot group of
1947 as the solar rotation carried it across the sun's disk in March and
in April. First series, March 3 through March 16; second series,
March 31 through April 13.

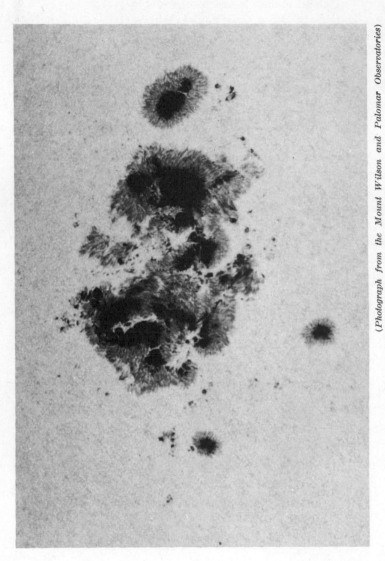

(*Photograph from the Mount Wilson and Palomar Observatories*)

Large sunspot group of May 17, 1951.

1248400

while to have different colours, Secchi's observations at Rome seeming to show that the visibility of very delicate details may depend on the tint. In the absence of a proper screen, smoked glass may be used : it is said to intercept heat very perfectly, by Prince, who places it within the eye-piece, close to the 'stop,' or circular opening, which bounds the field ; but thus it can have only one degree of depth, and must be taken out to view other objects. A strip of glass may be smoked to different densities in different parts, and held between the eye and eye-piece ; but it should be protected from rubbing by a similar strip of glass placed over it, and kept from touching by bits of card at the corners, the edges of the two strips being bound round with gummed slips of paper, or tape.[1] Where expense is not regarded, an optician will provide a delightful graduated screen with two wedges of glass, plain and coloured. A more complete command may be obtained by two such wedges sliding behind one another in a brass cap. In any case we should not begin with too faint a shade, but try the deepest first, and change it if necessary. The thickness of any external screen will contract the field much, unless the eye is brought as close up as possible. A pleasanter view is obtained by placing the screen within the adapter, but from its larger surface it will require to be worked very true.

To bring the Sun into the field, do not attempt to look for it with the finder unless it has a solar cap : point the telescope till the finder shows it centrally on the hand, or on a paper held behind it ; or bring it to shine through the eye-piece *before* the dark cap is screwed on.

With these precautions, there need be no fear for an ordinary sight, though long and uninterrupted observation is

---

[1] Gum-water or mucilage should always be made with *cold* water. It is far stronger, and keeps for a long time without growing mouldy.

not desirable, from the heat of the screen so near the eye; on which account, when not in actual use, the telescope should be pointed a little on one side. Should the light or heat be still unpleasant, the aperture may be contracted as recommended for defective glasses,[1] or, for a very sensitive eye, or a whole company at once, the image of the Sun may be received direct from the eye-piece, without any screen, on card. Choose a field large enough to take in the whole disc, and alter the focus till the image on the card is *quite* sharp, and at a convenient distance as to size; any spots then visible will be easily and, with due precaution, very fairly seen. And so will specks of dirt in the eye-piece; but these may be detected by moving the tube, as the true spots alone will keep their places in the image. If the eye-piece includes only part of the Sun, do not mistake the edge of the field as shown on the card for the Sun's limb; both are circular, but the latter only will move so long as the telescope is fixed. If a circle of suitable size is drawn on the card, and crossed by lines forming small squares, the image may be adjusted to coincide with it, and the progress of the spots may be marked and recorded day after day.[2] Noble has found that plaster of Paris, smoothed

[1] Schwabe used a contracted aperture and light screen; Herschel I. and Dawes preferred full apertures and deep screens, for sharper definition A small aperture has, however, one material advantage in preserving the screens from cracking. I have known a double screen demolished in a few seconds; partial fusion also, or blistering, may be produced by a large aperture.

[2] A simple method of determining the heliographic latitude and longitude of spots has been invented by Professor Thompson. It consists of a set of cardboard discs, 8 inches in diameter with lines ruled on them to correspond with the varying positions of the sun's axis at different times of the year. They require to be used with an equatorially mounted telescope, and should be attached by a light frame to the eye end of the instrument in order that the sun's image

while wet on plate-glass, gives a most beautiful picture; he
fixes a disc of it inside the base of a pasteboard cone, black-
ened within, 1 foot long, and 6 inches across the large end:
the small end being opened so as to fit close on the eye-
piece, with a hole in the side of the cone to look at the
image. Howlett prefers the projected picture to a direct
view.[1] It has at any rate the advantage of avoiding the
tinge given by a screen-glass. In either mode of observation, if an achromatic is employed, it is an excellent plan to
shade the face in the one case, or the screen in the other,
by a large piece of pasteboard with a hole in it, through
which the tube passes.

All being arranged, we shall find four points especially
worthy of attention: 1, the dark spots; 2, the faculæ; 3, the
mottled appearance ; 4, the transparent atmosphere.

1. The *Dark Spots.* These are not always visible; the
disc is occasionally entirely free from them, but more frequently one or more will be in sight. Unless very small,
they generally consist of two perfectly distinct parts—a dark
' umbra,' usually termed the ' nucleus ' by the older observers,
often very irregular in its outline,[2] which resembles, as Secchi

may be projected on the disc, and made to coincide with the 8-inch
circle. The necessary data for reducing the Observations and finding
the position angle of the sun's axis, and its inclination to the ecliptic
are given in the "Companion to the Observatory" for every fifth day,
the intervening days being easily calculated. These discs can be
obtained from Messrs. Casella & Co., 11, Rochester Row, Victoria
Street, S.W.

[1] It is impossible, however, to obtain by projection a picture of the
mass of detail procurable by direct vision in a large spot or group of
spots.—(D.)

[2] A double flexure, like that of the letter S, is not unfrequent.
It was noticed by Messier in the great spot of 1759 (the colour of
which, he says, was ' brun foncé '); and in modern times by Chacornac
and others. Howlett remarks this curve in the grouping of small spots.

remarks, the creeping of a very dense luminous material over an extremely rough surface; and a surrounding 'penumbra' (the 'umbra' of former days), a fainter shade with an equally definite, but in general less angular boundary, usually, according to Schwabe, in proportion to the umbra as 2 to 1, or as 7 to 3. The umbra appears black from contrast, but is not quite so, as is evident when Mercury in transit, or the limb of the Moon in an eclipse, passes near it. In such a juxtaposition, during the eclipse of July 1860, Dembowski found the lunar disc perfectly black, the umbra 'brun foncé.' Frequently the umbra is slightly and unequally illuminated, as if partially overspread by a thin haze, which Secchi compares to cirri, or mare's-tail clouds, and finds to be the harbinger of its decrease and extinction; sometimes it is intersected by narrow white veins, or bridges; these Huggins has occasionally found of especial brilliancy, and in one of them Secchi detected by the spectroscope a different constitution from that of the photosphere. In Dawes's very ingenious solar eye-piece,[1] a sliding plate, or wheel, of metal contains a series of holes gradually decreasing in size, each of which may limit the field in turn, while the whole is insulated by ivory, so as to prevent the eye-piece from getting heated; thus most of the luminous part may be shut off, and the spot alone viewed with a very light screen-glass. In this way, he detected in all large[2] and many small umbræ, a perfectly black spot, or opening, of much smaller size, which he termed the 'nucleus,' and the presence of which, he believed,

---

[1] A similar idea has been entertained by Professor Wilson, of Glasgow, in the last century, who thought a screen would not be necessary. But Langley says that even the darkest part would be insupportable to the naked eye.

[2] He mentions, however, one large and unusually changeable spot, in which he could detect no nucleus (1859). Brayley observes that they had been already figured by Herschel II. at the Cape.

might point out an important difference in the origin of the spots. Secchi, who concurs in this discovery, finds that holes in a glazed visiting-card (which may be burnt with a red-hot needle) answer well : the card, however, should be placed a little way from the focus, or the edges of the hole may be charred. A Barlow or even common concave lens, interposed before the rays reach the focus, will divert a great portion of the heat, and an excellent amateur arrangement may be made by a combination of concave lens, card diaphragm, and screen-glass. Howlett and others have occasionally perceived the nuclei without any such assistance, and Buffham has seen them frequently with a $2\frac{9}{10}$-in. object-glass; often multiple; once (1870, June 20) 5 in a single umbra : Huggins finds frequently 3. The feeble illumination of the umbra Dawes ascribed to the presence of a 'cloudy stratum' beneath the photosphere : this Secchi, with Merz's polarising apparatus, finds tinged with a rosy hue. The most diligent of solar observers, Schwabe of Dessau, has seen an occasional reddish-brown colour in spots, whose immediate contiguity to others of the ordinary greyish-black precluded deception; in one instance, three telescopes, and several by-standers, agreed as to this fact. Capocci, in 1826, perceived a violet haze issuing from each side of the bright central streak of a great double umbra : Secchi, during the eclipse, 1858, March 15, remarked a rose-coloured promontory in a spot visible to the naked eye. Schmidt records many tints, chiefly violet umbræ and yellowish penumbræ, especially as cast on paper; Howlett and others have noticed brown, and Lockyer copper-coloured and violet, tints in umbræ.[1]

---

[1] Miss Brown saw red tints occasionally, but never copper-colour or violet. An 'over-corrected' object-glass might possibly cause a violet tinge; and the strong influence of contrast must, at least in some cases, be taken into account.

Birmingham has also seen a red cloud suspended, apparently, across an umbra and nucleus. The penumbra—which in most cases encompasses considerable umbræ, occasionally comprises a group of them, and frequently [1] outlasts them— is made up, according to Schwabe, of a multitude of black dots usually radiating in straight lines from the umbra. Secchi, with greater optical power, finds these radiations to be alternate streaks of the bright light of the photosphere and dark veins converging to the umbra. The penumbra, Herschel II. observes, occasionally shows 'definite spaces of a second depth of shade;' it is generally darkest at the outside ; [2] an appearance which is proved by photography to be no illusion from contrast; sometimes it includes brilliant specks, or streaks, even close to the umbra. Schmidt describes one of these insulated specks as the brightest portion at that time visible. They have been frequently seen to disappear in floating over the umbra. Sun-spots are of all shapes and sizes, up to enormous dimensions, the umbra frequently surpassing the earth greatly in magnitude. The penumbra, especially of a group, is often much larger. Herschel II., at the Cape of Good Hope, estimated the area of one to be 3,780,000,000 square miles. Schwabe and Schmidt speak of groups which have extended across more than a quarter of the disc. The length of one, observed by Hevel in 1643, is said to have occupied one-third of it. Spots exceeding 50″, Schwabe finds visible to the naked eye through a fog, or dark glass : he has often recorded such instances, sometimes repeatedly in 12 months; and Dawes

[1] Miss Brown's long series of careful observations do not confirm this.

[2] This was figured by La Hire as far back as 1700. Dawes found it to be the case with his cloudy stratum also, but only in opening spots. Buffham and Andrews have seen a nucleus encompassed by a narrow grey ring.

states that a year seldom, if ever, passes without them.
When thus perceptible they surpass the earth at least 3
times—if conspicuous, much more. A gregarious tendency
is obvious, and the groups are apt, especially in certain
seasons, to be nearly parallel with the solar equator.
Herschel II. says that, if they converge, it will be towards
the preceding side of the disc. They are absent from the
poles, and infrequent and of short duration for about $10°$ on
each side of the equator : beyond this region are two fertile
zones, reaching as far as $30°$ or $35°$ each way ; sometimes
they exceed these bounds. Peters (U.S.) saw one (June,
1846) in $50° 55'$, La Hire in $70°$, of solar latitude (if correctly reduced, which Carrington thinks questionable). The
observations of Peters and Carrington tend to unsettle
these limits, which may be subject to change : the latter
astronomer has ascertained that, previous to the minimum
epoch, the spots break out nearer to the equator, and the
reverse afterwards.[1] The numbers are said to be greater in
the N. than S. hemispheres. Schwabe finds that the W.
members of a group disappear first, and new ones are apt to
form on the other side, on which are the greatest number
of minute companions, and on which the spots themselves
generally increase, decreasing the opposite way ; also that
the small points are usually arranged in pairs; and that,
near the edge of the Sun, the penumbræ are much brighter
on the side next the limb. Herschel II. saw the penumbræ
often best defined on the preceding side ; and Capocci found
that the principal spot of a group leads the way, and that

[1] This is now an established fact, the spots not only breaking out,
but gradually approaching the equator as the minimum period draws
near. When it has passed they suddenly appear in high latitudes,
showing that a new cycle has commenced. So that after the minimum
there are for a time, as it were, two spot zones, one in the high
latitudes and one nearer the equator.

the umbræ are better defined in their increase than diminution.
Peters and Carrington observe a remarkable tendency to
divergence in adjacent umbræ.[1] Groups are frequently
elliptical, curvilinear, or bifurcated. The extraordinary
mutability of the spots will be obvious; frequently they are
in continual change, varying from hour to hour, and even
more rapidly. Herschel I. lost a group while merely
turning away his eye for a moment : Biela has found spots
disappear while he looked at them : Krone has observed
them to form within a single minute : Schwabe saw a
penumbra increase from $1'\ 3''$ to $5'\ 2''$ in 24^{h}. Lubbock has
seen spots with the naked eye, of which a telescope would
show no trace next day. Capocci noticed the temporary
reduction of an umbra, four times as large as the earth, to
the dimensions of Europe, ' under his eyes :' an unfortunately
vague expression, as the Académie des Sciences has remarked,
but characteristic of that surprising fluctuation which must
strike every observer. Dawes has alluded to the probability
that the state of our own atmosphere may be concerned in
many of these apparent variations.

The inquiry into their nature is very perplexing, from the
absence of terrestrial analogies, the Sun evidently belonging
to a wholly different and entirely unknown class of bodies.
The theory of Professor Wilson of Glasgow, modified by
Herschel I., has been very generally adopted, that the spots
are openings[2] in a blazing envelope or 'photosphere,'[3]
through which we see, in the penumbra, a deeper and less

[1] Miss Brown divides spots into eleven classes : (1) Normal; (2)
Compound; (3) Pairs; (4) Clusters; (5) Trains; (6) Streams; (7)
Zigzags; (8) Elliptical; (9) Vertical; (10) Nebulous; (11) Dots.

[2] According to Klein, this was first suggested by Schülen in 1770.
Lynn has, however, shown that Klein was mistaken.

[3] Schröter used this very appropriate and now universally-admitted
term as far back as 1792.

(Courtesy of Mr. Walter Semerau, Kenmore, N.Y.)

Amateur backyard solar observatory equipped with electronic servo guiding for time-lapse photography; 4 angstrom quartz monochromator for observing prominences; small Ebert type grating spectrograph for studying solar spectra; and a miniature spectroheliograph for studying features on disk of sun.

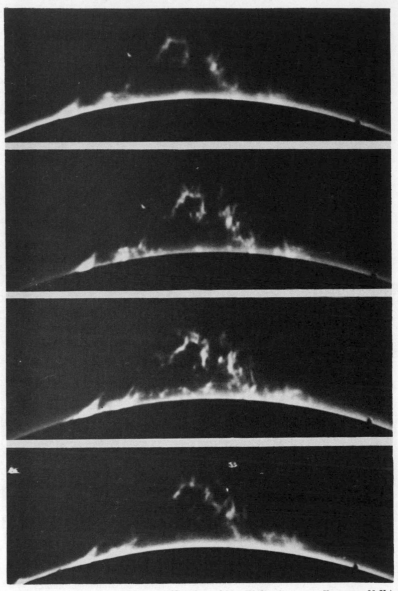

(Courtesy of Mr. Walter Semerau, Kenmore, N.Y.)

Prominence series. June 15, 1958. Series starts 13:27 UT, ends
14:00 UT NW limb, one fifth second exposure at one frame per minute
on 4EH alpha film, monochromator centered on hydrogen alpha line.

brilliant region; at a still greater depth, in the interior of the umbra, a feeble luminosity, marking the ' cloudy stratum' of Dawes (or ' cirri' of Secchi); and below both these, in the nucleus, the non-luminous body of the Sun. This view rests on the perspective appearance of the penumbra, when near the limb, which usually[1] is more contracted on the side next the Sun's centre; and the depression has been supposed to be corroborated by several observations of actual notches in the limb.[2] Herschel I. thought these openings might be caused by invisible elastic vapour, rising from the dark body of the Sun, and expanding in its ascent; such is also the view of Secchi, Chacornac, and Dawes, who refer the brighter edges of the openings to their being ' folded back,' as it were, by the rush from beneath. On two occasions, in 1861, Schwabe found the limb faint and indistinct beyond spots recently entered. Herschel II. inclined to the idea that a transparent atmosphere above the luminous stratum may be subject near its equatorial regions, like that of the earth, to hurricanes forcing their way downwards to the surface. Circular movements are occasionally traceable :

[1] De la Rue, Stewart, and Loewy have found, in longitude, 75 cases having the penumbra equal on both sides, 456 giving the perspective of depression, 74 the reverse; in latitude, 72 cases for, 17 against, depression, which they consider sufficiently established. It has been said, however (Klein, *Anleitung*, 60), that larger instruments and higher powers do not confirm the idea.

[2] An indentation on a globe will disappear in profile, unless its breadth and depth are considerable : hence such observations would be rare; they have been recorded by La Hire, 1703; Cassini, 1719; Herschel I., 1800; Dollond and others, 1846; Lowe, 1849; Newall, 1850, 1859; observers at Kew and Dessau, 1868; but some of these may have been due to inferiority in optical means. If the spots were masses suspended above the photosphere, as Kirchhoff and a few others still maintain, they would, as Howlett well observes, be often seen as notches in the limb.

they were noticed by Silberschlag a century ago; Elvins
and Knobel observed them in 1867 ; and Dawes detected
them in two nuclei, óne rotating through 100° in 6^d, the
other through 70° in 24^h. Secchi has also perceived, besides
several cases of rotation, a spiral structure in the penumbræ
and nuclei of certain spots. Something of the kind has
likewise been twice delineated by Birt, and noticed by
several other observers, especially Lohse in 1872; and,
though Spörer thinks it deceptive, it deserves careful attention. The excentricity or lateral deficiency occasionally
noticed in the penumbra seems to indicate an oblique
direction of disturbance. Secchi has revived Wilson's idea,
that the penumbræ may slope inwards : he calculates that
their depth is about $\frac{1}{3}$ the semi-diameter of the earth, or
upwards of 1300 miles—a depression which the subsequent
computations of Faye have extended through a space of
from 2000 to 3800 miles. From the nature of the photosphere, we might conjecture that of the spots, were it not
equally unknown. Dawes, Huggins, and Schwabe, like
Herschel I., infer an irregular distribution of luminous
clouds : Arago's polariscope experiments were thought to
have shown that the light is that of flame, not of white-hot
solid or fluid matter; but the result is questionable. Secchi
and Henry have shown that the spots are relatively cool.[1]
Herschel II. deduced the partial removal of definite films,
floating on a dark or transparent ocean, rather than the
melting of mist or mutual dilution of gaseous media, and
the analogy of the Aurora Borealis has also been alluded to

[1] Measurements at Mount Wilson show that solar radiation
increases with increasing number of sun-spots, whereas the temperature, which directly depends upon the solar radiation, falls with
increasing number of sun-spots. The radiation has also been found
to vary in short periods irregularly.—(Es.)

by him and his father. At present, however, the idea seems
to be obtaining currency that the darkness results from the
absorption of the light of the photosphere in traversing
vapour below a certain degree of temperature, and that the
spots are produced by descending currents of gaseous
material which have become cooled from their propulsion
into a higher region. It is known at least that an intimate
connection exists between the number of spots and the
number and magnitude of the upward currents which cause
the prominences surrounding the solar limb. It does not
fall within our province to treat of these marvellous appendages, at once beautiful in tint, fantastic in form, and
astonishing in mutability. The spectroscope, through which
alone they can be studied (excepting during a total solar
eclipse), is very seldom attached to 'common telescopes';[1]
and those inclined to pursue this most interesting branch
of research would find far better guidance than could be
given in these pages in Schellen's 'Spectrum Analysis'
translated by Miss Lassell, Roscoe's 'Spectrum Analysis,'
Secchi's 'Le Soleil,' or Schellen's enlarged German edition
of it 'Die Sonne,' or Proctor's 'Spectroscope.'

In confirmation of the theory last referred to, it is
observed that the prominences on the Sun's limb in the
vicinity of spots appear to curl over towards them; but
there is still much unexplained; the prominences occur in
all latitudes, even in the neighbourhood of the poles; but
the spots are chiefly confined, as we have seen, to much

---

[1] The spectroscope is now much more frequently found in the
hands of amateurs than was formerly the case, and valuable records
of prominences have been made with quite moderate apparatus.
Thorp's replicas of Rowland gratings have greatly reduced the cost
of an efficient spectroscope, and a telescope of a few inches aperture
is sufficient with such an instrument for the observation of the
prominences.—(P.)

narrower limits : and on the whole we are far from any satisfactory knowledge of the processes by which they are formed and maintained; our interest, however, in the phenomena is increasing, since there is now more than a suspicion that they influence the whole dependent system. The extraordinary perseverance of Schwabe[1] has shown that the spots have regular maxima and minima, with a period averaging about 10, or, according to Schmidt and Wolf (from a much more extended comparison),[2] 11·11 years;

[1] The President of the Astronomical Society, Mr. Johnson, thus refers to the presentation of their Gold Medal to this observer:—'It was not . . . for any special difficulty attending the research, that your Council has thought fit to confer on M. Schwabe this highest tribute of the Society's applause. What they wish most emphatically to express is their admiration of the indomitable zeal and untiring energy which he has displayed in bringing that research to a successful issue. Twelve years, as I have said, he spent to satisfy himself— six more years to satisfy, and still thirteen more to convince, mankind. For thirty years never has the Sun exhibited his disc above the horizon of Dessau without being confronted by Schwabe's imperturbable telescope, and that appears to have happened on an average about 300 days a year. So, supposing that he observed but once a day, he has made 9000 observations, in the course of which he discovered about 4700 groups. This is, I believe, an instance of devoted persistence (if the word were not equivocal, I should say, pertinacity) unsurpassed in the annals of astronomy. The energy of one man has revealed a phenomenon that had eluded even the suspicion of astronomers for 200 years!'

[2] An abstract of Dr. Wolf's results may be found in *Memoirs of the Royal Astronomical Society*, vol. xliii., showing that though the average length between successive *maxima* is 11·11 years, a period of 16·1 years is found between those of 1788 and 1804, while only 7·3 years elapsed between those of 1829 and 1837. The intervals of remarkable auroral displays correspond fairly with those of sun-spot *maxima*, and Wolf finds evidence for a longer period,—56 years, in the latter ; and that their increase is more rapid than their decrease, with a second subsidiary *maximum* a year or two after their greatest development.

which corresponds so exactly with the period of all magnetic variations, that both, as well as auroræ and electrical earth-currents, are now ascribed to the same unknown power, and the spots are no longer objects of mere curiosity, but indications of a mighty force, one of the prime laws of the universe.[1]

The revelations of the spectroscope, which, according to Balfour Stewart, have indicated the existence of 23[2] terrestrial elements in the Sun, are among the most surprising of modern astronomical discoveries, and stand on evidence which seems incontrovertible;[3] but they still leave much to be investigated; much that we can never reasonably hope to explain.

Concurrent authorities have justified our assuming that the spots are at least depressions, if not openings; yet observations exist, looking another way; and it may be well to insert them from their curiosity, as well as their being seldom referred to. Dr. Long, who published a Treatise on Astronomy in 1764, states that he, ' many years since, while he was viewing the image of the Sun, cast through a telescope upon white paper, saw one roundish spot, by estimation not much less in diameter than our earth, break into two, which immediately receded from one another with a prodigious velocity.' Dr. Wollaston says: ' Once I saw, with a 12-inch

[1] In 1913 for seven months the Sun was nearly always free from spots.—(Es.)

[2] This number has been very greatly increased in recent years.—(P)

[3] The probability resulting from one or two coincidences in the position of lines would of course be but slight, but it rises rapidly with the multiplication of comparisons. Kirchhoff says, that about 60 lines are common to the vapour of iron and the light of the photosphere, and the consequent chance in favour of its presence is more than 1,000,000,000,000,000,000 to one. Yet this is but one set out of a combination of corresponding lines.

reflector, a spot burst to pieces while I was looking at it. I could not expect such an event, and therefore cannot be certain of the exact particulars; but the appearance, as it struck me at the time, was like that of a piece of ice when dashed on a frozen pond, which breaks to pieces and slides on the surface in various directions. I was then a very young astronomer, but I think I may be sure of the fact.' It is also stated that Bayley, who sailed twice with Captain Cook, saw a spot split in two.[1] From such appearances, an observer, unacquainted with the ordinary theory, might easily have inferred the solidity, from the disruption, of the dark object. On chemical grounds, connected (but not as a necessary consequence) with spectrum analysis, Kirchhoff and Bunsen have deduced a constitution analogous to floating clouds; an opinion adopted by Donati and Spörer. Zöllner ascribes to them a scoriaceous character. Raschig (1816), Weiss (1864), Hallaschka and Haag (1869), observed what they considered a passage of one spot over another.[2]

Notwithstanding their changeable nature, the larger spots are possessed of some permanency.[3] After describing straight lines about June 11 and Dec. 12,[4] but elliptical paths at other times, in consequence of the position of the Sun's equator towards our eye,[5] they go out of sight at the W. limb, and, if not dissipated, return at the E. edge after about

[1] Some strange separations and oscillations of umbræ, recorded at Lawson's observatory in 1849, were probably due to the unsteadiness of our atmosphere; but a better observer, Robinson of Armagh, saw a luminous bridge shot across some thousands of miles of umbra in a few minutes.

[2] Schellen, *Spectrum Analysis*, 273.

[3] Howlett has also found some of the smaller and more isolated ones very persistent.

[4] So Herschel II., *Outlines of Astronomy*, § 390. But in the next paragraph they stand as July 12 and Dec. 11.

[5] Inclination 70° 15', Carrington; 6° 57', Spörer.

$13\frac{2d}{3}$ to run the same course. Some have thus persisted through many revolutions.[1] In 1779, a large spot continued visible for 6 months, and in 1840 and 1841 Schwabe observed 18 returns (though not consecutive) of the same group : the most permanent, he says, are usually round, of moderate size, and not sharply defined. Carrington thinks there can be no question of their occasional re-appearance in the same places; as indeed had been supposed by La Hire as far back as 1700 :[2] and this reduces within certain limits their proper motion which was perceived at an early period by Schröter and others, and micrometrically established in a lateral direction by Challis in 1857. Carrington has subsequently made known his very interesting discovery that the period of rotation varies with the latitude; the backward drift of the photosphere in the higher latitudes causing a difference of more than 2 days between the respective periods derived from spots in latitudes $\pm$ 50°, and those situated near the equator; so that the period of rotation of a spot may be determined by its latitude, if unchanged : in this respect, however, it may exhibit slight deviation.[3] With these

[1] Miss Brown, however, finds that it is the exception rather than the rule for even large spots to return more than two or three times.

[2] Maunder and Cortie have investigated numerous cases of recurrent spot groups and persistent areas of disturbance of the solar surface, and have traced their association with magnetic storms. These storms appear to take place when the Earth enters rays of negatively charged electrons emanating from the disturbed region on the Sun. It is thought that these rays are extensions of the coronal streamers such as are observed at the time of a total solar eclipse.—(P.)

[3] Peters (1846) ascribed to all the spots a *set* towards the equator; Laugier, from it. Carrington's valuable results were the fruit of unwearied perseverance through 11 years in the use of a very simple apparatus, consisting only of cross wires in an equatorially mounted

shifting landmarks, it is not surprising that the Sun's period of rotation should have been variously estimated. Laugier's value, 25^d 8^h 10^m, was formerly adopted; Spörer has given 24^d 14^h 59^m, Carrington 24^d 23^h 18^m 23^s, for spots in latitude $15°$. Possibly, as the latter suggests, the anterior mass may revolve with greater speed. Relative displacement in groups would be an interesting study, requiring neither micrometer nor clock, only careful drawing. The application of photography to solar delineation is not likely to be within the reach of our readers: it is, however, too important to be passed over in silence. Howlett and several others have found that spots near the limb require a different focus from those in the centre; arising, no doubt, as Dawes says, from the effect on the retina of very different degrees of brightness.[1]

telescope, without driving-clock or micrometer. It is to be regretted that his work has not been continued by some possessor of 'a common telescope,' which, with the requisite command of time, would be quite sufficient. A full account of his method is given in Carrington's *Observations of Solar Spots* (1863)—often to be met with second-hand.

[1] Professor Hale gives the following tentative working hypothesis of Sun spots :—

'As the result of an eruption, or some other cause tending to produce rapid convection, a gaseous column moves upwards from within the Sun toward the surface of the photosphere. Vortex motion is initiated by the difference in velocity of adjoining surfaces, or by irregularities of structure and is maintained by convection. The circulation in the vortex is vertically upward, and then outward along the photosphere, as in a terrestrial tornado. Expansion produces cooling at the centre of the vortex, and a comparatively dark cloud (the umbra) results. A rapid flow of negative ions sets in towards the cooler gases at the centre from the hotter gases without. These ions whirled in the vortex produce a magnetic field. The descending gases (especially hydrogen) in the higher atmosphere are drawn towards the pole of the magnet along the lines of force, thus accounting for the configuration of the hydrogen (Hα) flocculi. The typical spot-group is double, and the polarities of the two principal spots are

2 The *Faculæ*, or bright streaks. Less obvious than the dark spots, and requiring more power, these are not difficult objects, and were detected by Galileo : they are to be looked for in the spot-bearing regions, but only near the limbs.[1] They are irregular, curved, and branching, considerably more luminous than their vicinity, but not, according to Secchi, than the centre of the Sun. He observed one in 1858, at least 60° in length. They are proved to be what they appear, ridges in the photosphere, by an observation of Dawes, who once saw a facula projecting above the limb as it turned across it into the other hemisphere, and at another time the luminous border of a large spot which had just entered, forming an irregular low ridge upon the limb : Secchi also has seen a similar appearance. We seldom, however, find them visible close to the limb,[2] or far from it, as they are changed in the centre into bright tufts and specks ; an effect, as Secchi has pointed out, of perspective, if their height much exceeds their breadth ; or of the elevation of their crests above an absorbent atmosphere. Howlett sees them beautifully projected on a screen, and thus detects them in the centre of the disc. They are nearly as variable as the spots, and are probably connected with them, surrounding them usually near the limb, and sometimes as they cross the centre, attending their development,[3] and succeeding their

opposite, and the hydrogen (Hα) flocculi surrounding a bipolar group resemble the lines of force about a bar magnet' (Mt. Wilson Annual Report, 1912). An interesting diagram showing the radial velocities in Sun spots is given in *Contributions from the same Observatory*, No. 69, by St. John.—(Es.)

[1] They were observed by Carrington and Noble nearer the centre than usual in 1870, a maximum spot-period.

[2] Miss Brown saw them often very near the limb, but finds that there is sometimes an intervening space without any.

[3] The greatest authorities are now inclined to think that faculæ do not precede spots.

dissolution ; as though they were temporary accumulations of the displaced matter of the photosphere. Secchi compares them to immense waves raised by the outburst of the spots, of which they are commonly the harbingers. Schwabe thinks them rather more obvious when spots are few,[1] and suspects that one at least, consisting of 5 to 7 connected ovals, and enclosing occasionally a great group of spots, may be a permanent or recurring feature. The authors of 'Solar Physics' consider them (and probably the whole photosphere) as consisting of solid or liquid bodies suspended or slowly sinking in a gaseous medium. They find that on an average they follow the accompanying spots, and infer that they have probably been uplifted out of them, and have fallen behind from being thrown up into a more swiftly rotating region.[2]

3. The *Mottled Surface*. An object-glass of only 2 inches will exhibit a curdled or marbled appearance over the whole disc, caused by the intermixture of spaces of different brightness. The earliest mention I have noticed of this mottling is during the solar eclipse, 1748, July 14 (O.S.), when it was clearly described by Mr. J. Short (the eminent optician?), to whom it was quite new : since that time it has been a familiar object ; and it must have been this coarser mottling

[1] He afterwards adopted an opposite opinion.—*Monthly Notices*, xxvii. 286.

[2] In recent years the solar surface has been assiduously studied by Hale, Deslandres, Evershed, and others with the spectroheliograph. With this instrument photographs are taken in monochromatic light such as that of one of the lines of hydrogen or calcium, the remainder of the spectrum being cut off by a second slit. With such apparatus the faculæ are shown extending across the disc in bands corresponding with the spot zones in the two hemispheres. Moreover, by utilizing the middle or edge of such a spectral line the distribution and forms of the clouds of the element concerned at various levels are conveniently and successfully investigated.—(P.)

which Schwabe described in 1831, as showing itself strongest
in the spotted zones, like two freckled girdles round the Sun.
Should this marbled appearance not be at once detected, a
slight shaking of the image by tapping the telescope may
render it perceptible.   Increase of magnifying power, however, brings out a far more delicate mottling overspreading
the coarser irregularity, and occasioned by the juxtaposition
of minute patches of greater brightness on a greyer ground.
This was first observed by Herschel I., and described in two
very valuable but not perhaps sufficiently known papers on
the Sun ('Phil. Trans.,' 1795, 1801), in the former of which
the whole solar surface is said to have 'the appearance of a
mixture of small points of an unequal light,' and in the
latter is described as 'studded with nodules,' which are also
referred to a stratum of self-luminous clouds of unequal
thickness, of which the higher and lower regions tend
respectively to form faculæ and penumbræ.   It has more
recently been interpreted by Nasmyth (1861) as the inter-
lacing of a multitude of lenticular masses resembling willow
leaves in form, the length of each being ten times its breadth.
Considerable discussion has arisen as to the point; but the
supporters of this idea are few, and the prevalent opinion is
that of Dawes, who had been familiar with the phenomenon
since 1830; and found, from very careful examination of the
photosphere, that it was composed of minute 'granules,' or
luminous clouds, irregular in form and size, and separated
by less brilliant interstices; thus agreeing precisely with
the view given in 1792 by Herschel I.   The less luminous
interstices are frequently stippled with dusky or nearly
black points, seldom circular and often arranged in rows.
In the faculæ and round the penumbræ, where the photosphere appears to be heaped up or rolled together, these
interstices usually disappear, and the compressed and

elongated granules, like very slender faculæ, extend over
the penumbra, and often project, like irregular thatch, on
to the outer border of the umbra ; or, many being joined
together, cross the umbra and nucleus as luminous bridges.
The grey interstices were thought by Herschel I. to be
portions of a lower stratum; but, as he remarked, the depression must be very slight, since they are visible in
extreme foreshortening towards the limb.　This view is
adopted by many of our best observers, including Fletcher,
Lockyer, Huggins, and Knott ; and is supported by O. Struve,
Secchi, and Le Verrier.　Huggins adds his impression, that
the general surface on which the granules are strewed is
itself ' corrugated into irregular ridges and vales,' not unlike
a stormy sea ; and coincides with the idea of Herschel II. as
to ' a luminous medium intermixed but not confounded with
a transparent and non-luminous atmosphere.'　In the use of
a 13-inch achromatic of very fine definition, Langley has
found that each of these granules is composed of a varying
number, 3 to 10, of brilliant points (*his* granules), which on
the whole occupy less than $\frac{1}{5}$ of the Sun, and are the chief
source of its light.　He thinks that they are the upper ends
of elongated filaments, the length of which is seen in an
inclined position in the penumbræ ; and he finds evidence
in the spots not only of cyclonic action, frequently right and
left-handed whirls in juxtaposition, but also of horizontal
currents.　The same structure is also shown in some fine
photographs by Janssen.

　　4. The *Transparent Atmosphere*.[1]　That this exists, and

―――――――

[1] It may be well to note that astronomers divide this atmosphere
into the Corona and Chromosphere (though the term ' atmosphere ' is
not strictly applicable to the former.　The size and shape of the
Corona differs with the maximum or minimum of Sun spots).　Professor Young thus describes them.　' It (the atmosphere) is divided

is of far greater proportionate extent than planetary atmospheres, is demonstrated in total eclipses by the red prominences which then surprise the spectators, and which
may, as Janssen and Lockyer have discovered, be detected
at any time by the spectroscope : but the presence, and the
comparative shallowness, of an absorbent envelope forming
its interior stratum is at once evident from the faintness of
the limb compared with the centre of the disc. This was
early remarked at Rome by Luca Valerio, called by Galileo
the Archimedes of his time : it was denied by the inventor
of the telescope,[1] but may be easily perceived when the
image is cast on paper ; and its effect is evident in the
Kew and especially the Rutherfurd photographs.[2] By
means of a doubly refracting prism, Secchi has found the
limb not more luminous than the penumbræ of spots in
the middle of the Sun—that is, deprived of about half the
light;[3] and his previous discovery of a similar decrease of

into two portions, separated by a boundary as definite, though not so
regular, as that which parts them both from the photosphere. The
outer, and far more extensive portion, which, in texture and rarity,
seems to resemble the tails of comets * * * * is known as the
" coronal atmosphere " since to it is chiefly due the corona or glory
which surrounds the darkened sun during an eclipse * * *. At its
base and in contact with the photosphere is what resembles a sheet
of scarlet fire * * * *, this is the chromosphere.'

[1] It seems desirable to point out here that Galileo was not actually
the first to make a telescope, though he constructed one independently, and was probably the first to apply the instrument to the
study of celestial objects.—(P.)

[2] Arago's polariscope failed to exhibit this difference; it has been
shown by the latter observations of Schwabe, that it does not invariably exist, and that when it is not perceptible, there is also an absence
of faculæ, 'scars,' and pores. Spörer, however, is disposed to refer
such observations to dew or hoar-frost on the object-glass.

[3] He has subsequently reduced this to $\frac{1}{3}$ or $\frac{1}{4}$, and finds the limb
of a very decided smoky red tint. Elger has seen a portion of the

heat confirms the existence of such an absorbent stratum. Hence also may result the inferior distinctness of the solar limb as compared with that of the Moon in eclipses : a fact remarked by Airy, and exhibited by photography ; and Secchi has observed that the occasional bad definition of the spots may be due to the solar atmosphere instead of our own. Some measures of his, and observations by Spörer, seem to indicate a refractive power in this atmosphere, producing an apparent displacement of the spots towards the limb.

Something must be said of the Sun as a background for the exhibition of intervening bodies. Partial solar eclipses seldom gain much interest in the use of the telescope, excepting from the occasional projection of mountains on the Moon's limb. The total eclipse is so wonderful and so fugitive as to require special preparation, and is too rare in England to require notice here. The transits of Mercury will be found under the head of that planet: those of Venus are too uncommon and distant to be admitted in our limited space; the next visible in England not occurring till 2004. Comets, from the endless diversity of their paths, must occasionally traverse the solar disc [1] and the opportunity of such a background would be most valuable for acquiring more information as to their nature. If anything unusual should ever be noticed on the disc, it should be carefully watched ; and should its rate of progress show that it is not an ordinary spot, its appearance ought to be most critically examined with various powers and screen-glasses, and information telegraphed instantly, where practicable, to some of our principal observatories.

disc near the limb intensely brown, where large spots have disappeared.

[1] Comet Halley when in transit on May 18, 1910, was invisible according to Ellerman.—(E⁸.)

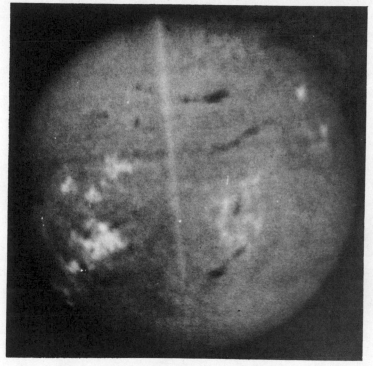

Spectroheliogram. July 28, 1959; 1901 UT three-second exposure,
4EH alpha film, 50 micron slit width, 30 inch fl. objective, 1½ inches
diameter. 30,000 lines per inch grating, 45 inch fl. spectrograph.

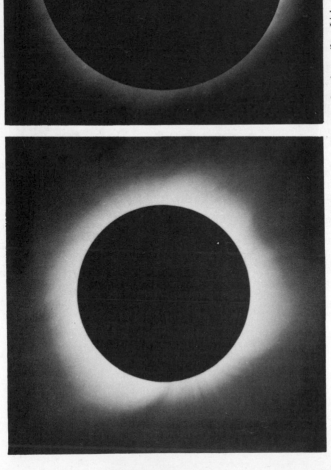

Eclipse of the sun, September 22, 1928, Wallal, Australia. *Left* Long exposure showing the outer corona. *Right* Short exposure showing the inner corona and prominences.

It may never be granted to our readers to witness such a wonderful outburst of light in front of the Sun as was observed by Carrington and Hodgson, 1859, Sept. 1 ; and repeated, according to Brodie, on a minor scale, 1864, Oct. 1.[1] But should any of them be so fortunate, the propriety need scarcely be mentioned of the greatest care in the record, and readiness in the publication, of such an event.

MERCURY.

THIS planet, though at times readily visible [2] to the naked eye, is but seldom seen from its nearness to the Sun, and often lies too near the horizon for the telescope. A well-adjusted equatorial stand will find it by day, but its small diameter of about 3060 miles subtends at a mean only $7\cdot5''$; and it was sometimes missed, as well as once noticed extremely faint, even by the experienced Schröter.

Ordinary observers will not see much, where professed astronomers have usually found little ; but, as these pages may possibly fall into the hands of some whose advantages or enterprise may lead them to attack a neglected object, the following points may be specified :—

1. The *Phases.* These will be easily seen, and are only remarkable because the breadth of the enlightened part has been sometimes found less than it should have been from

---

[1] And to Hale and others, July 15, 1892 ; and by Aiyar at Kodaikánal Observatory, Sept. 28, 1909, attended by magnetic disturbance.

[2] Often seen by Schröter and Heis with the naked eye 'lucenta sole.' Brightest from 10 to 14 days before greatest eastern (evening) elongations, much fainter at actual elongations.

calculation. Schröter noticed this: Beer and Mädler confirm it; but their explanation of a dense atmosphere en-
feebling the terminator, or boundary of light and darkness,
is inadequate, as their observation was before sunrise, when
even the dullest part of the disc would be very luminous.
See this again in Venus.[1]

2. The *Mountains*. At the close of the last and beginning of this century, Schröter, of Lilienthal in Hanover, a
most diligent observer, and his assistant Harding, obtained
what they deemed sufficient evidence of a mountainous
surface in the alternate blunting of the horns,[2] some minute
projections from the limb, and an irregular curve of the
terminator; they gave the inferred elevations a height of
nearly 11 miles.

3. The *Atmosphere*. The decrease of light towards the
terminator, and the occasional presence of dark streaks and
spots, indicated to the same astronomers a vaporous envelope,
where they even imagined traces of the action of winds.
From a combination of their observations Bessel deduced a
rotation in 24^h 0^m 53^s on an axis inclined about $70°$ to the
ecliptic of Mercury. A bright spot with faint lines diverging from it, N.E. and S., was seen by Prince a little S. of the
centre, in unusually clear air, 1867, June 11; Birmingham
was pretty certain that there was a large white spot near E.
limb, 1870, March 13; and Vogel at Bothkamp observed
spots, 1871, April 14 and 22. In De La Rue's Newtonian,

[1] According to Trouvelot the terminator becomes straight at eastern
elongations before, and at western elongations after, the calculated
times, as is found in the case of Venus.

[2] Noble also has suspected this (1864) as to S. horn, and Burton;
and both saw an ill-defined terminator. Franks has seen (1877) the
S. cusp blunted. Trouvelot confirms (1876–81) the blunting of the
S. horn, and the irregular curve of the terminator. Guiot at Soissons
has observed the S. horn rounded with a $3\frac{3}{4}$-in. refractor.

10-ft. focus, 13-in. aperture, constructed by himself, and now at Oxford, the planet has a rosy tinge, noticed also by Burton, and once by Harding; Franks, however, sees it very white. Secchi has remarked that the disc is always very ill-terminated, and very faint at the edges, but Burton's admirable silvered specula give a sharply defined limb. Venus in the same field appeared to Nasmyth fully twice as reflective as Mercury.[1]

[1] Recent observations have not added much that is certain to our knowledge of this planet. In 1888 Denning published an important series of observations made with a 10¼-in. With-Browning reflector. In the autumn of 1882 he obtained some good views of Mercury, and saw the markings on the disc so pronounced as to suggest an analogy to those of Mars. His observations also led this observer to conclude that the rotation period of the planet must certainly be longer than that usually accepted from Schröter's observations. Schiaparelli at Milan, whose observations were made usually in the daytime, and chiefly with an $8\frac{6}{10}$-in. refractor between the years 1881–89, in the latter year made the rather startling announcement that the planet performs a rotation in the same time that it completes a revolution round the sun (88 days). So that as the axis of Mercury is apparently nearly perpendicular to his orbit, if Schiaparelli's period is correct, the planet must always turn the same face to the sun. But owing to a considerable motion of 'libration,' resembling that which occurs in the case of the Moon, as much as $\frac{5}{8}$ of the planet's surface will be at times exposed to the sun's rays, the remaining $\frac{3}{8}$ remaining for ever in darkness. Schiaparelli also found the markings on the disc so definite and of such a degree of permanency, that he was able to construct a map of them. Lowell, Jarry Desloges, and others have also deduced a rotation period approximately equal to that of the planet's revolution; but Denning, comparing his observations of the markings, 1882–1906, with those of Molesworth and other observers, has obtained a period of 24^{h} 42^{m} 24^{s}.—(P.)

According to Zöllner's photometric researches the 'albedo,' or reflecting power of Mercury is very low, only 13 per cent. of the incident light being reflected. In 1890 the disc of Venus appeared to Denning like newly-polished silver, whilst that of Mercury was of a dull leaden hue. The planets were only $2°$ apart at the time.

Transits of Mercury are comparatively frequent. The planet breaks in upon the Sun as a dark notch, sometimes preceded, it is said, by a penumbral shade ; but the earliest impression will be missed, unless the exact point of ingress is known, and kept central in the field. As it advances, the part of Mercury not yet entered may become visible by being projected upon the ' corona,' which is so conspicuous in total solar eclipses, and has been known to relieve dark bodies in front of it, such as an inferior planet, or even a portion of the Moon (Pratt, 1873).[1] On finally entering the Sun, or beginning to leave it, the planet has been seen lengthened towards the limb from irradiation : fully on the disc, where Mercury appears intensely black, some astronomers have given it a slight dusky border, others a narrow luminous ring : both, probably, deceptions from the violent contrast and the fatigue of the eye,[2] especially as others have remarked nothing of the kind. A similar explanation may be applied to a whitish or grey spot on the dark planet, seen by Wurzelbauer, 1697 ; Schröter, Harding, and Kohler, 1799 ; Fritsch and others, 1802 ; Moll and his assistants, 1832 (when Harding *clearly* distinguished *two* spots, and Gruithuisen suspected one); and recognised in England and America, 1848, and by Huggins and Elger, 1868, when Browning perceived *two* spots again. In 1878 also a bright speck was noticed by several English and Belgian observers (in one case, *two* specks), though others entirely failed to detect it; and every attempt to recognise it in America was unsuccessful. No terrestrial analogy will explain a

[1] At the transit of 1914, Nov. 7, Fowler at South Kensington, making use of the spectroscope, saw the planet projected on the chromosphere fully a minute before it reached the sun.—(P.)

[2] Pratt, however, in 1868, saw the ' halo ' finely by projection in a darkened room.

luminosity thus visible close to the splendour of the Sun; and it seems natural to refer it to the exhausted state of the retina: an artificial disc, however, subsequently tried by Huggins, showed nothing of the kind. And everything that is seen, however improbable, should always be recorded: an opposite procedure would have effectually precluded many an important discovery. We may remark that Schröter and Harding ascribed to these spots a motion corresponding with the rotation which they subsequently inferred from other indications.[1]

VENUS.

Fairest of stars, last in the train of night,
If better thou belong not to the dawn,
Sure pledge of day, that crown'st the smiling morn
With thy bright circlet, praise HIM in thy sphere.

MILTON.

THE most beautiful of all the heavenly bodies to the unaided eye is often a source of disappointment in the telescope. For the most part it resists all questioning beyond that of Galileo, to whom its phases revealed the confirmation of the Copernican theory; an important discovery which he

---

[1] A similar phenomenon was observed on Venus in transit in 1761 (*Append. ad. Ephem. Astron.* 1766, 62); and by some observers in 1874. Many of the appearances of Mercury above described have been reported at recent transits, but it is generally agreed that they are illusions. At the 1914 transit many of the best observers using the finest instruments saw nothing abnormal, though the phenomenon of the '*black drop*,' which proved so troublesome in transits of Venus, was recorded by some.—(P.)

involved for a season in the following ingenious Latin transposition—

"Hæc immatura à me jam frustra leguntur, o. y."

the letters in their original order forming the words

"Cynthiæ figuras æmulatur mater amorum."

Observers in general will subscribe to the experience of Herschel II., who says it is the most difficult of all the planets to define with telescopes. 'The intense lustre of its illuminated part dazzles the sight, and exaggerates every imperfection of the telescope : yet we see clearly that its surface is not mottled over with permanent spots like the Moon ; we notice in it neither mountains nor shadows, but a uniform brightness, in which sometimes we may indeed fancy, or perhaps more than fancy, brighter or obscurer portions, but can seldom or never rest fully satisfied of the fact;' and he infers, like his father, and Huygens long before, that ' we do not see, as in the Moon, the real surface of these planets' (Venus and Mercury) ' but only their atmospheres, much loaded with clouds, and which may serve to mitigate the otherwise intense glare of their sunshine.[1]

[1] Chacornac was of the same opinion, from the absence of polarisation in the light of Venus. His apparatus showed her brightness to be 10 times greater than that of the most luminous parts of the Moon. The reduction of her light to $\frac{1}{2000}$ perceptibly diminished the image from removal of irradiation. Jupiter the same. Zöllner makes the ' albedo' of Venus 0·50, so that the planet reflects about half the light that falls upon it. This high reflective power favours the view of a cloud-laden atmosphere. On July 26, 1910, the occultation of η Geminorum by Venus was observed by several astronomers, the planet being at the time similar in phase to the moon two days before the last quarter. At the time of reappearance the star took upwards of two seconds to recover its full light. An atmosphere of 80 to 100 kilometres was deduced. The photo. of the transit of Venus at Puebla gave 126 kilometres for the height of the atmosphere.—(Es.)

Notwithstanding, however, the authority of this opinion, perseverance has of late years rendered it doubtful : moderate-sized instruments have proved of service : and the silvered reflector, from its colourless image, is here greatly superior to the achromatic. The following are the chief points to be noticed :—

1. The *Phases*. With a mean diameter of $18''\cdot8$, these are of course easily seen, and very beautiful, excepting the dull gibbous form in the *superior* or farther part of the orbit, where the disc is also small ; near the greatest elongation from the Sun towards the E. when she is an evening, or W. when a morning star, Venus puts on a beautiful shape—that of the moon in quadrature ; between these points in the *inferior* or nearer part of the orbit, she is a most elegant crescent, larger, sharper, and thinner in proportion as she is nearer really to the Earth and apparently to the Sun. This crescent has been seen even with the naked eye in the sky of Chile,[1] and with a dark glass in Persia, and a very small telescope will show it. When quite slender it should not be looked for after sunset or before sunrise, as it lies too low in the vapour ; but an equatorial stand will find it in the middle of the day—an exquisite object ; and thus, or in a transit instrument, it has been many times traced as a mere curved thread extremely near the Sun. Ordinary observers may succeed without an equatorial mounting in seeing it a very delicate crescent soon after it has passed its inferior conjunction, by watching for its earliest appearance

" Under the opening eyelids of the morn,"

setting the finder, or the telescope with the lowest power,

[1] Theodore Parker saw it in America when 12 years old, and ignorant of its existence, and when no one else could perceive it.

[2] Dawes considers that, with due precaution, Venus might be seen in her upper conjunction within $1'$ of the Sun's limb.

upon it, and following it at intervals sufficient to keep it in
the field, till it has cleared the vapours of the horizon ; in
this way it may be readily viewed for hours. In fact, the
planet is best seen for many purposes in the daytime; its
light, unpleasantly dazzling [1] in a dark sky, so as to bear a
screen-glass, is subdued by day to a beautiful pearly lustre.
Nor is it very difficult to find. For some time about its
greatest brightness, at 40° from the Sun in the inferior part
of the orbit, it not merely casts a shade by night, but is
visible to the naked eye at noon-day : if its position is pretty
well known, a little careful steady gazing will bring it out
as an intense white point, when in good air it will be a
charming telescopic object. At other seasons, a little hand-
telescope with a large field will show it much sooner in the
evening or later in the morning than might have been expected.[2] Like that of Mercury, the phasis often disagrees
with calculation ; at its greatest elongations it ought to be
exactly ' dichotomised ' as a half-moon ; but in August, 1793,
Schröter found the terminator slightly concave in that position, and not straight till 8 days afterwards ; and Beer and
Mädler fully confirmed this by many observations in 1836,
proving that the apparent ' half-moon ' takes place 6 days
earlier or later than the computed, according to the direction
of the planet's motion. They found also that there is a
similar defect in the breadth of the crescent-phasis. Neither
their explanation of this, through the shadows of mountains,
nor Schröter's, through the fading of light towards the termi-

[1] Olbers at brightest 19 to 23 times above Aldebaran; Bond 5 times
brighter than Jupiter at mean opposition; Plummer 9 times brighter
than Sirius.

[2] Trouvelot concludes that in the pure atmosphere of Cambridge,
U.S.A., Venus is visible to the naked eye in full sunshine in all parts
of its orbit, provided its angular distance from the sun is not less than
10° at inferior, or 5° at superior, conjunction.

nator, is satisfactory as far as night observations are concerned. In 1839 De-Vico and his assistants at Rome found
a similar discrepancy of about 3 days. This curious phenomenon is so easily seen, that I perceived it with an inferior
fluid achromatic, on Barlow's plan, 1833, March 6, before I
knew that it had been noticed by others.[1]

    2. The *Mountainous Surface.* La Hire, in 1700, with
an old 16-ft. refractor, power 90, professed to have seen on
several occasions in the crescent, when very narrow, 'des
inegalitez beaucoup plus considerables que celles de la
Lune;' and Briga not only described an indented terminator, but unjustifiably altered Cassini's figures accordingly.
Fontana is also stated to have perceived it in earlier days.
But Schröter's observations at the end of the last century
are far more trustworthy. With several fine reflectors and
a very good achromatic, he and others found the boundary
sometimes slightly jagged, sometimes irregular in curvature,
so as to vary the relative thickness of the horns; and these
would occasionally pass through such changes as to show a
rotation in $23^h 21^m 8^s$. At the quadrature, the N. cusp would
frequently project, while the S. was blunted, with sometimes
a minute point cut off from it by a narrow black line, the
shadow apparently of a lofty ridge; some of these mountains
Schröter supposed to be 27 or 28 miles high, but of course
with great uncertainty. Herschel I. attacked these discoveries in the 'Philosophical Transactions' for 1793, in
what Arago justly terms 'une critique fort vive, et, en
apparence du moins, quelque peu passionnée.' Schröter
calmly and satisfactorily vindicated himself through the
same medium in 1795; and Beer and Mädler, in 1833 and

---

[1] From observations of 9 elongations, Trouvelot found that
'dichotomy' occurred at east elongation 4 to 8 days before, and at
west elongation 6 to 11 days after the time of greatest elongation.

1836, have fully established his accuracy as to an irregularly curved terminator, causing great and rapid changes in the shape of the cusps. They also saw an occasional bending off of the S. horn, corresponding with Schröter's flattening of the limb in that direction,[1] as Langdon has done at the other cusp. Gruithuisen in 1847 saw the S. horn blunted. Fritsch, in 1799 and 1801, witnessed several of these appearances with small telescopes. Gruithuisen and Pastorff have drawn an indented terminator; Flaugergues and Valz noticed its irregularity, but deny its changes. Breen, with the Northumberland telescope at Cambridge, of 19½-ft. focus, and 11½-in. aperture, has often seen the unequal curve of the terminator and the blunted S. horn, and so have several recent observers : either cusp being at times blunted, or nearly or quite cut off. Pratt especially with a fine 8⅐-in. 'With' mirror has fully confirmed Schröter's projections and indentations on the terminator. Safarik has also seen them, 1868; and in 1876 Baron van Ertborn repeatedly observed a bright point detached from the S. horn.[2] But the most curious observations are those made by De-Vico and his assistants at Rome, in April and May, 1841. An achromatic by Cauchoix, 6¼-in. aperture, with powers sometimes up to 1128, enabled them to trace the approach towards the terminator, night after night, of a

[1] It is a pity that the figures in their 'Beiträge' are so bad. Schröter's, though not good, are more intelligible. The Roman observers also have noticed this strange temporary flattening of the circular limb near the S. horn, and consider it a profile view of one of the large grey spots, which, if so, must be deeply depressed.

[2] In 1886 a bright narrow line of light, about $\frac{1}{20}$ of the diameter of Venus in length, was observed by I. G. Lohse in prolongation of the lower horn, but perfectly separated from it. Trouvelot, who between the years 1876 and 1891 made 744 observations of the planet and 295 drawings, fully confirms the irregular curve of the terminator.

valley surrounded by mountains like a lunar crater, 4"·5 in
diameter. The crescent was narrow, and near the N. horn
they first saw an oblong black spot, which afterwards was
bordered with stronger light, in the sequel encroached with
half its ring upon the dark side, and ultimately formed a
black notch between two bright projections, giving the
appearance of a triply-pointed horn ; a longer black streak
was seen near the other cusp at the same time. Gruithuisen
and Pastorff seem to have noticed in part the same irregularity. Secchi, in 1857, with the 9$\frac{6}{10}$-in. Merz achr., when
the crescent was only o"·4 broad, observed it to be still
further contracted in one part. Safarik and Lyman have
seen two contractions ; Buckingham has found it when very
thin not merely irregular, but interrupted at 3 points ; and
Arcimis at Cadiz saw an indentation at the S. horn in 1876.

3. The *Spots*. These have occasioned much controversy,
from their indistinctness, which is such that the Virgilian
' aut videt, aut vidisse putat ' is often the observer's conclusion.[1] There have been, however, many exceptions. In
1645 Fontana detected a dark spot:[2] in 1666 and 1667
Domenico Cassini, at Bologna, repeatedly saw one bright
and several dusky spots, the former giving a rotation in
23^h 21^m ;[3] subsequently, in the air of France, he never could
recover them, nor were J. J. Cassini or Maraldi at Paris
more successful afterwards. In 1726 and 1727 Bianchini,
at Rome, observed spots many times with a 66-ft. refractor,
aperture a little more than 2$\frac{1}{2}$-in., power 112, like the

[1] In 1911 Quénisset at Juvisy photographed the spots.

[2] The spot observed by Fontana was, however, probably due to
the optical imperfections of the telescope used by him, as Flammarion
has pointed out.

[3] So almost invariably stated, but Schiaparelli has pointed out
that the period of rotation actually found by Cassini himself from his
observations is 23 *days*.

' seas ' in the Moon to the naked eye, though less distinct ; and not till after sunset, from want of light in his glass. His figures show them surrounding the equator of Venus, forming, as it were, three oceans—one tolerably circular, the others much lengthened, and each of the latter subdivided into three portions connected by narrower openings ; besides two spots, one occupying the S. polar region, the other forming a horseshoe round the N. pole. He did his work well, but, for want of *sky-room*, did not perceive the rapid motion of the spots, and gave a wrong rotation of $24^d 8^h$. A copy of this diagram is here given which the student may easily transfer to a small globe. Schröter and Herschel I., half a century later, with much finer instruments, but in less pellucid skies, could only make out through many years a few faint markings, with suspicions of motion. Bode saw some dark spots in 1788 ; at last, 1801, Aug. 29, Schröter

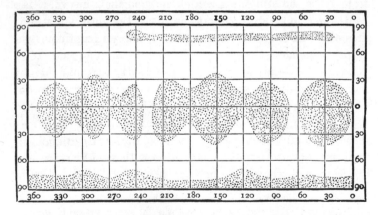

detected a dim oblique dusky streak, like one on Mercury, giving a rotation in about 24^h. Several other astronomers had occasional glimpses of darker shadowings ; Gruithuisen perceived repeatedly long vertical shades, and minute brilliant round specks, and Schumacher a dusky spot in the twilight, which in half an hour was lost in increasing glare : others, visible with a small telescope, he found effaced in a larger one—a caution for future observers. Lamont failed entirely with an 11-in. achr. at Munich in 1836 : but more effective results were obtained at Rome, 1839–1841, by De-Vico, who had been instigated by Schumacher to verify Bianchini's assertions in the same atmosphere. He used the Cauchoix achromatic chiefly by day, since in a dark sky the glare overpowered the spots so much as to render the micrometer useless, and account for Bianchini's erroneous rotation : the drawings of the latter were, however, found, save in the omission of one small spot, remarkably exact. Of 6 observers, the most successful in seeing these faint clouds were those who had most difficulty in catching very minute companions of large stars ;[1] but all agreed in the figures, and witnessed a progression, giving a rotation in $23^h\ 21^m\ 22^s$ on an axis greatly inclined, though less so than Bianchini had supposed.[2] They have given no less than 145

[1] De-Vico assigns no reason, but it seems obvious enough, and worthy of notice. A very sensitive eye, which would detect the spots more readily, would be more easily overpowered by the light of a brilliant star, so as to miss a very minute one in its neighbourhood. There is abundant industry in these Roman observations : Palomba, the assistant, made 11,800 measures in 1839, of which 10,000 were employed in determining the rotation. But De-Vico's style wants explicitness, and there are strange traces of inexperience or inattention in the Jesuit College, rendering the memoirs of that date far less satisfactory than those of the succeeding and now to be lamented Director, Secchi.

[2] The question of the duration of the rotation of Venus is still a disputed one, and several very elaborate though contradictory investigations upon the subject have been published within the last few years. In 1890 Schiaparelli came to the conclusion after a very exhaustive discussion of all the existing material, including some observations of his own, that the rotation of Venus is very slow ; and

delineations ; many of these are very coarsely executed, but, as they are little known in England, copies of a few of the more characteristic are given here. Of late these spots, invisible at Greenwich and to several of our first observers,

that whilst being very probably equal to the time taken by the planet in making one revolution round the Sun (225 days), it is certainly not less than 6 months or greater than 9 months. Perrotin confirms this slow rotation from observations of the markings on the disc made by him at Nice in 1890, and fixes it at from 195 to 225 days. In the same year Terby published a number of observations made by him in 1887-89, which appeared to him to still further confirm the slow duration of the rotation. But in 1891 appeared an important memoir by Niesten, giving the results of many observations made by himself and Stuyvaert at Brussels between 1881 and 1890. These observers, instead of supporting the slow rotation, strongly confirm the short rotation period of De-Vico. They also found the markings so evident and apparently permanent, that they were able to construct a map of them. This map, however, does not bear the slightest resemblance to that of Bianchini. More recently still Trouvelot has discussed the subject, and decides that the rotation is performed in about 24 hours. His observations of a large dark spot are referred to below. Lowell and his assistants in recent years, in the pure climate of Arizona, have recorded many markings on Venus of extremely well-defined character, and have given representations of them. They are straight, spoke-like features of unusual aspect and quite invisible to other observers, many of whom question their objective existence. Lowell deduces from them a rotation period about equal to that of the planet's revolution. Markings of a linear nature have also been drawn by G. and F. Fournier at Jarry Desloges's Observatory at Massegros, but they are entirely different in their arrangement from those of Lowell, and are mostly very elusive and fugitive. Jarry Desloges does not consider it possible to decide for or against a quick rotation of the planet. It seems possible, as suggested by Antoniadi, that certain features which apparently retain their positions unchanged relatively to the terminator may be merely phase effects. If so, any deductions of the rotation period from them are, of course, quite misleading.—(D. and P.) Recent spectroscopic results are contradictory : Slipher accepts the period of Schiaparelli, but Belopolsky's results suggest a day and a half.—(Es.)

have been recognised by others—De la Rue, Huggins, Worthington with a 13-in. mirror, Seabroke with the $8\frac{1}{4}$-in.

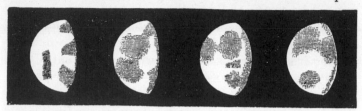

achr. belonging to Dawes, Terby, Denning, Safarik, Baron van Ertborn, and others, and described as bright patches and specks, and cloudy and crater-like markings of different forms and sizes; according to Ormesher, much like the spots of Mars.[1] With describes the disc (April 6, 1868) as marbled or veined all over, and on the same occasion perceived with a $12\frac{1}{4}$-in. unsilvered mirror, a small bright projection on the circular limb,[2] about 40° from S. cusp : this was confirmed by Key, at about 36°, April 12 and subsequent days, with granulations towards a terminator more deeply serrated than that of the Moon : March 15, Browning had seen a bright patch of some extent 80° from that cusp, so luminous as to show projection like the snow on Mars. Could we but see these features more readily, what an interesting object would this lovely planet become, especially as in point of size it is the only companion to the

[1] Trouvelot recorded a number of greyish or whitish spots between the years 1876 and 1891. They were usually of small size and little permanence, and generally only visible near the terminator. But in 1876, and again in 1891, he observed a large dark marking of comparatively well-defined nature and characteristic form, which remained visible for a number of days. In 1891 the spot was observed to arrive at the same position on the disc at a later and later hour on each succeeding day. This circumstance indicates a rotation period slightly longer than 24 hours.

[2] Compare Schröter and Harding on *Mercury*, p. 60.

Earth in the whole system![1] And the possessors of even common telescopes need not despair, though their chances may not be great: at Rome the spots have been seen even with a little telescope of 2-in. aperture, and the following recital shows that the chief difficulty lies in our own atmosphere; it is so curious that it must be given entire from the 'Philosophical Transactions':—'January 23, 1749–50, there was a splendid Aurora Borealis. About 6ʰ P.M., the Rev. Dr. Miles, at Tooting, had been viewing Jupiter and Venus, and showing them to some friends, with one of Short's reflectors, greatest power 200, when a small red cloud of the Aurora appeared, rising up from the SW. (as one of a deeper red had done before), which proceeded in a line with the planets, and soon surrounded both. Venus appearing still in full lustre, he viewed her again with the telescope, without altering the focus, and saw her much more distinctly than ever he had done upon any occasion. All his friends were of the same opinion as to the sight they had of her on that occasion. They all saw her spots plain, resembling those in the Moon, which he had never seen before, and this while the cloud seemed to surround it as much as ever; but whether the vapour might be rarer nearer the planet, no judgment could be made, because of her too powerful light.' In curious accordance with this, Langdon saw the irregularity of the terminator beautifully through an Aurora in 1873.[2]

4. The *Atmosphere.* The bright border noticed by some observers as attending the circular limb may be a deception; and so probably were the polar snows which Gruithuisen imagined that he frequently saw; but there is very sufficient

[1] Diameter, 7850 miles.
[2] A light green shade is helpful in looking for these spots.—(Es.)
[3] But Trouvelot, from a great many observations, confirms these

proof of the existence of a vaporous envelope. Schröter's dusky belt, already mentioned, indicates it.[1] He has ascribed to it the great decrease of light towards the terminator and cusps; and he and Herschel I. agreed as to the extension of the horns beyond a semicircle, which may be due in part to the penumbra, or additional daylight caused by the Sun's not being a point but a great disc, but more to refraction through an atmosphere. Schröter also perceived in 1790 a faint gleam along the limb beyond the horns, a true twilight produced by an atmosphere which must be denser than our own. In May, 1849, Mädler at Dorpat found the horns projecting to 200° and even to 240°, showing a refraction about $\frac{1}{6}$ stronger than ours; and Lyman with a 9-in. achromatic in America obtained a similar result; but from the calculation of Neison, who detected an error in the formulæ they employed, the true density comes out 1·892, or nearly twice as great as that of our atmosphere. From this cause Cassini in 1692, and Drew in 1854, found the crescent too broad near the conjunction. Secchi, in 1857, saw in that position the cusps much prolonged, and the twilight extending 19½°, even through our strongly

white polar spots, and has also pointed out that they have been seen in some form or other by a great many observers. According to Trouvelot they consist of brilliant white spots nearly always visible close to the two cusps, and never departing much from these positions. From their nearly invariable position he concludes that they mark the poles of rotation, and that the equator is only inclined 10° or 12° to the plane of the planet's orbit. He considers them to be elevated mountain masses, ice or snow covered; and that to their presence are due the deformations frequently observed in the horns. Under favourable conditions the margins of these polar spots appear formed of minute brilliant points, or detached mountain peaks.

[1] Similar ones have been detected by Buffham, and a long, narrow line, possibly atmospherical, by De La Rue and Lord Rosse in the great Melbourne Cassegrain reflector.

illuminated atmosphere. Noble has seen the whole disc so bordered in almost every inferior conjunction; it had been recorded in the transit of 1769; and in 1864 and 1866, and at the recent transit, in common with several other observers, Lyman found the delicate ring complete, and considers that it will always be so within 1° 50′ from the Sun's centre; a segment only, of an extent proportioned to the distance, being visible beyond that limit. When entering the Sun in 1875, this light was especially conspicuous in one spot.[1] Tacchini considers that this atmosphere contains traces of aqueous vapour.

5. The *Phosphorescence of the Dark Side*. This truly unaccountable appearance[2] is remarkably well attested; though it is but fair to state that it has been questioned by several good observers, even Dawes himself. It was noticed as far back as 1715, in the 'Astro-Theology' of Derham, who says that ' this sphæricity, or rotundity, is manifest in our Moon, yea and in Venus too, in whose greatest Falcations the dark part of their Globes may be perceived, exhibiting themselves under the appearance of a dull, and rusty colour.' 1721, June 7, Kirch, junior, believed that he saw it, the crescent being then extremely narrow; and again, with two others, 1726, March 8. Herschel I. perceived traces of it. In

---

[1] At the transit of 1882 the atmosphere very beautifully revealed itself, when the planet was about half on the sun, in the form of a brilliant half ring of light, marking the outline of that portion of Venus not yet entered on the sun. This semi-ring gleamed with a beautiful silvery or pearly light, and was of uneven brightness and breadth, probably owing to the planet's atmosphere being of varying degrees of opacity at different parts of the limb.

[2] Arago's 'negative visibility' is but a perplexing attempt at solution. The faint illumination which renders some of our terrestrial nights lighter than others, remarked by Schröter, Arago, and, I think, by myself, scarcely affords an adequate comparison. Humboldt gives a striking instance, *Cosmos*, I., 131 (Bohn).

1806 it displayed itself beautifully to Harding three times
(once with a companion), and to Schröter once, within five
weeks. Pastorff also witnessed it twice. Guthrie and others
noticed it in 1842, with small reflectors, in Scotland;
Purchas, at Ross, in England; De-Vico and Palomba, many
times, in Italy. Berry at Liverpool saw it in 1862 with no
previous recollection of its visibility; it was remarked in
that year, and especially in 1863, by many observers in
England, and by one in 1865, as well as by four at Leipzig
with the 8½-in. achromatic. To these we may add Petty,
1868; Winnecke, 1871, Nov. 6; Elger, Erck, 1873; Banks,
Grover, Arcimis, 1876; Mills, 1878. On Jan. 31 of that
year, after having many times looked for it in vain in former
years, I saw it, without specially thinking about it, with
powers of about 90 and 212 on my 9·38-in. mirror, coming
out at intervals rather paler and browner than the twilight
sky, and equally visible when the bright crescent was hidden
by a field-bar. Strange to say, it has been seen even in the
daytime, by Andreas Mayer, 1759, Oct. 20, through merely
a transit instrument, 44^m after noon: 'etsi pars lucida
Veneris tenuis admodum erat, nihilominus integer discus
apparuit, instar lunæ crescentis, quæ acceptum a terrâ lumen
reflectit:' and Winnecke records a similar observation,
though very faint, 1871, Sept. 25, a little before noon.[1]

[1] Langdon and several others perceived it by day a little before
inferior conjunction, 1870, Feb. 5; but this, as well as some other
instances, may have been merely the atmospheric ring of Lyman and
Noble; and such appears to have been the case in some day-observa-
tions of Baron van Ertborn in 1876. A curious observation of my
wife's may be cited here, made June 30, 1880, 7^h 30^m A.M., between
the Lago Maggiore and Domo D'Ossola. The waning Moon, 21½^h
past Last Quarter, was still at some height in W., but pale in the
strong sunshine, when she noticed that the circle appeared complete,
the dark side being smaller than the bright, of a more lilac tint than

Von Hahn also says he made it out repeatedly, by day as well as by night, and with several instruments; he was, however, an inferior observer. Gruithuisen saw it once at sunrise; Mad. Safarik in a broad crescent, 1871, Aug. 9, 11^h A.M.; Browning many times, 1870, Feb. and Mar. with 10$\frac{1}{4}$-in. silv. mirror, very distinct, brighter than the bright twilight of 5^h P.M., and even when gibbous Baron van Ertborn saw it in 1876. The dark side is often too small in proportion (as I saw it), like that of the crescent Moon to the naked eye; and from the same cause,—the irradiation of the luminous part; it is sometimes described as grey, sometimes reddish. It would be well worth looking for when the crescent is narrow, but Venus should have high N. latitude to clear the vapours of the horizon: the bright part should be put behind a bar in the field; and it should be noted whether the dark side is lighter or darker than the background. Noble has repeatedly seen the latter, projected, perhaps, on the solar corona.

the deep blue Italian sky, and irregularly shaded, being brighter towards the S.W. limb, as it would be, though she was not in the least aware of it. The phenomenon was confirmed to her by a good binocular glass; but neither I nor her servant could perceive it. She was not thinking at the time of the *lumière cendrée*, and still less of the dark side of Venus.

THE MOON.[1]

(Abbreviations :—Schr., *Schröter.*—G., *Gruithuisen.*—L., *Lohrmann.*—B. & M., *Beer* [2] & *Mädler.*—Ne., *Neison.*—Schm., *Schmidt.*—B.A.A., *British Astronomical Association.*—L.A.S., *Liverpool Astronomical Society.*—Sel. Journal., *Selenographical Journal.*)

THE comparatively small distance of our satellite, 240,000 miles,[3] renders it the easiest of telescopic objects. Its shadowed and irregular surface, visible to the naked eye,[4] is well brought out even with a low magnifier; hence Galileo readily comprehended the nature of what his new and imperfect invention disclosed to him, and the smallest instrument will show that freckled aspect, arising from numberless craters, which he compared to the eyes in a peacock's tail. Many a pleasant hour awaits the student in these wonderful regions; only let him not expect that what he sees so plainly will be equally intelligible, excepting in its unquestionable relief from the effect of light and shade. Greatly overstrained ideas, as to the possibility of making out the minute details of the surface, have been entertained, not much more reasonable than those of the islanders of Teneriffe, whose simplicity led them to imagine that the telescope of Piazzi Smyth would show their favourite goats in our satellite; a very little consideration, however, will

[1] The notes supplied for this edition are the work of Goodacre. In an appendix will be found his additional notes on the various lunar formations.

[2] This name is retained, as originally associated with the work, which, however, is known to have been chiefly executed by his colleague.

[3] More accurately 238,840, varying, from its elliptical orbit, between 252,972 and 221,614 miles.

[4] Klein observes that an immense amount of detail may be made out in the Full Moon with the naked eye, especially if the light of a flame enters it at the same time.

detect the absurdity of such anticipations. The first 'Moon Committee' of the British Association recommended a power of 1000; few indeed are the instruments or the nights that will bear it; but when employed, what will be the result? Since increase of magnifying is equivalent to decrease of distance, we shall see the Moon as large (though not as distinct) as if it were 240 miles off, and any one can judge what could be made of the grandest building on earth at that distance: very small objects, it is true, are discoverable there with the finest instruments, possibly 150 feet broad, or from their shadows one-third as much in height; but their nature remains unknown. Much difficulty, too, arises from the want of terrestrial analogies. It may be reasonably supposed that Venus or Mars, at the like distance, might be far more intelligible. We should certainly not find them mere transcripts of our own planet, for the conditions of existence as to temperature and air, if not in other respects, are very different, and, as Schr. often remarks, variety of detail in unity of design is characteristic of creation; but we might have a fair chance of understanding something of what we saw. It is quite otherwise with the Moon. It is, in B. and M.'s words, no copy of the Earth; the absence of seas, rivers, atmosphere, vapours, and seasons[1] bespeaks the absence of 'the busy haunts of men;' indeed of all terrestrial vitality, unless it be that of an insect or reptile. Whatever may be the features of the averted hemisphere, on which, as G. and Hansen have suggested, other relations may exist, we perceive on this side a mere alternation of level deserts and craggy wildernesses. The hope which

---

[1] This assertion must be limited to the subject in hand. It is not intended to deny the possibility of some kind of atmosphere, or fluid; and a trifling change of seasons would result from the slight inclination of the lunar axis (1° 32' 9").

cheered on G. and others, of discovering the footsteps of human intelligence, must be abandoned.[1] If it should be thought probable, as it very reasonably may, that the lunar surface is habitable in some way of its own, we have reason to suppose that, where the conditions of life are so extremely dissimilar, its traces would be as undecipherable by our experience as a brief inscription in a character utterly unknown. We ought not, in fact, to be surprised at such a difference between bodies belonging to distinct classes: it would have been unreasonable to have looked for a duplicate of a primary planet in its attendant. Waiving, then, any disappointment from this cause, we shall find the Moon a wonderful object of study. It presents to us a surface convulsed, upturned, and desolated by forces of the highest activity, the results of whose earliest outbreaks remain, not like those of the Earth, levelled by the fury of tempests, and smoothed by the flow of waters, but comparatively undegraded from their primitive sharpness even to the present hour. The ruggedness of the details, as old Hevel anticipated, becomes more evident with each increase of optical power, and we cannot doubt that we look upon the unchanged results of those gigantic operations which have stereotyped their record on nearly every region of the lunar globe.[2]

[1] The existence of many natural wonders on our own globe—for example, the *cañons*, or river-gorges, of NW. America, one of which has a length of 550 miles, an extreme depth of 7000 ft., and a closest contraction of 100 ft.; or the obelisk of limestone, near Lanslebourg, 360 ft. high with a base of 40 ft. (Weld., *Auvergne*, etc., 305), shows how cautiously inferences should be drawn as to the artificial origin of extraordinary appearances.

[2] This is sufficiently correct as a popular view of the subject; but a more careful examination may require it to be somewhat modified. The varieties of colour, if not arising from vegetation, may indicate

A brief general description of the phenomena of the Moon will prepare us for an examination of its topography. We have then—

1. The *Grey Plains*, or *Seas* as they were formerly believed to be, and are still termed for convenience.[1] These are evidently dry flats—if the term 'flat' can be applied to surfaces showing visibly the convexity of the globe—analogous to the deserts and prairies and pampas of the Earth. B. and M. find that they do not form portions of the same sphere, some lying deeper than others: they are usually of a darker hue than the elevated regions which bound them, but, with a strong general resemblance, each has frequently some peculiar characteristic of its own.

2. The *Mountain Chains*, *Hills*, and *Ridges*. These are of very various kinds : some are of vast continuous height and extent, some flattened into plateaux intersected by ravines, some rough with clouds of hillocks, some sharpened into detached and precipitous peaks. The common feature of the mountain chains on the Earth—a greater steepness along one side—is very perceptible here, as though the strata had been tilted in a similar manner. Detached masses and solitary pyramids are scattered here and there upon the plains, frequently of a height and abruptness paralleled only in the most craggy regions of the Earth.[2] Every gradation

an amount of 'weathering' which must be great from the distance at which it is perceptible : nor can we confidently affirm that with powerful telescopes no traces can be detected of the hand of time.

[1] Riccioli, when he recast the lunar nomenclature, and substituted the names of philosophers for the feeble geographical analogies of Hevel, retained the generic titles of 'seas,' though he altered their designations. The reform attempted by G., who would have had them called 'surfaces,' has never taken effect.

[2] Schm. ascribes less rapidity to the gradients than is here supposed ; very seldom exceeding 60°, never attaining in any extent 90°. Phillips was of an opposite opinion ; but Ne. concurs with Schm.

of cliff and ridge and hillock succeeds : among them a large
number of narrow banks of comparatively slight elevation
but surprising length,[1] extending for vast distances through
level surfaces; these so frequently form lines of communication between more important objects,—uniting distant craters
or mountains, and crowned at intervals by insulated hills,—
that Schr. formerly, and B. and M. in modern times, have
ascribed them to the horizontal working of an elastic force,
which, when it reached a weaker portion of the surface,
issued forth in a vertical upheaval or explosion. The fact
of the communication is more obvious than the probability
of the explanation.

3. The *Crater-Mountains*, comprising both the mound
or wall, and the included cavity. These are the grand
peculiarities of the Moon : commonly, and probably with
correctness, ascribed to volcanic agency : yet differing in
several respects from the foci of eruption on our own globe:
on the Earth, they are usually openings on the summits or
sides of mountains—on the Moon, depressions below the
adjacent surface, even when it is a plain or valley ; on the
Earth, the mass of the cone usually far exceeds the capacity
of the crater—on the Moon, they are much nearer equality ;
on the Earth, they are commonly the sources of long lava-
streams—on the Moon, traces of such outpourings are rare ;
on the Earth, their number as well as dimensions are comparatively inconsiderable—on the Moon, M. considers that
there are upwards of 1000 visible with a breadth of 9 miles,

---

[1] Schr. gives a length of 630 or 640 miles to a ridge connecting the
spots Copernicus and Kirch. The great serpentine ridge, traversing
the M. Serenitatis on the western side, is one of the most prominent
of these features, and is fully 300 miles in length. That they usually
appear to take the direction of the meridian is simply due to the
E. or W. projection of the shadows which make them prominently
visible.

and Schm. has drawn nearly 33,000 in all, so that they are
the greatest characteristic of its surface, and, the grey plains
excepted, among the largest of its features. When, however,
allowance has been made for the inferior power of gravity
on the Moon, through which a six-fold displacement in
height or distance would be caused by the same amount of
force,[1]—for the possible difference of materials,—and for
the more rapid cooling produced by radiation in the absence
of an atmosphere, it is quite conceivable that volcanic force,
similar to that on the Earth, may have been the real agent,
though in a greatly modified form. Any one may see, with
the ingenious Hooke, a strong resemblance to the rings
left by gaseous bubbles;[2] but to this impression mechanical
difficulties arising from the cohesion of materials have been
opposed, and a more consistent explanation sought in the
idea that the larger craters may be the remains of molten
lakes; in these, left for a while unfrozen in the general
cooling and crusting over of the once-fiery globe, an alternate shrinking and overflowing of lava, from a fluctuating
pressure from beneath, might gradually produce the existing
forms. This theory has been extended and advocated
with much ingenuity in the 'Selenographical Journal'
by Green, who would substitute erosive for eruptive agency,
even in the smaller craters; the undermining and re-dis-

[1] Mount Tongariro in New Zealand was, in 1875, throwing stones
8 miles from the crater.

[2] Scrope has suggested a somewhat similar hypothesis. He thinks
that the lunar craters have derived their peculiar features 'from the
explosions of vapour that produced them, breaking through a surface
of soft and semi-liquid matter in successive bubbles, whose bursting
would throw off all round a concentric ridge formed of repeated layers
of this substance.'—*Volcanoes*, 2nd Ed., 1872, p. 233. Pickering, by
blowing air through liquid paraffin wax, has obtained excellent
reproductions of the peculiarities of lunar craters.—(Es.)

solving power of fluid lava pressed upwards through the surface, and subsequently in many cases receding, being substituted for actual explosion. On this hypothesis the brighter and more elevated parts of the globe would, as a rule, date from a more ancient epoch than the darker and once fluid plains.

We have nothing on the Earth to be compared with the gigantic scale of the greater circles, though an extinct crater-plain, 20 miles in diameter, with peaks on its ring, is said to exist on the island of Mauritius : and the craters of the Sandwich Islands, Kilauea and Haleakala—the one a fused, the other a frozen, lake of lava,[2] with the small 'blowing-cones' which eject only cinders and ashes—afford an analogy,[3] the striking nature of which will be apparent from the following representation of the latter, taken from a view in Elwes's 'Sketcher's Tour.'[4] Difficulties no doubt

---

[1] Mr. S. E. Peal of Assam advocates, very ingeniously, 'A Theory of Lunar Surfacing by Glaciation,' in which he contends that the walled-plains, ring-plains, etc., 'have all been lakes or lagoons left for a time in a slowly glaciating crust, kept liquid by quasi-volcanic orifices;' and that the aqueous vapour rising from these areas, forming a local and dome-shaped atmosphere, ultimately condensed round the margin as snow and formed the ring.

[2] Dana has shown in the case of Kilauea that the whole floor slowly rises till the weight of the lava column becomes too great for the sides of the volcano to bear. It then breaks out in a lateral eruption, when the floor immediately sinks. The two active vents Mauna and Kilauea are both Basaltic volcanoes.—(Es.)

[3] The craters of Java are also said to bear out this comparison.

[4] Haleakala, 'the house of the Sun,' in E. Maui, is of an oblong form, with two great openings in the wall, more than 30 miles in circumference, 10,000 feet above the sea, and about 2000 feet deep. On the floor are 12 or 13 small red or yellow cones. The highest summits in the view are the two snowy volcanoes of Hawaii, seen over the clouds in a very faint distance : our sketch gives only the general effect.

remain; but we can hardly wonder at them, while geologists are still so little agreed about 'elevation-craters' and submarine volcanoes on our own globe. The circular cavities of the Moon are arranged in three classes,—*Walled* (or *Bulwark*) *Plains, Ring-Mountains,* and *Craters:* a fourth includes little pits without, or with scarcely a visible ring. The second and third differ chiefly in size; but the first have a character of their own;—the perfect resemblance of

Extinct Crater of Haleakala.

their interiors to the grey plains, as though they had been originally deeper, but filled in subsequently with the same material; many of them, in fact, bearing evident marks of having been broken down and overflowed from the outside. Their colour is often suggestive of some kind of vegetation, though it is difficult to reconcile this with the apparent deficiency of air and water. It has been ingeniously suggested that a low stratum of carbonic acid gas—the frequent product of volcanoes, and long surviving their activity—may in such situations support the life of some kind of plants:

and the idea deserves to be borne in mind in studying the changes of relative brightness in some of these spots.[1] The deeper are usually the more concave craters; but the bottom is often flat, sometimes convex; and frequently shows subsequent disturbance, in ridges, hillocks, minute craters, or more generally, as the last effort of the eruption, central hills of various heights, but seldom attaining that of the wall, or even, according to Schm., the external level. The ring is usually steepest within (as in terrestrial craters),[2] and many times built up in vast terraces, or in parallel walls, frequently lying, Schm. says, in pairs divided by narrow ravines. Nasmyth refers these terraces—not very probably—to successively decreasing explosions; in other cases he more reasonably ascribes them to the slipping down of materials piled up too steeply to stand, and undermined by lava at their base, leaving visible breaches in the wall above: they would be well explained on the supposition just mentioned of fluctuating levels in a molten surface. Small transverse ridges occasionally descend from the ring —chiefly on the outside: great peaks often spring up like towers upon the wall; gateways at times break through the rampart, and in some cases are multiplied till the remaining piers of wall resemble the stones of a huge megalithic circle.[3] A succession of eruptions may be constantly traced,

[1] The supposition, however, is said to be incompatible with the law of the diffusion of gases.

G. thought he perceived, in the grey tints of depressed surfaces, some of which vary with the amount of solar light, traces of several kinds of vegetation, comprised between 65° N. and 55° S. latitude, and preserving the correspondence observed on the Earth between increasing latitude and elevation.

[2] Schm. gives 4° to 15°, and 20° to 50°, as the respective average inclinations without and within.

[3] Or Druidical Avenue, as, for example, between Guerike and Parry.

in the repeated encroachment of rings on each other, where, as Schm. says, the ejected materials seem to have been disturbed before they had time to harden : the largest are thus pointed out as the oldest craters, and the gradual decay of the explosive force, like that of many terrestrial volcanoes, becomes unquestionable. The peculiar whiteness of the smaller craters may indicate something analogous to the difference between the earlier and later lavas of the Earth, or to the decomposition caused, as at Teneriffe, by acid vapours : in the grey levels we thus perhaps obtain an indication of the superficial character of their colouring.[1]

4. *Valleys*, of ordinary character, are not infrequent ; some of grand dimensions ; others mere gorges. The most contracted of these latter are entitled to be classed apart as

5. *Clefts* (or *Rills*[2]). These were discovered by Schr. : G. and L. added to their number, which B. and M. raised to 90 in the text of their work ; but the latter astronomer, on taking charge of the noble Dorpat achromatic, $9\frac{6}{10}$-in. aperture, perceived more than 150, and thought it might be possible to descry 1000. Schm. published in 1866 a catalogue of 425, the greater part discovered by himself ; and has since brought the number up to nearly 1000. These most singular furrows pass chiefly through levels, intersect craters (proving a more recent date), reappear occasionally beyond obstructing mountains, as though carried through by a tunnel, and commence and terminate with little reference to any conspicuous feature of the neighbourhood. Ne. observes that they are frequently connected with valley-systems open-

---

[1] In addition to these more prominent objects, traces of obscure and ancient rings are found in almost every part of the lunar surface, but perhaps more commonly on the Maria.

[2] An incorrect term adopted from the German, in which it does not imply, as in English, the presence of water.

ing out of high lands, and often run down the centre of
valleys. Klein says they are not common in the great plains.[1]
The idea of artificial formation is negatived by their magnitude;[2] they have been more probably referred to cracks in
a shrinking surface; a process which M. and others think
may even now be in operation. The observations of Kunowsky, confirmed by M. at Dorpat and Schm., seem in
some instances to point to a less intelligible origin in rows
of minute contiguous craters; but a more rigorous scrutiny
with the highest optical aid is yet required.[3] To these we
may add

6. *Faults,* or closed, not open, cracks, sometimes of considerable length, where the surface on one side is more elevated than on the other. These familiar geological features
have been recognised in abundance by Birt and With, and
are more readily traced on the Moon than on the Earth,

---

[1] Klein's statement is surely inaccurate. Some of the most extensive and best known systems are found associated with the great
plains. On the S.W. side of M. Serenitatis from Plinius, along the
margin of the Mare, and stretching to Haemus are a number of these
objects, so on the E. and W. sides of M. Humorum. If Gassendi,
Atlas, Cleomedes be classed as plains, the inaccuracy is more manifest. The extraordinary thing is that the vast majority are found
only on the N. Hemisphere, very few are found in the broken surface
towards the S. Pole.—(G.)

[2] Schm. gives them 18 to 92 miles long, $\frac{1}{3}$ mile to $2\frac{1}{10}$ miles broad,
and 100 to 430 yards deep. G., following out his strange theory
that the Moon was once surrounded by an immense ocean which has
wholly disappeared, considered the larger of these furrows as the
beds of dried-up rivers; the smaller he referred to artificial clearings
in the forests, answering the purpose of roads. It is to be regretted
that the extravagance of his fancy should in many instances have
brought discredit upon the unquestionable precision of his sight.

[3] Klein, with a very sharp image and power upwards of 400, finds
their breadth much more irregular than would be suspected with
inferior means.

from the absence of superincumbent alluvial deposits and denudation.

Wonders are here in abundance for the student : but he will find it impossible to pursue them far from the terminator,—they must be viewed under the oblique rays of a rising or setting Sun. As the angle of illumination increases, a fresh aspect of things creeps in, and extends itself successively over the whole disc, and in its progress the inexperienced observer will find himself astonished at the change, and frequently bewildered in the attempt to trace out the landmarks of the surface. Objects recently well recognised under the relief of light and shade will become confused by a novel effect of local illumination, and the eye will wander over a wilderness of streaks and specks of light, and spots and clouds of darkness, where it may sometimes catch the whole, sometimes a portion, sometimes nothing of many a familiar feature; while unknown configurations will stand boldly out defying all scrutiny, and keeping their post immovably till the decreasing angle of illumination warns them to withdraw. Nothing can be more perplexing than this optical metamorphosis, so complete in parts as utterly to efface well-defined objects ; so capricious as in some instances to obliterate one, and leave unaffected the other, of two similar and adjacent forms.   G., carrying out an idea of Schr.'s, referred some of these changes to the progress of vegetation which, if existing, will naturally, in default of a change of seasons, run its whole course in a single lunation : even the cautious B. and M. have admitted that some variations of colour may possibly point in this direction ; and photographic results seem to indicate the presence of green light not cognisable by the eye : but the general change demands a more universal solution ; and probably a wide range of colours in the soil may be concerned in the effect. The subject calls for careful study, but would involve much laborious application.[1]

The most obvious features of the Moon under a high illumination are the *Systems of Bright Streaks* which issue, though in widely differing proportions, chiefly from seven different centres : all craters, few inconsiderable, but none of the very largest class. In some cases the streaks proceed from a circular grey border surrounding the crater; in others they cross irregularly at the centre. They pass alike over mountain and valley, and even through the rings and cavities of craters, occasionally reach the terminator,[2] and seem to defy all scrutiny.[3] Nichol asserts that in some contiguous systems, the order of formation may be detected from the mode of their intersection ; [4] a statement well deserving the notice of those whose telescopes will carry them through the inquiry. But one thing is certain, that they are very seldom accompanied by any visible deviation in the superficial level ; a fact irreconcilable with Nasmyth's conjecture, that they are cracks diverging from a central explosion, filled up with molten matter from beneath ; trap-dykes on the Earth are, indeed, apt to assume the form of the surface, but the chances against so general and exact a restoration of level, all along such multiplied and most irregular lines of exposure, would be incalculable ; many of the rays are also

[1] The polarisation of light by the Moon was found by Secchi to be entirely different in the lowlands and in the mountainous parts. Birt sees a greenish tint in the plains under very oblique lights.

[2] Ne. remarks this, in opposition to B. and M., and says that some of the Tycho streaks shift a little with varying libration.

[3] A very ingenious theory is that of H. G. Tomkins. He suggests that they are composed of layers of salt left by the drying up of the oceans. Vast tracts of salt are found in the Punjab, and elsewhere in India, which he has personally examined.—(G.)

[4] The following, according to him, is the chronological order of three great systems: *Copernicus, Aristarchus, Kepler.*

far too long and broad for this supposition, or for that of B. and M., that they may be stains arising from highly heated subterraneous vapour on its way to the point of escape.[1] The extraordinary brilliancy of some portions of the Full Moon is less difficult of explanation, when we bear in mind

[1] Schwabe suggests that they may be due to contrast; a shade being formed in their intervals as the day increases by a multitude of thin converging or parallel grey lines, which may be seen by a good instrument, and which may possibly result from some kind of vegetation.

In a paper recently published in the *Astronomische Nachrichten*, Professor Pickering gives the results of his observations of the bright streaks with a 13-inch telescope at Arequipa. He finds: (1) That the streaks round Tycho do not radiate from the apparent centre of this formation, but point towards a multitude of minute craterlets on its SE. or N. rim. Similar craterlets occur on the rims of other great craters, forming streak-centres. (2) Generally speaking, a very minute and brilliant crater is located at the end of the streak nearest the radiant point, the streak spreading out and becoming fainter towards the other end. The great majority of lunar streaks appear to issue from one or more of these minute craters, which rarely exceed a mile in diameter. (3) The streaks which do not issue from minute craters usually lie upon or across ridges, or in other similarly exposed situations, sometimes apparently coming through notches in the mountain walls. (4) Many of the Copernicus streaks start from craterlets within the rim, flow up the inside and down the outside of the walls. (5) Though there are similar craters within Tycho, the streaks from them do not extend far beyond the walls of this formation. All the conspicuous streaks about Tycho originate outside its walls. (6) The streak-systems of Copernicus, Kepler, and Aristarchus are greyish in colour and much less white than that associated with Tycho. Some white lines extending SE. from Aristarchus do not apparently belong to the streak-system. In the case of craterlets lying between Aristarchus and Copernicus, the streaks point away from the latter. (7) There are no very long streaks. They vary from 10 to 50 miles in length, and are rarely more than a quarter of a mile in width at the crater. From this point they gradually widen out and become fainter. Their width, however, at the end farthest from the crater is seldom more than 5 miles.

the effect of chalky strata, or that peculiar kind of granite which on the loftiest peaks of the Himalayas may readily be confounded with the adjacent snow.[1] In many cases the form of the surface gives us no key to the distribution of this vivid reflection; in others it occupies a marked position, as on the summit of rings and central mountains: the idea of a mirror-like glaze [2] reflecting an image of the Sun, though entertained by such authorities as B. and M., seems difficult to be reconciled with the ever-varying angle of illumination.

A scale of reflective power has been adopted from Schr. by later selenographers, in which (blackness being o) the darkest grey shades rank as 1°, the brightest portions 10°. This is of some use, though merely arbitrary. A more reliable plan, especially in combination with such a scale, would be the mode of comparative values, in which the light of any given spot is referred to others above and below it in brightness. Changes are more than suspected in the reflective power of portions of the lunar surface, and it would be interesting to examine it in that aspect; but we have no good map of the Full Moon, and if we had, it never could

[1] Trachyte is nearly white, and when acted upon by hot vapours, as in the case of the Solfatara, is of the colour of chalk. The Rhyolites of Antrim are also very light in colour. Basalts on the contrary are generally nearly black. In volcanic regions there is usually a strange mixture of acid and basic rocks, and an active vent sometimes ends in the slow protrusion of pasty lava forming a dome like the Puy de Dôme in the Auvergne. The terrible eruption, in 1902, of Mt. Pelée ended in the protrusion of a mass of pasty lava, which has been called Pelée's cork. Wood, by photographing the moon first in yellow, and then in ultra-violet light, found a large deposite dark to the latter, close to Aristarchus, and notices that of two specimens of volcanic tuff which appears exactly alike in yellow light, one appears in ultra-violet light much darker than the other.—(Es.)

[2] The extraordinary brilliancy of some of the gneiss and micaschists under full sunlight in Switzerland is possibly somewhat similar to the vivid reflection from some parts of the full moon.—(Es)

adequately express the various gradations of brightness, which must be the object of topographical study.

A few *peculiarities of arrangement* deserve to be mentioned here. The remarkable tendency to circular forms,[1] even where explosive action seems not to have been concerned, as in the bays of the so-called seas, is very obvious; and so are the horizontal lines of communication already mentioned. The gigantic craters or walled plains often affect a meridional arrangement: three huge rows of this kind are very conspicuous, near the centre, and the E. and W. limb. A tendency to parallel direction has often a curious influence on the position of smaller objects; in many regions these chiefly point to the same quarter, usually N. and S. or NE. and SW.;[2] thus in one vicinity (between G, L, and M on the accompanying map) B. and M. speak of 30 objects following a parallel arrangement, for one turned any other way; even small craters entangled in such general pressures (as round L) have been squeezed into an oval form; and the effect is like that of an oblique strain upon the pattern of a loosely woven fabric: an instance (near 27, 28) of double parallelism, like that of a net, is mentioned, with crossing lines from SSW. and SE. Local repetitions frequently occur; one region (between 290 and 292) is characterised by exaggerated central hills of craters; another

---

[1] It has been pointed out by Elger that the borders of a large number of formations are polygonal in shape, and that many exhibit a tendency to a hexagonal figure, *e.g.* Copernicus, Langrenus, Vieta, Ptolemæus, Wargentin, Hevel, Hansteen, etc. (see *Journal B.A.A.*, vol. iii. p. 314).

[2] The N. and S. arrangement is also found in the case of volcanoes on the Earth. It is very noticeable in the Auvergne. In Italy the volcanic focus of activity has apparently shifted from N. to S., and the present active vent of Vesuvius is S., and not in the centre, of the older volcano, Somma.—(Es.)

(A) is without them; in another (185), the walls themselves
fail. Incomplete rings are much more common towards the
N. than the S. pole; the defect is usually in the N., seldom
in the W., part of the circle; sometimes a cluster of craters
are all breached on the same side (near 23, 32).[1] Two
similar craters often lie N. and S. of each other, and near
them is frequently a corresponding duplicate. Two large
craters occasionally lie N. and S., of greatly resembling
character, S. usually ¾ of size of N. from 18 to 36 miles
apart, and connected by ridges pointing in a SW. direction
(20, 19: 78, 77: 83, 84: 102, 103: 208, 207, 204: 239,
242: 261, 260: 262, 263: 340, 345). Several of these
arrangements are the more remarkable, as we know of
nothing similar on the Earth.

The question as to the *continuance of eruptive action* on
the Moon is one of great interest.[2] It is now well known
that the volcanoes, which Herschel I. and others thought
they saw in activity on the dark side, were only the brighter
spots reflecting back to us the earth-shine of the lunar night
with the same proportional vivacity as the sunshine of the
day. No valid reason, indeed, has been assigned for the
fact, witnessed by many observers, especially Sm., that one
at least of these spots—Aristarchus—varies remarkably in
nightly luminosity at different periods,[3] nor for the specks

---

[1] Compare Elwes's account of the small cones on the floor of the
great extinct crater Haleakala, some of them 'broken down at the
side, nearly always on the NE.'—*Sketcher's Tour*, 214.

[2] Prof. W. H. Pickering claims to have detected changes in connection with Eimart, which he attributes to volcanic agency.—(G.)

[3] Elger saw a spot on the dark side, apparently Aristarchus,
1867, April 12, 7ʰ 30ᵐ to 8ʰ 30ᵐ, nearly as bright as a 7 mᵍ star, with
a 4-in. aperture, and too conspicuous to be overlooked by the most
careless observer. It was much fainter during the last 15ᵐ, and
scarcely perceptible at 9ʰ. The Moon was 1ᵈ 5ʰ after I. Qu. He had

of light which more than once Schr. caught sight of on the
dark side for a short time:[1] but in these cases there has
been no subsequent perceptible alteration of surface; and
they furnish no reply to the inquiry respecting present
changes. Such were abundantly recorded by Schr. in his
day, chiefly variations in the visibility or form of minute
objects; but a great majority of them he, and subsequently
G., who witnessed many such appearances, referred to the
lunar atmosphere: and B. and M. are disposed to discard
them all as the result of inaccuracy or varying illumination.
The extraordinary influence of the latter upon the aspect of
distant and unknown objects may be estimated by any one
who will sketch the changed effects of light and shade on
any familiar terrestrial object at different times of day;
still there seems to be a residuum of minute variations not
thus disposed of, and in some cases possibly indicating actual
local change. Terrestrial analogy is in favour of the idea
that disturbing agency may have greatly diminished without
having become extinct: but observation, not assertion, must
decide the point. There are no traces of any grand convul-
sion since the date of the first lunar map; and we are only
now becoming possessed of the means of detecting smaller
changes. Schr.'s drawings are very rough; the much more
careful ones of L., and B. and M., would be too recent to
warrant great expectations, even were they more reliable—
especially the latter—as to minute details; and they are sub-

seen something similar on former occasions. Schr.'s conjecture that
the variations, which he observed in a minor degree in several parts
of the disc, may be due to atmospheric condensation during the
lunar night, is more elegant than probable: it may, however, deserve
consideration.

[1] Such a phenomenon, more extended, but very faint, was seen,
or fancied, by G.; and witnessed in our own day, with great distinctness, by Grover and by Williams.

ject to the same material drawback as the recently published great map of Schm.—admirable as it is in its own way— that of representing objects in only one aspect, and that a conventional one. This defect is of course inherent in every general map, and can only be supplied by topographical sketches, after the manner of Schr., giving repeated views of the same object under differing angles of illumination and reflection. As yet, this has been only partially attempted. We have no monograph representing any one spot for each successive night of its visibility, and in varied conditions of libration : but such a series would be very instructive, as well as valuable for the future. But we must not omit to do justice to the indefatigable as well as accurate labours of Birt, continued through many years, and adding very materially to our knowledge of lunar detail; and much is to be hoped from the researches of the Selenographical Society, established in London in 1878, which, comprising many eminent English and foreign astronomers, has for its object the collection and preservation of observations, and the indication of the most promising lines of research.[1]

Little of a satisfactory nature can be said as to a *Lunar Atmosphere*. That its density cannot amount to $\frac{1}{150}$ of that of our own is demonstrable from theory, and proved by observation, which shows us a sharp outline, and detects no change in the aspect of stars in contact with the limb:[2] and hence its entire absence has been maintained by great astronomers: Schr. asserted its existence from many changes

[1] This Society was dissolved at the close of the year, 1882, but its work was subsequently resumed by the Liverpool Astronomical Society, and is now being actively carried on by the Lunar Section of the British Astronomical Association.

[2] It has been ascertained of late years that the Moon's observed diameter exceeds by 4″ that computed from occultation of stars. This appears too much to be explained by irradiation.

of aspect in minute objects, and from a very dim twilight which he traced through 9 years beyond the points of the horns; his inferences are supported and in part exceeded by G., who frequently saw—or imagined—fogs and clouds

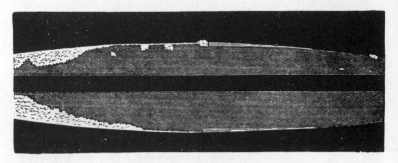

resting on the surface; nor is Klein disposed to deny the probability of such obscurations, especially in deep places.[1] The defined limb and the absence of refraction are accounted for by Schr. by limiting the sensible atmosphere to the inferior regions. B. and M., while explaining away—not very satisfactorily—Schr.'s twilight, which they could never distinctly find, do not deny the possibility of a very rarefied gaseous envelope.[2] Those traces of twilight, which have

[1] A list of temporary obscurations in M. Crisium Pierce A, Cleomedes A, Posidonius, Piton, Messier, Plato, Schroeter's Valley, Picard, Tycho, is given in the sixth report, Lunar Section, B.A.A.—(G.)

[2] Some very curious photographic experiments by De la Rue have been thought to tend the same way. It seems hardly probable that oxygen, which forms $\frac{1}{3}$ of the weight of terrestrial earths, should be entirely absent from the Moon; and the whiteness of the small craters in the grey plains is a suggestive fact. Schm. has in a few instances (to which he might have added one from Schr.) seen a grey border to the black shadow in craters, but this he ascribes to its being thrown from a very ragged edge. Schr. and other observers have noted occasional want of definition in certain spots as compared with others. In a few cases M. and Schm. have perceived a blue tint

been confirmed by G. and recently by MM. Henry with a large telescope at Paris, and which I imagined I saw, 1855, June 20, but only doubtfully from want of better optical means, might well engage the student's attention : in order to assist him two figures are here given from among Schr.'s numerous delineations. They represent the cusps of the Moon as seen by him, 1792, Feb. 24, with a 7-ft. reflector by Herschel I., powers 74, 161.

Occultations of planets or stars, which are important to the professed astronomer, are interesting to the amateur as bringing out distances and motions of which the naked eye takes little cognisance : the comparative nearness of our satellite becomes self-evident, and its orbital movement is made apparent from minute to minute. A grand effect is produced by the visible sailing of this ponderous globe through immeasurable space; and it may well convey a deep impression of the omnipotent Power and consummate Wisdom which orders its undeviating course. The instantaneous extinction, too, and sudden flashing out of a large star in these circumstances are very striking, though less instructive than might have been expected as to the question of an atmosphere : the immersion and emersion are usually as sudden as if none existed ; but this may be accounted for by the rapid motion of the Moon, or, on Schr.'s theory, by the elevation of that portion of the limb : the gradual extinction sometimes recorded may be only due to irregularities on the edge : the distortions or flattenings occasionally noticed in the shape of planets at occultation are too extensive for any such cause, and must be referred to optical

round bright points on the terminator, probably, as Schm. says, due to the 'secondary spectrum' of all achromatics. De la Rue's remark is important, that it is difficult to conceive any chemical formation of matter without an atmosphere.

illusion.[1] All occultations of importance are predicted in the Nautical Almanac; the most beautiful are *immersions* behind the *dark* limb when the latter receives a strong earth-light, as between New Moon and I. Quarter.[2]

The *projection* of a star upon the Moon, just before immersion, as if it advanced in front of it, is very difficult of explanation. South, after a careful examination of the instances on record, was unable to come to any satisfactory conclusion : it is an occurrence of the most capricious kind, which can never be predicted for any star, eye, or telescope ; and is evidently an optical, not astronomical, phenomenon.

Libration must be well understood before proceeding to topography. This is an apparent displacement of the spots with respect to the limb (or centre), arising in one direction (that of lunar longitude) from the equable rotation of the Moon on its axis combined with its unequable velocity in an elliptical orbit, in another direction (that of latitude) from the inclination of its orbit to the ecliptic in conjunction with a slight inclination of the axis to the plane of the orbit : it completes its changes in about four weeks, though an exact restoration of the position called 'mean (or medium) libration' does not take place till the end of three years. Hence, the usual statement that we see always the same hemisphere is only approximately true. The spots are constantly swinging a little backwards and forwards, and those near the E. and W. limbs going alternately out of sight ; while, as our eye rises successively above each pole, a little more or less of those regions is seen,—the whole

---

[1] See Proctor's very ingenious illustration of such deceptions under the head of *Saturn*.

[2] Kunowsky has seen the dark limb sharply defined 3^d 4^h after I. Quarter. G. professed that he was able to trace the larger seas on the dark side with the naked eye.

area thus concealed and exposed by turns amounting to $\frac{2}{11}$ of the surface of the globe.[1] No map of the Moon, therefore, can correctly represent its whole aspect on two following nights, and they are of course constructed to correspond with a state of mean libration. The displacement of the spots, which amounts at a maximum to 6° 47′ N. and S., 7° 55′ E. and W., and 10° 24′ from a concurrence of both, in either direction from a normal position, produces little effect upon the aspect of the central parts, which are merely shifted with regard to the Moon's equator or 1st meridian; but in the foreshortened neighbourhood of the limb its results are very obvious. Fresh regions constantly take the outline of the disc, and the mountainous projections of to-night may be all out of sight to-morrow. One effect of libration is, that the spots have no fixed position with respect to the Moon's age, being sometimes earlier, sometimes later, on the terminator, so that no precise instructions can be given when to look for them; it may be useful, however, to know that, as Birt has pointed out, the terminator passes through very nearly the same part of the surface at recurring intervals of 59d 1h 28m. A few approximations alone will be found in these pages, especially as a little practice with the map will render identification easy : the following considerations, however, may be useful to the beginner :—

The relief of the surface will be stronger as it is nearer to the terminator, and all delicate and difficult objects are best seen near the sunrise or sunset of the Moon, which, like the corresponding times of the Earth, abound with grand and beautiful effects of light and shade. Every little irregularity then assumes temporary importance ; inconsiderable hillocks, minute craters, low banks, narrow canals, become visible in the horizontal ray ; rising grounds or soft valleys

[1] Proctor, *The Moon*, 197.

seem to start into existence, the outer slopes of craters
advance into the surrounding levels, larger masses appear
in exaggerated prominence,

> Majoresque cadunt de montibus umbræ.

These broad and deep shadows often taper off to such slender
points, that a caution may be requisite, not to infer anything
extravagant respecting the sharpness of the form which casts
them.   It may be questioned whether anything in the Moon
exceeds the acuteness of the Swiss Finsteraarhorn, or the
abruptness of the Pic du Midi d'Ossau in the Pyrenees.   An
oblique light cast upon a rough surface, modelled in clay
or dough, will show how disproportioned oftentimes is the
shadow to the reality; and the same experiment will prove
to us that in many cases the true relief will be unknown till
the shadow on either side of the object has been examined.
The intense blackness of the lunar shadows gives an effect
which must be strangely contrasted with a distant prospect
of our Earth.   Here, a highly reflective and vapour-charged
atmosphere surrounds all objects with a constant illumination, beginning before sunrise and outlasting sunset; there,
the Sun goes up and down in noonday strength, and the
shadows are unrelieved by any reflection from a sky which
must be almost black all day: every mountain produces
utter darkness where it intercepts the Sun; and every crater,
while its ring is glittering like snow in the rising or setting
beam, is filled with midnight shade.   Dawes, alone, by employing the contracted field of his solar eye-piece, has
traced a very faint glimmering in these depths, produced
by reflection from the opposite sunlit cliffs.[1]   The termi-

---

[1] Schm. twice saw the innermost cavity of the peculiarly shaped
crater 399 feebly illuminated at sunrise, as though filled with mist.
He prefers an explanation identical with that of Dawes; but qu. as
to its adequacy under the circumstances? Another large crater near

nator is, indeed, marked through the grey plains by a narrow shadowy border, and the tops of the mountains just appearing or vanishing in the night-side are somewhat deficient in brightness; but this is the 'penumbra,' or partial illumination, due to a portion of the Sun's disc, while the rest is beneath the horizon. In other respects the glittering sharpness of the Moon's sunrise, or sunset, is widely contrasted with the softness of our own skies. But though it is then that we must watch for minute details, for large objects we shall find the relief too broad and partial; unbroken night conceals the greater cavities, and the shade of loftier summits renders lower ranges invisible. Not till day descends among the terraces of the one, or creeps down over the shoulders and along the slopes of the other, does their true structure come out; and their distinctness increases while their minuter neighbours decline into insignificance.

L.,[1] and B. and M., have done admirably well in their delineations. Yet a little experience will show that they have not represented all that may sometimes be seen with a good common telescope. My own opportunities, even when limited to a $3\frac{7}{10}$-in. aperture, satisfied me, not only how much remains to be done, but how much a little willing perseverance might do, provided there were some knowledge of the laws of perspective and shadow, and a due attention to the direction of the incident and reflected light: some facility in design would also be very desirable, and, if

S. pole also twice showed a similar internal twilight.—Compare appearance of 132, *Eng. Mech.* 1871, Dec. 25; 1872, Mar. 15.

[1] His general map is valuable, and not expensive; but the scale, $15\frac{1}{4}$ inches, is rather small, and the deviations from circularity in the craters exaggerated. The discontinuance of his 'Sections,' on a 3-ft. (French) scale, from failing sight, was long a serious hindrance to selenography; but the missing portions have been recovered, and recently published under the careful editorship of Schm.

proportion is tolerably preserved, a number of rough sketches under varied lights taken at the eye-piece, and carefully compared with the original, would be more serviceable than one or two finished drawings. Detail being the great object, a small portion only should be attempted at once; this will not merely be easier and more pleasant, but will avoid the change in the shadows, which is considerable near the terminator during a long-continued delineation. The record, to be of value, must possess four data: 1. *Hour of Observation;*—2. *Moon's Age*, reckoned from or to the nearest change;—3. *Position of Terminator* referred to well-marked spots, some nearly in the latitude of the observed region; others a good way N. and S. of it, so as to show the direction of illumination, which is seldom exactly at right angles to the lunar meridian;—4. *Libration*, indicated (i.) in longitude, by time reckoned to or from nearest perigee or apogee; or both may be specified; (ii.) in latitude, by Moon's latitude at the time; these particulars being taken from 'Nautical Almanac,' and the last reduced to the hour of observation. More than this cannot be ascertained without a micrometer or calculation; but this is enough for the comparison of delineations. If the last two data are nearly coincident in any observations, the angles under which the landscape is illuminated and viewed differ so little that any variation in its details must be referred to either (1) inadvertence or mistake in the observer; (2) actual change in the Moon's surface; or (3) obscuration or deception in her atmosphere. Schr. relates so many instances of the latter kind that, even if we reject the confirmation of the keen-eyed but fanciful G., it seems difficult to follow B. and M. in disposing of them all as errors of observation; nor does Klein, a very accurate observer, think the inquiry by any means unworthy of special notice. One important caution seems not to

(*Photograph from the Mount Wilson and Palomar Observatories*)

Moon, region of Copernicus. 200-inch photograph.

(Photograph from the Lick Observatory, Mount Hamilton, California)

Moon, age 7 days (first quarter).

Moon, age 22 days (last quarter).

(Photograph from the Lick Observatory, Mount Hamilton, California)
Moon, age 14 days (full).

have occurred to Schr. : the change of lunar seasons, slight as it is, somewhat affects the direction of the shadows; and the variations of foreshortening from libration may make them more or less visible; and thus some apparent discrepancies might be reconciled. With large apertures, a lightly tinted screen-glass works well; possibly the use of different colours might bring out some curious result.[1]

The map in the present edition is that of W. Goodacre. This was originally drawn on a single sheet 77 inches in diameter, and subsequently reproduced in 25 sections on a scale of 60 inches to the Moon's diameter. It depends for its accuracy on more than a thousand measured points made by the late S. A. Saunder. This map represents the results of the author's own observations extending over 30 years, and incorporates much of the work of every known observer published during the same period. A photographic atlas of the Moon was published in 1904 by W. H. Pickering. The photos. were taken with a 12-in. O. G., and a focus of 135 ft. The tube was fixed, and the image reflected from an 18-in. mirror, driven by electric motors. The image of the Full Moon is 15·7 in. in diameter. The aperture of the O. G. was usually reduced to 6 in.

The points of the *Lunar Compass* must be mastered before we can use the map. Astronomers have fixed these from their relative, not intrinsic, position; that is, the several portions of the disc are named from the adjacent quarter of the sky when the moon is on the meridian. Hence N. and S. occupy the top and bottom, but E. and W. are reversed, as compared with terrestrial maps: the former being to the left, the latter to the right. But maps of the Moon usually represent its telescopic—that is, inverted—

[1] See De la Rue, on increased distinctness during advance of lunar eclipse, *Monthly Notices*, xxv. 276.

appearance, so that we shall find S. at top, N. at bottom, E. to right, W. to left. The meridians and parallels of latitude have been omitted, except the 1st Meridian and Equator, which divide it, like the original, into Four Quadrants: these are called by B. and M., the 1st or NW., 2nd or NE., 3rd or SE., 4th or SW. Quadrant. A selection of the most interesting objects in each follows, from materials furnished by the 'Mond' of these astronomers and retaining their arrangement: additions are made from other sources; but all statements not otherwise authenticated depend upon their authority. In the more remarkable instances, their measures of height and depth are given; these were ascertained by the lengths of the shadows—a method previously employed with less accuracy by Schr.; capable of much precision on favourable ground, but elsewhere uncertain. For our present purpose round numbers will be a fully sufficient approximation.[1]

First, or North-West, Quadrant.*

MARE CRISIUM (A). We begin with a conspicuous dark plain, the most completely bounded on the Moon, and visible to the naked eye: apparently elliptical from foreshortening, but really oval the other way, being about 281 m. from N. to S., 355 from E. to W., and containing about 66,000 square m., or $\frac{1}{94}$th part of the visible hemisphere—more than half as much again as the area of England and Wales. Its grey hue has a trace of green in the Full; this has also been represented by the late talented Astronomer Royal for Scotland, C. Piazzi Smyth,

---

[1] Minuteness of numerical detail in astronomical results should not be misunderstood. It represents no natural fact, but only the care bestowed upon measurement.

* [An Index Map of the Moon, divided into quadrants, is given between pages 158 and 159.—M.W.M.]

in two beautiful figures taken during the increase and wane.
On rare occasions it has been seen by Schr., and in part by
B. and M., speckled with minute dots and streaks of light:
something of this kind I saw with a fluid achromatic, 1832,
July 4, near I. Quarter. A similar appearance was noticed
by Slack, and Ingall, 1865. It would be difficult to say
why, if these are permanent, they are so seldom visible—a
suggestive, though at present unintelligible, phenomenon.
The surface is deeply depressed, lower than Mare Fœcunditatis and M. Tranquillitatis. Many low ridges cross it in a
N. and S. direction; but in this, as in many other cases, it
must be remembered that those lying E. and W. would be
imperceptible for want of shadow. The boundary mountains are in part very steep and lofty. The PROMONTORIUM
AGARUM (1) rises about 11,000 ft.; a mountain SE. of Picard,
15,600 ft., rivalling our Mont Blanc. On W. edge, Schr.
delineated a crater called by him ALHAZEN, which he constantly employed to measure the existing libration : he saw
in it after a time unaccountable changes, and since, it has
been said, it cannot be made out. B. and M. think he
confounded it with a crater (2) lying farther S.; G., however, drew it in 1824; the question which was debated
among Kunowsky, Köhler, and others, has been cleared up
by Birt, who has recovered Schr.'s crater, between two lofty
mountains; the cause, however, of its greater obviousness in
Schr.'s earlier days still offers some difficulty. The plain
contains several moderate-sized craters—the largest, PICARD
(4), S. of which G. saw some curious regular white ridges
like ramparts : while on the W., Birt and Ingall have
pointed out a remarkable bright patch, which subsequently
faded to a great extent, and which, according to Espin,
marks a depression. The next crater N. (PEIRCE) has
a very minute interior craterlet, discovered by Schm.—a

test-object. The next crater N. of this (PEIRCE A) Birt has sometimes been unable to find. There are also several very minute craters in the level. Near the E. edge where there is a pass in the great surrounding ridge between **450** and **451**, lie several small, but in part lofty mountains,[1]— islands, as it were ;—among these Schr. describes singular changes, which he refers to an atmosphere ; B. and M. consider them merely varied illumination, or pass them by as unworthy of attention. Succeeding observers may revise, even if they ultimately acquiesce in, this summary decision. Schr. was a bad draughtsman, used an inferior measuring apparatus, and now and then made considerable mistakes ; but I have never closed the simple and candid record of his most zealous labours with any feeling approaching to contempt ; and though there may be truth in the assertion of B. and M., that he was biassed by the desire of discovering changes, they, possibly, were not themselves free from an opposite prepossession.

A long winding cleft is suspected to cross the centre of A.

Central hills seldom occur in craters here.

A may be well seen about 5^d after New, or 3^d after Full ; in the latter case it is a magnificent spectacle when crossed by the terminator and partially covered in by the vast shadows of the mountains, from which Schr. considered that those on NE. side must be at least 16,000 or 17,000 ft. high.

This astronomer has inserted in his work a marvellous observation by Eysenhard, a pupil of Lambert, 1774, July 25. The night being perfectly clear, he saw with a common 4-ft. refractor four bright spots in A, then intersected by the terminator, two of which only—those on the day-side—

---

[1] These are ill-figured in the great map, and B. and M. have given a separate representation of them in their *Mond*.

can be identified; after noticing them at times for 2ʰ, he found all at once that the part of the terminator in A had a slow reciprocating motion, completed in 5 or 6ᵐ, between these pairs of spots, each pair being touched by it in turn. Two other refractors of 7 and 12 ft. showed this appearance with equal distinctness, and it was observed for 2ʰ, the terminator in X remaining perfectly still. A very strange story, yet Lambert seems to have believed it ; and perhaps we cannot pronounce it wholly incredible in the face of an equally wonderful and perfectly well-attested retrogression in a satellite of Jupiter, to be described hereafter.

Between FIRMICUS (7) and the limb, halfway in mean libration, are some curved dark streaks (*Paludes Amaræ*, Hevel), in which B. and M. found singular variations, resulting, as they admit, possibly (not probably) from periodical vegetation.

CLEOMEDES (12), a walled plain 78 m. in diameter, includes a small crater (Cleomedes A), brilliant, but not always alike defined, in Full; Schr. had found it not always equally visible. He speaks of many variations in the interior level, which he represents rather differently from B. and M.—G. found its W. part marked out into many rhomboids—squares in perspective, since confirmed in part by Ne.

BURCKHARDT (19), 35 m. in diameter, lies 12,700 ft. below its E. wall.

GEMINUS (20), 54 m. broad, has a ring 12,300[1] ft. high on E., 16,700 ft. on W. side.[2]

---

[1] By a singular coincidence, in reducing as usual French to English measure, the resulting number was 1, 2, 3, 4, 5 with 6 in the first place of decimals. The chances against such a sequence must have been extremely great; but it exemplifies a principle, not always kept in mind, that so long as a thing is *possible*, it must *sometimes* occur.

[2] And two distinct clefts traversing the inner slope of the SW.

BERNOUILLI (21), equally deep, is very precipitous.

GAUSS (22) is a walled plain, 110 m. long. B. and M. describe the fine effect of sunset upon its ring. It has a grand central mountain, which must at times command a glorious view, across a plain of 50 m. covered with night, to illuminated peaks all round the horizon, above which the Sun on one side, and the Earth on the other, are slowly coming into sight.[1]

STRUVE (25), a slight depression, is remarkably dark in Full.

ENDYMION (27), a walled plain 78 m. in diameter, is, in some states of libration, very dark in Full; the irregular wall rises W. to more than 15,000 ft., overtopping all but the very highest peaks of our Alps. I have seen it in grand relief $3^d 7^h$ after New, $2^d 9^h$ after Full. Between 27, 28, and 29 is a curious double parallelism, objects all ranging SSW. or SE.

ATLAS (28), a superb amphitheatre 55 m. broad, 460 square m. in area; its ring rich in terraces and towers, rising 11,000 ft. on N.; a very dark speck in interior, where I have also seen some clefts with Bird's 12-in. silvered reflector.[2]

HERCULES (29), a worthy companion to it, 46 m. across. The ring, in places double, includes a small crater of subsequent date, and according to Schr. a central mountain, not seen by others. Look for this pair 5 or 6^d after New, $3\frac{1}{2}^d$ after Full.[3]

and NE. walls respectively, and extending for some distance on the floor.

[1] There is a long range of hills running in a meridional direction on the floor, and two large rings on the S. side of it.

[2] There is a drawing of Atlas (and Hercules), showing these clefts and other details on the floor, in *Sel. Journal*, vol. v. No. 53.

[3] There are two small contiguous craters on the SE. wall, another

FRANKLIN (32). Several incomplete rings lie hereabout, all open N.

DEMOCRITUS (38), a deep ring-plain, lies at the beginning of a region remarkable for net-like and often quadrangular forms. Craters and ring-plains are not, however, absent. Among the latter the dark and level interior of MOIGNO (408) bears a small but conspicuous crater.

MARE HUMBOLDTIANUM (B), discovered by B. and M.,[1] is rather more than half as large as M. Crisium, but close to the limb, above which the peaks of its W. border sometimes appear in profile, in one part 16,000 ft. high.

In this region, in certain states of libration, occur two singular flattenings of the limb, divided by a ridge. These, with another, were discovered by Key, 1863. One of them extends for 10°.

GIOJA (44) is the nearest visible formation to N. Pole, which, however, owing to foreshortening, is at some distance beyond it.

MOUNT TAURUS (51) is a lofty range, containing the terraced crater RŒMER (52), 26 m. wide, 11,600 ft. deep.

POSIDONIUS (54). This walled plain, nearly 62 m. across, includes several small details, in which Schr. found repeated

at the foot of the SW. wall, and many minute objects in the interior. See Plate xxii. vol. vi. *Journal* L.A.S.

[1] Part, however, is shown on Russell's Lunar Globe (1797), beautiful as a work of art, poor in detail. A larger globe by the same observer, in relief, is preserved in the S. Kensington Museum. Mme. Mädler modelled a lunar globe in wax. Mme. Witte, a Hanoverian lady, has completed a very perfect globe in relief, from B. and M.'s observations and her own. There is at Bonn a magnificent relief of the Moon, 18 Paris ft. in diameter, executed under Schm.'s direction by Dickert (1854). Sir Chr. Wren, when Savilian Professor at Oxford, made a lunar globe in relief at the request of the Royal Society and by command of Charles II., who placed it in his cabinet. We must hope that it has been carefully preserved.

changes : the shadow in the bright little crater was abnormal in length, and once replaced by a grey veil. B. and M. never saw anything unusual. Schm. found it once, but under bad circumstances, 1849, Feb. 11, shadowless : so G. 1821, April 7. It has been finely drawn by Gaudibert, *English Mechanic*, 1872, March 1. It contains 7 clefts. A good object about 6^d after New.

LITTROW (55) and MARALDI (56) show the SSW. parallelism of the vicinity : VITRUVIUS (57), with a very dark interior, lies in a mottled region, in one place slightly tinged with blue.

MOUNT ARGÆUS (58), a small range gradually rising from W. to a summit, ranked by Schr. as high as the loftiest of our Pyrenees (N. gives 8400 ft.), and then sinking, on its NE. face, in an amazing precipice, down to the wide plain. It is remarkable for the spire of shade which it casts at sunrise ; but it has been unfairly treated by B. and M. being omitted from their nomenclature, which contains many very inferior hills : as it is so interesting an object, I hope I am not guilty of presumption in assigning a name to it, chosen from its vicinity to 51. It requires close watching, as the shadow rapidly loses its slender point ; look for it when the ring of 61 just heaves in sight beyond the terminator. I have seen it thus 4^d 21^h after New.

MACROBIUS (59), nearly 42 m. broad, sinks almost 13,000 ft.

PROCLUS (60) has a ring, next to 148 the most luminous part of the Moon ; yet scarcely ever visible on the dark side ; very much less so than many duller objects. B. and M. ascribe this to the narrowness of the wall. It is the centre of several bright streaks, not very easily seen.

PALUS SOMNII (F), an uneven, defined, always distinguishable surface, has a peculiar tint, perhaps yellowish-brown, unlike the simple grey of MARE TRANQUILLITATIS (G). The latter in Full is sometimes strewed with very small bright points.

PLINIUS (61), a terraced ring, 32 m. in diameter, filled with hillocks. N. lies a broad cleft, with a smaller one farther out, and a very minute one between them.[1]

MENELAUS (70), a very steep crater about 6600 ft. deep; with a ring very brilliant in Full. All the ridges running from it trend SW., and this parallelism reaches over a great district, including most of 85, 68, L, and the vicinity. Several bright streaks issue from 70—one is a continuation of a ray from 180, extending in all more than 1850 m. Here was one of Herschel I.'s pseudo-volcanoes.

MARE SERENITATIS (H). This wide and beautiful plain is nearly circular, about 433 m. from N. to S., 424 from E. to W.; the interior appeared at Full to B. and M. of a clear light green, unnoticed by Schr. and L., and not easily seen even by its discoverers; it is set in a border of dark grey, and bisected by a straight whitish streak, invisible, like most of its class, near the terminator. Towards the W. edge of the plain is a curious long low serpentine ridge, discovered and figured by Schr., but only well seen from its shadow near the terminator. I have found it thus between 5 and 6[d] after New. A little E. of it I have seen a lower one with reverse flexures.

LINNÉ (74). A small crater, described by L. as 'very deep,' and by B. and M. as 'deep,' but discovered by Schm. to have entirely lost that character, and to resemble a *whitish cloud*, surrounding a most minute elliptic crater, which I have seen beautifully on rare occasions with 9⅓-in. mirror.[2] This

---

[1] There is a sketch of Plinius and the associated clefts in the *Eng. Mec.* 1882, Feb. 3.

[2] Small deep crater well seen at Bristol on Oct. 17, 1905, with

very interesting spot has undergone a rigorous scrutiny, and opinions are still divided, owing to some want of explicitness in the earlier records. The balance, however, seems decidedly in favour of actual change : and this and many other spots would have been more carefully observed, could it have been foreseen that questions would subsequently be raised about them.

CAUCASUS (75). This grand mountain mass rises into insulated peaks, suitably termed 'aiguilles' by B. and M., as lofty as any on the Moon, those on the limbs excepted, and reaching 18,000 or 19,000 ft. Their narrow shadows are drawn out into fine points—a superb spectacle, which I have seen about I. Quarter. Craters are very rare here.

EUDOXUS (77) and ARISTOTELES (78), a noble pair of craters, not easily found in Full, in a region sprinkled as it were with luminous dust. The terraced wall of 77, 11,300 ft. above the W. interior, is on that side crowned by two turrets of 15,000 ft. Etna, as Schr. observes, would stand in this great cavity. 78 is more than 50 m. broad, nearly as deep as 77, but with a much richer wall. The interior of both resembles the surrounding country more than is usual. I have seen a row of 4 or 5 craterlets in 78, running SW. from the central hill—a test-object. 78 is very remarkable for rows of minute hillocks lying NE., NW., and SW., in lines pointing to the crater—the finest specimen of this not uncommon arrangement : it is less distinct round 77. It requires very favourable light, and is difficult for the student. I have seen it, with wide SW. libration, about I. Quarter. S. and SW. of 77 the surface down to H is thronged with hillocks, and W. especially, craterlets innumerable ; on E. these mounds reach to 75. Many small craters and a little

12½-in. If the *white cloud* of Linné is 8 miles in diameter the involved crater would be about 2 miles in its greatest width.—(D.)

cleft (crater-row, Schm.) NE. of 78 are omitted by B. and M.

GREAT VALLEY OF ALPS. An extraordinary cleft, figured by Bianchini in his work on Venus; a circumstance unnoticed alike by Schr., B. and M., and Schm. About 83 m. long, and from $3\frac{1}{2}$ to $5\frac{3}{4}$ m. broad, it breaks in a straight line through the very loftiest Alps, with precipitous sides and a depth of at least 11,500 ft., in which Mont Perdu or the Vignemale of the Pyrenees would disappear. The bottom is very flat, but high powers according to Klein show landslips from the edges. It is always easily found. Between this valley, 79 and I, lies a curious region all sprinkled with hillocks: B. and M. estimated them at 700 or 800 at least. I once saw them finely developed at I. Quarter, in a 20-ft. achr. by Slater, of $14\frac{3}{4}$-in. aperture.[1]

ALPS (80), a lofty and exceedingly steep chain, rising into separate peaks : one of the highest, the Mont Blanc of Schr. (next to which our number stands), reaches, he says, to 14,000 ft. B. and M. reduce it below 12,000 ft. Close beneath its E. foot, Schr. perceived, 1789, Sept. 26, on the dark side of the moon, a small speck of light, like a 5 m^g. star to the 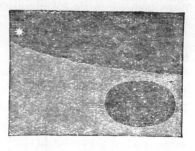 naked eye, which having been verified in position, and kept in view for fully 15^m, disappeared irrecoverably : the round shadow, sometimes black, at others grey, which he subsequently found in the day-side in or near its place, was

---

[1] The valley is crossed about midway by a cleft which is easily recognised, even under a high light. Detailed drawings of the formation will be found in the L.A.S. *Journal*, vol. iii. pp. 20 and 72.

probably nothing new. A copy of his figure is here given. Strange to say, 1865, Jan. 1, Grover recovered this bright spot, or one very near its site, with only 2 in. of aperture, and saw it unchanged like a 4 m^g. star to the naked eye, but rather larger, for fully 30^m.

PALUS NEBULARUM (I) and PALUS PUTREDINIS (K) are for the most part so level, that mounds of 50 or 60 ft. would be rendered visible by their shadows near the terminator.

CASSINI (81), a curious ring-plain; the narrow wall encloses a scarcely depressed space, and a deep ring-plain, which has a considerable irregularity within, unnoticed by B. and M., but not new, as I saw traces of it in 1826.[1] The ring casts long spires of shade about I. Quarter. An insulated mountain E. of it in the plain (477, *Mons Christi*, Hevel), usually very bright, was once seen by Schm. near lunar sunset of a remarkable dark grey. G. had noted many changes in its form and colour, which he ascribed to lunar clouds.

THEÆTETUS (82) would take in Snowdon twice over, with still depth to spare.

ARISTILLUS (83), a very magnificent crater, 34 m. broad, 11,000 ft. deep on E. side, has a fine central mountain, which I saw, with 5½ in. of aperture, as three parallel ridges. The ring stands up nobly from the plain, and is flanked on all sides (as Schr. perceived) by radiating banks resembling lava-streams, or currents of ejected blocks or scoriæ,[2] evidently posterior to the surrounding level: in suggestive

[1] There is also a conspicuous deep crater on the SE. side of the floor.

[2] The volcanoes of Java have all ribbed sides; but these are ascribed to erosion by torrents. The grand volcano in the island of Luzon ejects red-hot stones forced up over the edges of the crater, and rolling down amid showers of fire on every side of the cone.

contrast to 120. I have seen them well about 1ᵈ after
I. Quarter.[1]

AUTOLYCUS (84), its smaller companion, is nearly as deep,
with a similar but less evident radiation. This pair of craters
illustrates a not uncommon arrangement, of two rings in the
same meridian; very similar in every respect; if unequal
in diameter as 3 to 4, and the smaller lying S.; from 18 to
36 m. apart; and connected by low ridges running SW.

APENNINES (85). This very extensive chain is more like
the mountains of the Earth than is usually the case.[2] Its
length, according to Schr., is nearly 640 m., great part of it
lying in the next Quadrant. Its SW. side ascends gradually
—the opposite aspect breaks down at once in awful preci-
pices of stupendous height, casting a shade through 83 m.,
or losing the last ray as far beyond the terminator. Huygens (90), the loftiest peak, rises, according to Schr., no bad
measurer, to 21,000 ft. B. and M. think he confounded
two adjacent summits, and give 18,000 ft.; Schm. prefers
18,500 : in any case a superb elevation. On its apex is a
minute crater. Other summits, though inferior, are yet of
extraordinary height and steepness : Hadley (87), facing 75,
15,000 ft.—Bradley (89) 13,600 ft.—Wolf (92) 11,000 ft.
The gradual entrance of the range into sunshine about
I. Quarter is a glorious spectacle; and its projection into
the dark side, which may be seen without telescopic aid,
probably gave rise to the early idea mentioned by Plutarch,
that the Moon was mountainous : from its abruptness it
does not lose all real shadow till 3ᵈ before Full. With very
few craters, it consists of ridges and peaks not to be

[1] There is a large obscure ring a little N. of Aristillus, which is an
interesting object under a low sun.

[2] Schm. considers the resemblance not striking, and notes the
absence of depressions similar to terrestrial river-valleys. Ne., however, asserts the reverse.

numbered by thousands in large instruments : Schr. detected
this ; M. says it would take the opportunities of three or
four years to delineate all the details which a power of 800
or 1000 will show.

CLEFT OF HYGINUS. A fine specimen of these furrows
lies fortunately in an excellent position in the MARE VA-
PORUM (L), a tract of which the dusky streakiness has often
interested me about I. Quarter. The cleft is conspicuous
enough to yield to a power of 40 in a good telescope, under
any illumination. It begins from NE. at the foot of a long
low hill, as a flat valley about 1½ m. wide by 9 m. long,
where I have found (with 5½-in. aperture) that it receives a
branch from E. : having then contracted to about ¾ m. with
precipitous sides and great proportionate depth, it passes
through 4 minute craters (or, as Ne. and Klein think, mere
enlargements), bends a little, receives another short branch
from E., and traverses Hyginus (93), but at a lower level, and
as a bank. B. and M. once saw, in the wane, its edges bridg-
ing the black cavity as two narrow bright lines ; and Schm.'s
large map represents it so : in this position I have not seen
it well, but repeatedly in the increase with 5½-in. achrom.
and 9⅓-in. reflect., when the bank appears cut down before
reaching the E. side : once I saw the S. of these lines, but
cut off at its E. end ; at another time the N., perhaps continuous, while a similar line diverged from the same point
W. to the NE. side of the crater. A bay at the N. end of
93, shown by L. and G., but missed by B. and M., seems the
result of a smaller explosion. This curious spot should be
well examined with the most powerful means. B. and M.
describe and figure a wall to 93 ; Schr., L., G., and myself
(even with reflector) see none.[1]   The cleft then, after

---

[1] Schm. drew it, and thinks there are no lunar craters without banks.
Such 'explosion-craters,' however, exist in Java, the Eifel, and Auvergne.

touching on 5 very small craters and two broad hills, becomes wider and shallower, and ends after about 106 m. much as it began. S. of this cleft are two small dark spots, one larger, and one of a greenish hue: on the N. side is a region worthy of notice for its change of colour: in Full it is tolerably luminous: at Quadratures, there is near 93 a large blackish spot, covering two ranges of hills and the vale between. Here B. and M., most unprejudiced if not oppositely-prejudiced witnesses, admit a variation of colour not dependent merely on the angle of reflection, and possibly connected with changes like those of our seasons. Of late years a considerable depression, without ring, but full of shadow at the terminator, has become visible in this region, but is of difficult identification without the drawings in the 'Selenographical Journal.' It is called HYGINUS N.

CLEFT OF ARIADÆUS. This, discovered like the preceding by Schr., lies W. of it: it is longer, broader, and probably deeper than its neighbour, with which, as I found, 1866, April 21, it is connected by a branch N. of 102.[1] It seems to pass under the two mountains nearest its W. end, but others it cleaves visibly, though greatly narrowed by one lofty hill. The accurate L. saw it passing through them all, and traced it for 175 m. I have observed it interrupted, but not exactly as B. and M.: I find it also double for a short distance—two halves not in the same line, with overlapping ends. G. detected a minute prolongation of it far through Mare Tranquillitatis, subsequently seen by Kunowsky, Birt, and Freeman. This and the preceding cleft may be looked for about I. Quarter.[2]

[1] This was discovered by G.—a difficult object which Klein at times found invisible, at others very distinct.

[2] Some ancient crater-rings have been seen on the site of this cleft with the great Lick Telescope.

TRIESNECKER (94) is surrounded by several minute clefts intersecting and uniting with each other in a manner of which only one other instance is known (near 228 ; Schm.).[1] L. detected some of them, but G. drew a surprising number. With 5½-in. I found more than in B. and M.; one cleft double, with overlapping ends. Gaudibert has traced others. E. of this spot L. found some curious streaks and markings believed to be now changed in form.[2]

MANILIUS (95), a beautiful cavity, 25 m. in diameter and 7700 ft. deep, has a broad luminous terraced crater- and peak-besprinkled ring. Being visible on the night-side, it was one of Herschel I.'s imaginary volcanoes in eruption. Schr. has seen variations, not easily accounted for, in the relative visibility of this and 70 in the earth-shine.

JULIUS CÆSAR (96) [3] and BOSCOVICH (98) are very dark enclosures, DIONYSIUS (99) and SILBERSCHLAG (101) very brilliant crater-rings.

Near the two fine craters AGRIPPA (102) and GODIN (103) [4] (which exemplify the remark under 84), Schr. once saw for a short time on the dark side, a minute point of light.

RHÆTICUS (104), an irregular crater, marks exactly the Moon's Equator, and is one of the few spots to which

[1] The interior of 232 may be added.

[2] See drawing of Triesnecker and Hyginus clefts in *Journal* L.A.S., vol. iii. p. 20.

[3] The wide valley on the W. of this formation is very noteworthy at sunrise. It probably represents a row of large depressions, the division walls of which have been partially destroyed. The low ridges and mounds a little E. of Sosigenes, forming in part the S. boundary of Julius Cæsar, appear to exhibit indications of denudation.

[4] There is a trumpet-shaped valley on the SW. flank of Godin which is very conspicuous when the E. wall of the formation is on the morning terminator.

the Sun and Earth may both be vertical.[1] (See another
Rhæticus, in a note on 112.)

SECOND, OR NORTH-EAST, QUADRANT.[*]

SCHRŒTER (106). This imperfect crater in an intricate district
where the levels are bright, the hills and valleys very dark
grey, darkest at Full, is the guide to a remarkable spot a
little N., the number on the map standing between the two
objects. Here, in 1822, G. discovered the regular formation
which at first attracted so much attention, and subsequently,
from the fanciful character of the observer, fell into unmerited
oblivion. The object, which he called 'Schröter' (a name
transferred by B. and M., when they could not find it, to the
nearest crater), and which some have maintained, notwithstanding its size, to be a work of art, is described by him as
a collection of dark gigantic ramparts, visible only near the
terminator, extending about 23 m. either way, and arranged
on each side of a principal meridional rampart in the centre,
from which they slope off SE. and SW. respectively, at an
angle of 45°, like the ribs of an alder leaf; those to the SW.
abutting on a meridional side-wall, beyond which Schwabe
and himself subsequently perceived their continuation:
frequently, however, traces only of the figure could be
discerned, as though it were obscured by clouds: from this
cause he supposed it had been quite misrepresented by the
careful L., though he had studied it for 6 months: some
years afterwards it appeared to have undergone a sudden
change, and subsequently G. himself could scarcely make it

[1] A coarse cleft or narrow valley running round the outer slope of
the E. wall, and apparently connected with the Triesnecker rill-system,
is an easy object under a low morning sun.

[*] [An Index Map of the Moon, divided into quadrants, is given
between pages 158 and 159.—M.W.M.]

out on some occasions, though at other times quite distinct: B. and M., notwithstanding great pains, were altogether unsuccessful, till in 1838, subsequently to the date of their map, they surveyed and measured the region with the Berlin achromatic of $9\frac{6}{10}$-in. aperture; then at last, among a number of curious labyrinthine details, of which their 'Beiträge' contains a view, 5 parallel valleys appeared side by side, each about 9 m. by $3\frac{1}{2}$, sloping all to SW., with prolongations in the same direction, giving very fairly half of G.'s figure—a remarkable attestation from an unfavourable quarter. But he could call many earlier witnesses, having shown it to several German philosophers; Prince Metternich at Vienna found it sooner than any one else from his description, and it was beautifully seen by Schm. and Schwabe. In England it does not seem to have been looked for, as though to justify G.'s taunt, 'The scientific John Bull here has gone empty away, and behaved himself about it just as his natural disposition led him.' This is, however, no longer true. Knott saw it, 1861, March 19: I caught it with $5\frac{1}{2}$-in., 1862, Feb. 7, a long way from the terminator, which passed through 121; and could even trace it the next day. I have several times seen it since, but never on, or near, the terminator. It has been finely seen by Whitley, 1870, June 7 and 8; and somewhat differently by Birmingham, 1871, March 29. It is a curious specimen of parallelism, but so coarse as to carry upon the face of it its natural origin, and it can hardly be called a difficult object.[1] A line from 211, through 106, carried as far again, finds it a little N. of its place in the map. An interesting drawing by Gaudibert is in *English Mechanic*, 1874, March 13.

SINUS ÆSTUUM (N). The absence of even the minutest

---

[1] Birt has referred to a similar formation in Auvergne, described by Scrope, *Extinct Volcanoes of Central France*, 162 (2nd edit.).

crater here is remarked as unique : but L. had shown one,
and M. subsequently picked out a few with the Dorpat
telescope. I have found two easy with $5\frac{1}{2}$-in.

ERATOSTHENES (110) and STADIUS (111), neighbours, the
former more than 37 m. broad, the latter 5 m. broader,
connected by a steep mountain of 4500 ft. (higher than any
land in the British Isles), are curiously contrasted : 110 has
a fine central hill, 111 is nearly level.   110 has a widely-
terraced wall of very irregular height ; the surrounding
ground is also very uneven ; so that on E. side it is 16,000 ft.
above the inner, 7500 ft. above the outer surface ; on W.
only 10,000 ft. and 3300 ft.   111 has such an insignificant
ring, about 130 ft. high, that B. and M. did not notice it
till after a three-years' search for *Riccioli's* Stadius, which,
being only a spot of local colour, they missed after all.   I
found, however, little difficulty with this ring.[1] Its interior,
as pointed out by Dobie, is curiously speckled, especially
S. and W., with minute craters, which have been supposed
to be on the increase.   Schm. (1849) counted 50, and
with the 14-ft. Berlin achr. found this region perforated
with the minutest craterlets ' like a sieve.' [2] 110 is about
as large as the county of Hereford, and lies intermediate
between most dissimilar regions.   Its Full-Moon aspect is
very unlike the description of B. and M., and should be
drawn and watched.

COPERNICUS (112).   One of the grandest craters, 56 m.
in diameter.   It has a central mountain (2400 ft. Schm.), two
of whose 6 heads are conspicuous; and a noble ring composed

---

[1] It has been traced, together with some of the features it includes,
when the terminator has advanced as far E. as Herodotus.

[2] Seventy craters within and about the border were detected in
the years 1885–86 with an $8\frac{1}{2}$-in Calver-Reflector. For notes relating to these and other details see L.A.S. *Journal*, vol. v. p. 221.

not only of terraces, but distinct heights separated by ravines:
the summit, a narrow ridge, not quite circular, rises 11,000 ft.
above the bottom—the height of Etna, after which Hevel
named it. Schm. gives it nearly 12,800 ft. with a peak of
13,500 ft. W., and an inclination in some few places of 60°.
The shadow of this peak on the E. terraces he once saw
reddish-brown and obviously indistinct. Piazzi Smyth
observed remarkable resemblances between the conchoidal
cliffs of the interior and those of the great crater of Teneriffe.
A mass of ridges leans upon the wall, partly concentric, partly
radiating; the latter are compared to lava, and the whole
is beautifully though anonymously figured in Herschel II.'s
'Outlines of Astronomy.' There is also a much larger
drawing by Se.: but this grand object requires, and would
well reward, still closer study. It comes into sight a day
or two after I. Quarter. Vertical illumination brings out
a singular cloud of white streaks related to it as a centre.
It is then very brilliant, and Klein remarks that some
portions have a bluish tinge. The ring sometimes resembles
a string of pearls: B. and M. once counted more than 50
specks. Schm. found the whole neighbourhood, even as far
as 144, studded with the minutest craters. In the direction
of 113, a great number of blackish points come out under
a high light; and Klein remarks that processes may be
going on there, of which a superficial observation detects
nothing.[1]

[1] To the SW. of 112 Hevel has figured 3 contiguous round dark
spots under the name of 'Lacus Herculeus.' Of these the NW.
was named by Riccioli 'Dominicus Maria,' the SW. 'Stadius,' and
the E. 'Rhæticus.' B. and M., puzzled in identification, owing probably to there being *Full-Moon* markings (though easy ones), dealt
summarily with this nomenclature; ignoring Dom. Maria, notwithstanding its claim of neighbourhood to the site 111; transferring
Stadius across it, without any intimation, *per saltum*, to that position;

CRATER-RANGES NEAR COPERNICUS. Between 110 and 112 lies one of the most curious districts in the Moon. Here, in strange contrast with the undisturbed Sinus Æstuum, B. and M. have shown 61 minute craters, believe that more than twice that number might be seen, and question whether any level ground is left : it is pierced ' like a sieve ' according to Schm., who reckons about 300. The greater part are arranged in ranges ; one row is very evident, where they stand so close that but for their partitions it would be a cleft, which indeed its N. end resembles. The telescope at Dorpat showed M., after his removal there, great part of the Hyginus cleft as a chain of confluent openings,[1] thus strengthening the idea that these forms may have had a common origin. This region, strangely missed by Schr., was discovered by G., who estimated its minute craters at 400 or 500 ft. in diameter; B. and M. give them about 6 times that size. They are easily seen, but the suitable illumination is fugitive : they should be looked for while the sun is rising on E. side of the wall of 112.

TOBIAS MAYER (117), 9700 ft. deep towards W., has a fine specimen of subsequent eruption by its side.

MILICHIUS (118).   Remarkably luminous in Full.

MARE IMBRIUM (0).   The largest of the circular plains,

and removing Rhæticus to 104, at some distance. The latter transposition led to a mistake in the first edition, which Knott has enabled me to rectify. It is this original Rhæticus, not 104, in which G· discovered one of his curious ' rampart-works ; ' and I should have given a copy of his figure in *Astr. Jahrb.* 1828, had he not himself condemned it. It was something like his ' Schröter ; ' a slightly curved line, with a little crater at one end, and a mound at the other, crossed by 4 shorter straight lines. A year later he complained that it had been greatly obscured ' selenospherically,' and seldom visible.

[1] W. of 93 I have, however, seen its bottom apparently quite flat under high illumination, with Bird's 12-in. silvered reflector.

ill-defined E., 5 times as large as M. Crisium : one half dark
and flat, the rest very irregular.

ARCHIMEDES (120). One of the most regular walled
plains, apparently more ancient than the surrounding level,
which seems to have nearly filled up its interior, and overflowed the lowest slope of its ring : though 50 m. in diameter,
it is depressed only about 650 ft.; the wall, averaging 4200 ft.
above the interior, carries several towers, the highest nearly
7400 ft. The plain appears smooth as a mirror, according
to B. and M., but is divided into 7 nearly parallel stripes of
unequal brightness. Observations, however, by Knott in
1860, and Gray in 1880, indicate changes which deserve
special attention. There are minute craters in it : G. saw
one, Knott 6 or 7. The outer slope of the wall is very complex ; a magnificent object against the rising or setting sun.[1]

LA HIRE (123), a small solitary mountain 4900 ft. high
(Schr.), inserted in the map of B. and M., and in the index
of their 'Mond,' but strangely omitted in the text. There
is nothing striking in its usual appearance, but it was twice
seen by Schr. under very different illumination so brilliant
as to glitter with rays like a star : he noticed also changes
in its form. G. never saw its radiant aspect, and thought
its shape entirely altered, and its size reduced, since Schr.'s
time. Schm. detected a craterlet on the summit. I once
found it on the terminator, 2^d 7^h after I. Quarter, the
brightest object in sight, and radiating as described by Schr.
At another time I noticed a similar hill, about $\frac{1}{3}$ of the
distance from 122 to 121, glittering on the terminator like
a star with rays.[2] Gerling (1844) found the same phenomenon in a peaked hill on S. side of 80, and Brodie (1865)

[1] More than 50 small objects have been detected on the floor by Gray
and others, including 4 crater-cones on the E. quarter of the interior.
[2] This has also been seen by Hunt, 1862.

close to 149. I have also seen 131, and a hill S. of it,
very brilliant in the like circumstances. Future observation
may decide whether this depends upon a peculiar angle of
reflection and vision, or on some changes in a lunar
atmosphere ; and on this account these objects are especially
recommended to the student.

EULER (125), 19 m. across and nearly 6000 ft. deep, is
conspicuous for its bright streaks.

CARLINI (128). In this neighbourhood Williams and
two others observed for $1\frac{1}{2}^h$, 1865, Nov. 24, on the dark side,
a distinct bright speck like an 8 m^g. star with $4\frac{1}{16}$-in. aperture.
This region should be mapped with special care.

HELICON (129) and its neighbour Helicon A (now LE
VERRIER, 425) form a curious twin crater, each 13 m. in
diameter, and of vast depth. Schr. has given the latter of
them 13,600 ft. ; its complete disappearance in Full,[1] while
129 remains conspicuous, is a striking instance of this
peculiarity, and may account for the entire omission of one
of them in the maps of Hevel and Riccioli. Did two small
craters, on the wall of 129 and the slope of 425, exist in B.
and M.'s time ? They are plainer than another which they
have given here. I have seen with 9-in. refl. a craterlet in
the centre of 129,—a test-object.[2]

PICO (131) is a very fine specimen of an insulated pyra-
mid, rising from a narrow base to 9600 ft. according to
Schr., reduced by B. and M. to 7000 ft. (nearer 8000, Schm.) :
on any estimate a magnificent sight from the surrounding
plain. Schm., however, thinks the profile would not be
very striking, quite inferior to the steeper of the Swiss

[1] Brodie finds (1865) that this is incorrect, and Gaudibert and
Dennett have seen 425 the brighter of the two.

[2] Helicon is traversed by a ridge from N. to S., which has considerably disturbed the walls, and rendered it a very interesting object
when it is on the morning terminator.

Alps, or even the Niesen above the Lake of Thun. S. of
410, where that number stands in our map, is a small crater
Pico B. B. and M. show a longish white spot S. of it,
which Schm. could never find.

PLATO (132). A slight magnifier shows this ' steel-grey '
spot, lying as a lagoon at the edge of O, and foreshortened
into an oval whose proportions vary from (3 to 5) to (4 to 5)
in the extremes of N. or S. libration, its distance from the N.
limb being in one case half of its amount in the other : such
optical variations must always be allowed for in making or
comparing delineations of objects not far from the limb.
The rampart, not a very connected one, and failing, as Schm.
remarks, in terraces, averages 3800 ft. E., something less W.,
where 3 towers crown it, the loftiest nearly 7000 ft., another
somewhat higher bulwark surmounting the E. side (Schm.
gives it 9000 ft.). A large winding cleft unnoticed by B.
and M. issues from a crater on the W. side, and runs for
some distance nearly parallel to the great valley of the
Alps. The very level interior, about 60 m. broad, and containing 2700 square miles, was described by B. and M. as
crossed by 4 lighter streaks from N. to S., and containing
3 or 4 specks ranking among the minutest of lunar objects.
G. detected 8. The central one is not difficult under a high

light, and, with at least 10 others, is
evidently a craterlet. Two are quite
close, like a double star (Dawes) : to
which Pratt has added a third. A
copy from B. and M.'s map is given
here,[1] as the local shading, considered very variable by G., was
found greatly changed by me (1855), and is so still.
Bianchini, Short, and Elger have seen some longitudinal

----

[1] These streaks have been omitted in their 2nd edition.

bright streaks at lunar sunrise. The light-specks have
been of late years very carefully studied by Pratt, Gledhill,
Elger, and others. By the former observer 37 have been
recorded (27 the greatest, 15 the average number at once),
as well as 30 or more streaks; and Birt's most accurate
comparison of the whole series shows that the visibility of
many of them is affected at times by some local cause.[1]
The colour also of the interior, unlike almost all other
similar spots, is found to darken progressively with the
increasing angle of sunshine, and even beyond the lunar
noon, as though connected with heat. Klein saw several
times in 1878 something like fog in the E. portion.[2] There
is a large landslip at SE. end of ring, which Shaler (Cambridge, U.S.) thinks may have resulted from the great
changes of temperature, possibly 1000°, between noon and
midnight.[3]

HARPALUS (133) has a wall rising 2800 ft. above the
plain, nearly 16,000 ft. above the chasm below.

SINUS IRIDUM (P), styled by B. and M. 'perhaps the
most magnificent of all lunar landscapes,' is a dark semi-
circular bay, level almost as water, wrinkled only by a few
slight ridges scarcely exceeding 100 ft. and encompassed by
abrupt and colossal cliffs, the promontories being upwards
of 140 m. apart. The ridge is crowded full of minute,
usually round summits, with numberless other objects: the
height is not conveniently measurable, but a point by no
means the loftiest, W. of SHARP (139), reaches about 15,000

---

[1] Many additional light spots and streaks have been subsequently
recorded by Mr. A. S. Williams.

[2] A similar observation was made by Ne. and Elger in 1871.

[3] Recent observations of Plato by Professor Pickering, at Arequipa,
tend to show that changes have taken place in the appearance of
some of the spots since they were systematically observed in the
years 1869 and 1870. See *Observatory*, vol. xv.

ft., and the great cape LAPLACE (134) rises some 9000 ft. abruptly from the plain. Between it and 132 is a strong NW. parallelism. P is in noble projection 2^d or 3^d after I. Quarter.

KEPLER (144), nearly 22 m. in diameter, sinks 10,000 ft. in the deepest part beneath a very low bright wall. It is the centre of a great ray-system, connected with that of 112. G. thought its aspect not always alike in the same illumination.

MARIUS (147). The interior of this cavity is both drawn and described by B. and M. as quite uniform. It contains, however, a minute white crater, seen by G. in 1825, and rediscovered by me in 1864, conspicuous in the lunar morning, though invisible in the evening. There is also a trace of some other object. A similar crater E. of the ring is not in Schr.'s figure. More than 100 grey hillocks, the loftiest little exceeding 1000 ft., lie in a narrow space NE. In the plain S. is said to be a most curious winding cleft, like the *cañons* of NW. America.[1]

ARISTARCHUS (148). The most brilliant crater in the Moon; quite dazzling in a large telescope, the steep central hill being the most vivid part. The ring is 28 m. across, on W. rising 7500 ft. above its inner, 2650 ft. above its outer foot; on E. it becomes a plateau, which connects it with a smaller and steeper crater, HERODOTUS (149). A curious serpentine valley will be noticed here, nowhere exceeding $2\frac{1}{2}$ m. in width (about $\frac{1}{3}$ m. deep, Schm.), not unlike a dry river-bed.[2] The reflective power of 148 is extraordinary,

[1] A drawing of this formation, showing four objects in the interior (including 'the minute white crater'), and three depressions on the S. border, will be found in the L.A.S. *Journal*, vol. vi. p. 278.

[2] Ne. has seen the high mountain a little way N. of 149 blurred and of a violet tint, when the surrounding objects were all sharp and white.

rendering it visible even to the naked eye on the bright
side, and with the telescope on the dark : one of Herschel I.'s very few errors was his taking it for a volcano in
eruption. Schr. pointed out this, but the mistake has been
since repeated by others. There are, however, as already
mentioned, variations in its light, noticed by Schr., for
which Smyth, who has seen it of every size, from a 6 to a
10 m^g. star, says it is difficult to account.[1] The bright
streaks around it in Full Moon are no more of the nature
of lava than they are elsewhere ; but I have seen it on the
terminator surrounded by wavy radiating streams. Schm.
has repeatedly found the 'nimbus,' or darker space round
the wall, of a violet hue, a tint that he has seen also
occasionally in the interior of 272 as well as in other
places, and which I have independently noticed (1867), at
least a bluish glare, under high illumination, near 302 and
325.[2] About 45 m. WNW. begins a little group of
mountains (490), the highest nearly 7800 ft. : these coming
into light about 3^d after I. Quarter are the 'harbingers' of
the great spot, conspicuous a day later. Birt remarks that
489, a mere ring in the map of B. and M., wears a very
different aspect now.

HEVEL (154), a walled plain 70 m. across, contains a
straight ridge, and an extensive convexity of surface; also
a small crater, considered by Schr., but on inadequate
ground, to be new. There are some remarkable cross clefts
on its floor and W. wall.[3]

[1] See p. 93, *antea*.

[2] There could be no suspicion of secondary spectrum, as the reflector was employed. Schm. has sometimes found blue light on the
peaks of mountains beyond the terminator, as well as in the interior
of 112 and 180, and in other situations.

[3] These clefts are on the W. of Lohrmann (153), a smaller ring
immediately S. of Hevel.

ANAXAGORAS (168), 31 m. broad, and very white, includes a great mountain not in the middle. It is a streak-centre.

Between TIMÆUS (170) and FONTENELLE (171) is a good deal of parallelism, and adjoining 171 on W. is one of the most curious instances of it: a nearly square enclosure foreshortened into a lozenge, whose rampart-like boundaries, according to B. and M., 'throw the observer into the highest astonishment.' They are very unequal in height, and one is little more than a light-streak; yet they are so regular that it is scarcely possible to imagine them natural, till we find that they are 64 m. long, 250 to 3200 ft. high, and 1 m. or more thick. There are parallel ridges in the interior, and in one place the form of a perfect cross: unfortunately, it lies in such a position that years, as B. and M. observe, may pass without a good view of it. I have often looked for it in vain. Birmingham has been more successful.

E. of the table-land ROBINSON (413), are 3 curious *dark* mountains, about 5900 ft. high.

PYTHAGORAS (176) is the deepest walled plain in the Quadrant, nearly 17,000 ft. on SE. side.

THIRD, OR SOUTH-EAST QUADRANT.

THIS includes the metropolitan crater of the Moon, TYCHO (180), a most perfect specimen of the lunar volcano, visible even to the naked eye in Full, and roughly figured by Galileo in the earliest telescopic representations. Its diameter is 54 m., its depth 17,000 ft. or nearly 3 m., so that the summit of our Mont Blanc would drop beneath the ring: the height of its fine central hill, 5000 ft.[1] (6000 Schm.),

---

[1] A smaller hill close to it on the W. is omitted by B. and M., though readily seen. Birt rediscovered it, but it appears in D.'s

ranging nearly with the terraces, from 3 to 5 rows of which border the inner slope of the narrow wall. This noble object lies among so many competitors that it is not always immediately identified by an unpractised eye near the terminator, a day or two after I. Quarter; but as the Sun rises higher upon it, its pre-eminence becomes more and more evident. Its vicinity is thronged with hillocks and small craters, so that for a long distance not the smallest level spot can be found; further off, the craters increase, till the whole surface resembles a colossal honeycomb. At 180 commences the largest of the systems of rays, extending over fully $\frac{1}{4}$ of the visible hemisphere; one ray passes through H, almost to the opposite limb. Everywhere the visibility of the streaks is the converse of that of the shadows, so that many great ring-mountains which are overspread by these rays become totally imperceptible under high illumination. In photograms, however, they are less difficult of recognition —a singular fact. The streaks have no connection whatever with the form of the surface, are not in the least elevated or depressed, and resemble nothing on the Earth. In Full the central hill and wall of 180 are brilliant, the interior dark, as well as an exterior zone, beyond which a light cloud forms the base of the streaks. Their appearance reminds me of a vast net gathered up round a circular opening.[1]

HESIODUS (187) guides the eye to a cleft E. of it, in the M. NUBIUM (S).[2]

map. Gaudibert has detected a curious crevice passing along the inner NE. slope, crossing the crest, and running down the outer SE. face of the wall with a branch inside, and another outside the rampart. Birt had at one time great difficulty in defining the interior of Tycho, but subsequently found the mistiness disappear.

[1] A cleft on the inner slope of the SE. wall is easily traceable under a low morning sun.

[2] This object, which under favourable conditions is traceable in a

CICHUS (189), a crater in table-land, lies 9000 ft. beneath the plateau, 4000 ft. below the plain. In 1833 I perceived

I

that the small crater on its ring was twice as large as it had been represented 3 several times by Schr. On becoming possessed of the map of B. and M., I found it there also enlarged. Schr., though a clumsy, was a faithful draftsman ; his views have the appearance of being each independently drawn, and they are under different angles of illumination, which often vary the apparent size of small craters ; but, though the characteristic silence of B. and M. may be disregarded, a longer acquaintance with selenography leads to the

2

impression that such evidence of change is of little value. The two figures here given, of which 1 is a copy of Schr.'s design, 1792, Jan. 4, and 2 is taken from B. and M.'s map, may serve as specimens of the respective modes of delineation adopted by these observers.

LONGOMONTANUS (192), a great ring, 90 m. across, very deep : a peak on W. wall measures nearly 15,000 ft. The region is most wild and dislocated. 192, with HEINSIUS (190), a triangle of craters each highest W., as is common here,—and WILHELM I. (191), are admitted by B. and M. to be a little misplaced and out of proportion in their map.

CLAVIUS (193). One of the grandest cavities in the Moon, though ill-placed for observation ; tolerably circular, and more than 142 m. broad ; it is encompassed by a wall damaged by successive explosions, but still portentously high and steep, attaining 17,300 ft. in one of its W. peaks, and

4-in. achromatic from the NE. of Hesiodus to the region SW. of Ramsden, is an interesting example of a cleft striking across a mountain-range (the Cichus—Mercator range) nearly at right angles.

covering the gulf with night amid surrounding day. On
and within the ring Schm. counts at least 90 craters. 'In
a good telescope,' we are told by B. and M., 'the prospect
of a sunrise upon the surface of Clavius is indescribably
magnificent.' The shaded side, they justly remark, cannot
be in perfect darkness when exposed to the reflection of
such an enormous mass of enlightened cliffs. The bottom
of the small included crater lying farthest W. falls nearly
24,000 ft. below the peak already mentioned—an interval
greater than the height of Chimborazo. Well may these
observers express their astonishment that of this gigantic
bulwark not a trace can be discovered in the Full Moon![1]
About 1ᵈ after I. Quarter, Schr. remarks that its shadow
blunts the S. horn to the naked eye.

MAGINUS (195). The ruin of a vast complex ring, with
an interior depressed 14,000 ft. Some minute hillocks and
a little hollow in its centre form a good test. There is an
admirable drawing of it in Ne.'s work. The Sun rises
grandly upon it a little after I. Quarter, but ' the Full Moon
knows no Maginus!' S. of its W. side lies a hollow, the
only dark spot under high lights in all this wild region.

SAUSSURE (196) bends into a curve one of the streaks of
180—a solitary instance, or nearly so, of such deviation. W.
of it the surface swarms with craterlets, some hardly 0″·5
in diameter.

NASIREDDIN (198) and Nasireddin a, just N., are two fine
craters ; the latter reaches 11,000 ft. The former I have
often wondered at, about I. Quarter, as the culminating
point of immense explosive energy.

The GREAT CRATER-RANGE of the 1ˢᵗ Meridian comprises
5 vast walled plains in almost uninterrupted succession,
which, like two other series near each limb, seem to have

---

[1] Scarcely to be taken literally, according to Ne.

been formed upon a long cleft running N. and S.: similar volcanic phenomena occur on the Earth—for example, the Andes, and the Puys of Auvergne. The 5 lunar circles greatly resemble each other in character. We begin at the S. end :

1. WALTER (200) has lofty peaks on its ramparts.[1]

2. PURBACH (202) is about 7500 ft. deep. NE. of it, out of the main line, lies

THEBIT (203), 32 m. broad, 9800 ft. below one part of its ring. The wall has been pierced by a smaller and deeper crater, against the ring of which a yet lesser mine has been sprung.[2] E. of it we find the

STRAIGHT WALL, a most curious formation, regular enough for a work of art, but more than 60 m. long, and of a very uniform height of about 1000 ft. (880, Schm.). To me it appears brownish. Ne. finds slope exceedingly gradual on W. side, and an irregular 'ditch' all along E. foot. At one end is a small crater; at the other a branching mountain, giving it, as B. and M. say, the appearance of a staff tipped with a stag's horn. It may be well seen from 1^d to 2^d after I. Quarter, or 1^d after III. Quarter. At a short distance E. is a minute cleft of varying breadth and all the character of a river, according to Klein, who considers it a test. We now return to the centre of our series :

3. ARZACHEL (204), 65 m. across. On W. side of ring is a peak of 13,600 ft. Its neighbour,

ALPETRAGIUS (205), is so deep—on W. 12,000 ft.—as to be only 5 or 6 days free from shadow. It contains one of the finest central peaks in the Moon—drawn too small by

---

[1] And a number of craters in the interior. One of these, nearly central, casts a prominent spire of shadow at sunrise.

[2] This has a central mountain, which is a good test for a 4-in. achromatic.

B. and M.—7000 ft. high (Schr.). E of it, and close to LASSELL (484), is a very brilliant little crater, Alpetragius B, 'light-encompassed' like 221. Farther E. in a line through the S. ring of 205, and the centre of 484, is a small round brilliant spot, described and drawn as a crater by B. and M., but level now. 484 was difficult to them in Full, but easy at present.

4. ALPHONSUS (207), 83 m. in diam., has a steep central peak of 3900 ft. (4500 Schm.), about the height of Vesuvius; under a high light two bright specks, and several defined blackish patches, vary the surface, in those places perfectly level. L. drew 6 dark spots; Schm. found but 3 dark and 1 faint. The latter sees 2 clefts in both 207 and 204.

5. PTOLEMÆUS (208) is the last and largest of the chain: its breadth (over-stated by Schr.) is 115 m.—a magnificent lake, whose surface at sunrise or sunset is occasionally seen all roughened with ridges like waves, not 100 ft. high. I have seen the shadows of the W. boundary of it drawn out into bundles of black filaments. Schr. on one occasion drew 4 deep pits in it, 2 of them equal to the obvious small crater: he had never seen them before, and in their position are only 2 minute craterlets now. Schm. gives part of its rampart 12,800 ft., and counted, with the Berlin achromatic, at least 46 minute craters in its interior; 12 in E. forming a chain.[1] He also found an innumerable multitude between this spot and 203.[2]

MŒSTING (211) has a vast depth of 7500 ft. beneath a wall only 1600 ft. high on the outside. A minute crater S., Mösting A, is very luminous. HERSCHEL (212), 9500 ft. deep, forms with 211 and 94 a triangle marking the Moon's centre.

[1] It is also traversed by a number of light streaks.
[2] See paper on Ptolemæus, *Journal* B.A.A., vol. i. p. 305.

BULLIALDUS (213), a grand crater 38 m. across, 9000 ft. deep, with a quadruple central hill of 3200 ft. bearing, according to Schm., a minute crater-row, is connected by a gorge with a little crater, and is the centre of a remarkable group. I have seen a large radiation round it, as of ejected matter. SW. of it Whitley has discovered several minute crater-chains.[1]

Three walled plains, of which one is PARRY (217), bear evidence of extreme antiquity, and have their rings very curiously split by as many clefts.[2]

EUCLIDES (221) is the best specimen of an infrequent variety, the 'light-encompassed' crater. There are 9 of these—all deep, regular, not large, bright, and closely surrounded by a luminous cloud not resembling the white streaks in character　Four of them lie near.

LANDSBERG (222), whose ring of 28 m., with a greatest height of 9700 ft., must command a boundless prospect over the dead level W. of it : it rises very gradually without, but is steep and terraced within.[3]

FLAMSTEED (223) is a crater combined with a circle of banks averaging only 320 ft. in height, which is complete in Full, and looks like an overflowed ring.

MARE HUMORUM (T) is a small circular foreshortened plain, about 280 m. across, which may be detected by a keen unaided sight. The greater part is as distinctly green as H, with, in most parts, a narrow grey border. It is sprinkled

---

[1] The fine ring-plain C, on the SE., is encircled by a silvery glow.

[2] The best view of the group (Parry, Bonpland, and Fra Mauro) is obtained when the E. wall of Copernicus is on the morning terminator.

[3] Among the seven conspicuous craters E. of this formation, four are 'light-encompassed.'

with innumerable craterlets requiring power and very steady air.[1]

CAMPANUS (226) contains an especially dark centre, and 2 minute craters not in B. and M.; E. of it and W. of HIPPALUS (225) is a most remarkable system of clefts: I have seen 3 readily, 2^d 3^h after I. Quarter.

RAMSDEN (228) is surrounded by a very fine system of branched and intersecting clefts discovered by Schm., having strangely escaped previous notice. In this case the ring-plain seems to have intercepted the clefts.

VITELLO (229) is almost unique in having, within a second concentric rampart, a central peak overlooking the whole ring.

GASSENDI (232), a conspicuous walled plain, 55 m. across, lies considerably higher than the M. Humorum. Its loftiest point is 9600 ft. above the interior, which contains many minute objects: one little hill shines brilliantly in Full. Schr. noticed several changes here; and there is a strange diversity in the drawings by different hands; but it has recently received much careful study and delineation, and would repay yet more. It must be remembered that its proportions vary considerably according to libration. Many curious clefts may be at times made out in it. Schm. mentions at least 14, Ne. 38. A monograph by the latter is contained in *Astronomical Register*, 1873, May, August, October.

MERSENIUS (231) has a convex interior, with several minute craters, hills, and clefts; L. gives but one craterlet; B. and M. omit everything: Schm.'s drawing is unsatisfactory. This should be well studied. Two little craters,

---

[1] The long undulating ridges, which originate near Vitello (229), and roughly follow the curvature of the W. side of the Mare, are noteworthy objects at sunrise.

Mersenius b (NE.) and o (NW.), are very luminous. Between 231 and 232 are two clefts, seen plainly by me 4^d 3^h after I. Quarter.

HAINZEL (237) is of great depth and steepness : the ring of CAPUANUS (238) is peculiarly irregular in height, and contains at least 7 craterlets.

SCHICKARD (239), an enormous plain, exhibiting a fine scene between 4 and 5^d after I. Quarter, is encircled by a complex wall, 460 m. in compass. Chacornac observes, that from the rapid rounding of the lunar globe, a spectator in the centre would think himself in a boundless desert; the ring, though in the N. more than 10,500 ft. high, being invisible in every direction. The interior is nearly level, but its colour strongly varied—a curious contrast to the monotony of its neighbour,[1] PHOCYLIDES (242). The latter I have frequently seen crossed by a grand shadow from a peak in the ring.

WARGENTIN (243) is a singular formation ; a circular elevated plain 54 m. across, which, excepting for a very slight rampart, resembles a large thin cheese. G. and Schwabe have drawn a similar formation N. of it, and E. of 239.[2]

BAILLY (245), like a small sea, lies near the limb ; its wall, probably almost as high as that of 193, seems to run back into the

DŒRFEL MOUNTAINS (246), a region of enormous elevation, whose 3 principal summits are occasionally visible in grand profile. B. and M. admit that Schr. did not overestimate them at 25,000 or 26,000 ft.

[1] There are a number of large depressions on the floor, and many craterlets, which, under good conditions, may be seen in a 4-in. achromatic. A well-marked dark area is conspicuous on the SW. quarter of the interior.

[2] Low ridges on the floor are traceable when the E. wall is on the morning terminator.

Great craters lie between 242 and S. pole. KIRCHER (252) is 18,000 ft. deep, among numberless small explosions. CASATUS (254) is still deeper; a dome upon its mighty wall rises to about 22,300 ft. KLAPROTH (255) is a wonder of flatness in these regions.

NEWTON [1] (256), an irregular crater, 142 m. long and about half as broad, is the deepest known: the height of its loftiest tower is probably about 23,900 ft. above the interior.

MALAPERT (258) is the nearest visible crater to S. Pole, 4° of lat. farther, among mountains where the sun never sets.

LEIBNITZ MOUNTAINS (259). Ranges of colossal elevation break up the limb here, more than rivalling 246, and far exceeding anything within the disc : several of the peaks measure nearly 30,000 ft. ; and Ne. gives a probable height of nearly 36,000 ft. to a huge mass, ϵ on his map, lying a little beyond the limb. They extend along a considerable arc of the 3rd and 4th Quadrants. In the crescent their summits frequently prolong the horn ; in Full, with suitable libration, they come out in striking projection on the sky,[2] while even their apparent basis may lie far above any lunar ' sea.' Their outline is rather rounded : some long ridges may be the profile of great rings. The E. extremity lies in the direction of the bright streak running S. from 180. I find a clear description and rough measure of them by Cassini, in 1724. Schr., who did not know this, observed

[1] B. and M. transferred this name from a spot so called by Schr. in 0 close to 132, which they thought unworthy of the designation There was some inducement in this instance; but the precedent should not be followed, as liable to produce confusion.

[2] We never see a *real* Full Moon; that is, she is never exactly opposite to the Sun except when centrally eclipsed; hence there is always a small deficiency at one or the other pole; and libration must be favourable, to show these mountains well, and *on a circular limb*.

them more correctly, and called them the LEIBNITZ MOUN-
TAINS. By some unwonted inadvertency, B. and M. have
interchanged the names of 246 and 259.[1] Ne. and myself
have preferred retaining them as given by the earlier discoverer. These and other ranges sometimes roughen the
limb during a solar eclipse, but Schr. found that their peaks
then appear much sharper from the irradiation of the Sun.

BLANCANUS (260), a noble crater 51 m. in diameter, with
a terraced and turreted ring, domineers 'like Etna over
Sicily,' bearing a peak of 18,000 ft. above the interior.

SCHEINER (261), larger and steeper, includes 10 craters
and a partition.

MORETUS (262), a very fine object, is 78 m. broad, but of
unequal height, 15,000 ft. on W. side, widely terraced within,
with a bright central hill, the loftiest yet measured—6800
ft., by which it is easily identified. Its sunrise or sunset is
very fine : it may be seen in noble relief about 1^d after I.
Quarter. I have seen with 9$\frac{1}{3}$-in. speculum a very minute
crater N. of central mountain.

GRUEMBERGER (265) has a central crater, whose bottom
is probably more than 20,000 ft. below a great peak in the
wall.

ZUPUS (268), a valley, very dark in Full. SIRSALIS
(270), a double ring, W. of which lies a very remarkable
cleft, figured by Gaudibert (*Eng. Mech.*, 1873, Dec. 19),
with Schm.'s continuation probably more than 400 m. long ;
the longest known, but requiring favourable libration.

GRIMALDI (272). The S. link of a chain of great craters
lying in the meridian. This grand spot, 147 m. long by
129 wide, has a darker interior than any portion of the
Moon of equal size ; it has sometimes been detected even

---

[1] Their groundless complaint of Schr.'s want of explicitness here
shows superficial acquaintance with his work.

without a telescope. G. perceived here a regular formation somewhat resembling the letter *H* much inclined.

RICCIOLI (273) is in part as dark; its ring is grand before the rising or setting Sun.[1]

The CORDILLERAS (274) and D'ALEMBERT MOUNTAINS (275), a series of great ranges, nearly 20,000 ft. in general height—much higher, according to Schr., in parts—rise along the E. limb. They extend far S., and this extremity is called the ROOK MOUNTAINS (276). Two valleys were discovered by Schr. in profile of this limb, of enormous depth, rivalling the height of the mountains. They have not been found by Ne.

BYRGIUS (279) has on its ring a small crater, Byrgius A, remarkably brilliant, and a centre of streaks. NE. of it stands a great mountain, of probably at least 13,000 ft.—as high as the Swiss Jungfrau.

FOURTH, OR SOUTH-WEST QUADRANT.

HIPPARCHUS (288), 92 m. across, contains all kinds of formations. Schr. has seen the shadow in its interior bordered on SW. by a fringe of fine lines, indicating a row of sharp and regular pinnacles on the wall. Three small craters, Hipparchus E, G, and C (reckoned towards S.), in and near W. wall, are very bright in Full.

ALBATEGNIUS (289). A walled plain, 64 m. wide, very level. Its rampart, 14 to 18 m. broad, has been all torn by explosions; B. and M. counted at least 33 of their results: a peak in NE. attains 15,000 ft. Its central hill, piercing a

---

[1] The dark area is on the N. of the centre, and has been estimated to be somewhat darker than any part of Grimaldi. There is a remarkable cleft between Riccioli and Lohrmann.

mass of shade, forms a noble spectacle, which I have seen 10^h before I. Quarter. Close on NW. is

HALLEY (458), a 21 m. ring. Here, on NW. part of floor, a photogram of 1865 shows a craterlet which Gaudibert could hardly find when he saw another very distinctly SE. not in the photogram, and, as he thinks, of subsequent formation. There are several instances of craters omitted by earlier observers, though now more obvious than others that they have drawn : indications, possibly of modern activity, but certainly of the great advantage of photography, in never missing anything visible at the time.

Craters with irregular walls and very large central mountains bend round from 289 through AIRY (291), to LA CAILLE (292). This last, with a wall of 9700 ft., is almost level.

WERNER (295), 45 m. across, is one of the loftiest rings; its narrow ridge ranging 13,000 ft. (the height of the Alpine Eiger) above the depth, and rising on the E. to 16,500 ft., nearly 1000 ft. loftier than our Mont Blanc. A spot on the SE. side of it is very bright—another, on the inner slope of the NE. wall, is stated to be as brilliant as 148, and more luminous than any other part of the Moon; but this ' starlike flashing point,' being only between 4 and 5 m. square, is said to be easily overlooked with low powers. I have several times readily seen it with two achromatics of $3\frac{7}{10}$ in., and powers 75, 80, 144, but *never of the specified brilliancy :* a careful study of it in 1864, with $5\frac{1}{2}$ in., confirmed with a 9-in. mirror in 1871, induces me to believe that *it has faded since the date of B. and M.* The reflector has shown in it a minute black pit (Ne., crater-cone) and very narrow ravine. It is not mentioned by Schr.

ALIACENSIS (296) is similar to 295, but larger.

THEON SEN. (297), THEON JUN. (298) ALFRAGANUS (300), are all luminous.

ABULFEDA (305), nearly 40 m. across, and ALMANON 306), have their walls united by a row of little craters like a cleft, visible about I. Quarter.

ABENEZRA (310) sinks more than 14,500 ft. PONS (313) has very dark spots in the ring.

ALTAI MOUNTAINS (315): This long range (name omitted in B. and M.'s map) is almost the only high ground in this Quadrant undisturbed by eruptive forces. Its rounded summits lie awkwardly for measurement, but seem about 13,000 ft. I have often seen the NW. face as a bright line of nearly 280 m. of cliffs, in the increasing Moon.

A group of 3 huge craters follows, forming a wild and gigantic region, very difficult to delineate. The details occupied B. and M. portions of more than 50 nights. It has since been effectively sketched by Phillips.

THEOPHILUS (319) is the deepest of all visible craters, if we regard the general line of the ring, which ranges from 14,000 to 18,000 ft. above the chasm, with a diameter of 64 m. No scene in the least approaching to it exists on the Earth. The central peak is 5200 ft. high (more than 6400, Schm., who gives the wall but 3200 ft. outside height, and finds it surrounded by radiating ridges: these I have seen with a $9\frac{1}{3}$-in. silvered speculum). CYRILLUS (320), equally large and terraced, approaches to a square. A small crater, Cyrillus A, on its E. side is very brilliant. CATHARINA (321) is rather the largest of the three, and more than 16,000 ft. deep, but irregular in character. Of this superb cluster, 319 first catches the rising Sun, and I have seen it far beyond the terminator, and even without the telescope, 5[d] after New: it is a grand object when filled with night, through which its glittering central peak comes out like a star. A wide valley connecting 320 and 321 is much better represented in the beautiful old map of Tobias Mayer, and by Russell, than by B. and M.[1]

Isidorus (323) and Capella (324) lie side by side, with a peak more than 13,000 ft. between them ; a broad cleft cuts down the ring of 324, open also in another direction. Schr. here saw traces of a line of little confluent craters. Double craters, too numerous not to have some special cause, abound in this region.

Censorinus (325), a minute crater, with its vicinity is very brilliant in Full.

Messier (327) and Messier A, a pair of small deep craters, exhibited to B. and M. such an entire similarity in size, form, depth, brightness, and even the position of some peaks upon the rings, that they say it must have been either a wonderful coincidence, or the result of some unknown natural process. This similarity does not now exist, but the evidence of physical change is not satisfactory. Two curious white streaks, slightly divergent, extend from Messier A for a long distance E., forming with the included shade—not always visible according to G.—the picture of a comet's tail. G., who imagined them to be artificial, states that they are totally unlike any other lunar streaks, being composed of a multitude of distinct lines, each possibly consisting of minute points. In consequence of an observation by Schr., who discovered this 'comet,' B. and M. examined the streaks, and could scarcely have avoided including the craters, *more than* 300 *times*, between 1829 and 1837, without noticing any change. Strange to say, however, G., who frequently examined this region, expressly states that on

[1] Between (319) and Beaumont (322) is a region which includes crater-cones, considered by Klein to be analogous to terrestrial volcanoes.

several occasions in 1824 and 1825 the W. crater was observed less distinct, or much the smaller, and in 1825 extended E. and W.: once only under very high illumination did it appear to surpass its neighbour in size;—as, in fact, Schr. had already drawn it in 1788. And without knowing anything of G.'s remarks, 1855, Nov. 14, I perceived with my $3\frac{7}{10}$-in. achr. that the E. crater appeared the larger of the two; and 1856, March 11, I found the W. crater not only the lesser, but, '*lengthened obviously in an E. and W. direction.*' I have since noted the dissimilarity with larger instruments; and, however difficult to be explained in accordance with B. and M., it is a matter of very easy observation. The figure is taken from a rough sketch, 1857, Feb. 28: the shadow is probably too broad in W. crater, which is that to the left in the inverted diagram.

G. also found, on one occasion, the 2 craters not standing as usual in the axis of the tail, but somewhat oblique;   and at another time the interior of the W. crater bright, and the wall open E., like a horse-shoe, while the E. crater was perfect and shadowed. Klein twice found the W. ring of the W. crater invisible, and its interior foggily shaded.

GUTTEMBERG (330), like many of its neighbours, is pearshaped. NE. are 3 considerable clefts. E. and S. of it lie the

PYRENEES [1] (331), two mountain masses, the N. portion 12,000 ft. high.

COLOMBO (333), a double crater: in the NE. cavity, Schm. once found a central hill, not seen by B. and M., or L., nor again by himself.

BORDA (337) has a lofty range on its W. side; a peak (Borda *a*) lying in the direction of the centre of 340, rises

[1] This name is omitted in the *Mappa Selenographica.*

at one spring 11,000 ft., as abrupt as the Alpine Wetter-
horn, or the two great Pics du Midi in the terrestrial
Pyrenees.

We come now to the last of the 3 great rows of craters
lying in the meridian, consisting of the 4 following objects,
which must be looked for in the crescent 3^d or 4^d old, or at
a shorter interval after Full :—

1. LANGRENUS (338) is a superb object under oblique
sunshine, with its terraced ring 9600 ft. high, raised in SE.
to more than 15,000 ft. by Schm., who gives 5800 ft. to its
brilliant central hill.[1]

2. VENDELINUS (339) is unequal to 338, though on the
Earth it would be esteemed a wonder of magnificence : it
contains a very dark speck in Full.

3. PETAVIUS (340) is one of the finest spots in the Moon :
its grand double rampart, on E. side nearly 11,000 ft. high,
its terraces, and convex interior with central hill and cleft,
compose a magnificent landscape in the lunar morning or
evening, entirely vanishing beneath a Sun risen but halfway
to the meridian. Gaudibert has drawn it in *Eng. Mechanic*,
1874, May 8. This, as well as 338, is according to Schm. a
centre of radiating ridges, and he finds the E. walls of these
3 great craters, as well as the neighbouring plain, all crowded
with craterlets and crater-rows.

4. FURNERIUS (345) has a central crater, N. of which I
have seen with 5½-in. a bent cleft : the deep little crater
Furnerius A at N. end of the wall is, in Full, a brilliant
point on a white streak, and with another streak E. of
STEVINUS (344) identifies this neighbourhood.

(NW. of KÆSTNER (347), in favourable libration, a large

---

[1] Beautiful enlargements of Langrenus, Vendelinus, and Petavius,
from the Lick lunar photographs, have recently been made by Dr.
L. Weinek of Prague.

grey.plain comes out from the limb, resembling A, and little, if at all, inferior to it in size. It was discovered, drawn, and described by Schr., and named by him Kästner, but strangely overlooked by B. and M., who appropriated his name to a ring (347) connected with it. This interesting region has received from the late Dr. Lee the appropriate name of MARE SMYTHII, in remembrance of one whose services to astronomy would, however, under no circumstances have been forgotten. Its position in mean libration is shown by a shaded space on the limb opposite W on the Map.)

(In various parts of the W. limb [I think from 6° to 9°, and from 11½° to 18½° S. lat., and on each side of 52° N. lat.,—towards E. for 10°], very remarkable flattenings are visible in certain states of libration. Those to the S. lie behind 347 and 424, with which one of them is identified by Ne. They had been in part previously known to Dawes, but were first described by Key, 1863, Sept. 21. Their most striking appearance is very transient.)

WILHELM HUMBOLDT (352), one of several huge rings on the limb, shows peaks of 16,000 ft. in profile.

STŒFLER (354), rising in one part to 12,000 ft., has a very level interior, crossed by two of the rays from 180, and containing at least 16 very minute craters. It is well seen about I. Quarter.

MAUROLYCUS (358). A noble walled plain, sure to be found in grand relief about I. Quarter, or 2ᵈ before III. Quarter. Its complex rampart is heaved up on E. side to 13,800 ft.; on W., though not according to B. and M. quite so lofty, I have often seen it more conspicuous in the increasing Moon; and Schm. gives it here 18,000 ft. B. and M. describe the plain as crossed by 12 diverging bright lines in Full.

BACON (360) has a peak on E. ring nearly as high as 358, and on the top of SE. side a row of 5 minute craters.

LINDENAU (370), a perfect ring, rises on E. by 4 stages.

PICCOLOMINI (371), a noble circle 57 m. in diameter, has a central hill and complex wall, bearing on E. a tower about the height of our Mont Blanc.

FRACASTORIUS (372), a partially destroyed ring, which has been seen complete by Birt and Simms, forms a bay of the MARE NECTARIS (V): a little crater on E. headland is brilliant in Full. There are good drawings of it in *Eng. Mechanic*, 1873, Jan. 31, Feb. 14, April 11 ; 1876, June 30; 1883, Nov. 16.

From W. side of REICHENBACH (375) towards RHEITA (376) extends one of the gigantic valleys peculiar to this region. 376 has a ring reaching 14,000 ft. Close under it on the side next METIUS (384), is another valley 186 m. long, and from 14 to 23 m. wide, bordered by steep walls; in one spot more than 9000 ft. deep. Along W. side of FRAUNHOFER (377) is another valley 7 m. wide, which may be traced through 345, though of very unequal depth, for 212 m.

STEINHEIL (385) is probably the deepest of the double rings, in one place sinking to 12,000 ft.

VLACQ (388), the leader of a colossal group, is 57 m. across.

A little crater E. of NICOLAI (393) called Nicolai A, is very bright in Full. Minute insulated craters abound here at the rate of 65,000 for the visible hemisphere.

ZACH (396), 13,000 ft. deep, is magnificently terraced.

CURTIUS (404) has a very complex and unusually steep wall, probably surpassing the elevation of our Chimborazo.

WEBB (456) marks very nearly the position of the lunar equator.

INDEX TO THE MAP OF THE MOON.

GREY PLAINS, USUALLY CALLED SEAS.

A. Mare Crisium
B. —— Humboldtianum
C. —— Frigoris
D. Lacus Mortis
E. —— Somniorum
F. Palus Somnii
G. Mare Tranquillitatis
H. Mare Serenitatis

I. Palus Nebularum
K. —— Putredinis
L. Mare Vaporum
M. Sinus Medii
N. —— Æstuum
O. Mare Imbrium
P. Sinus Iridum
Q. Oceanus Procellarum

R. Sinus Roris
S. Mare Nubium
T. —— Humorum
V. —— Nectaris
X. —— Fœcunditatis
Y. —— Smythii
Z. —— Australe

CRATERS MOUNTAINS, AND OTHER OBJECTS.

1. Promontorium Agarum
2. Alhazen
3. Eimmart
4. Picard
5. Condorcet
6. Azout
7. Firmicus
8. Apollonius
9. Neper
10. Schubert
11. Hansen
12. Cleomedes
13. Tralles
14. Oriani
15. Plutarchus
16. Seneca
17. Hahn
18. Berosus
19. Burckhardt
20. Geminus
21. Bernouilli
22. Gauss

23. Messala
24. Schumacher
25. Struve
26. Mercurius
27. Endymion
28. Atlas
29. Hercules
30. Oersted
31. Cepheus
32. Franklin
33. Berzelius
34. Hooke
35. Strabo
36. Thales
37. Gärtner
38. Democritus
39. Arnold
40. Christian Mayer
41. Meton
42. Euctemon
43. Scoresby
44. Gioja
45. Barrow

46. Archytas
47. Plana
48. Mason
49. Baily
50. Burg
51. Mt. Taurus
52. Römer
53. Le Monnier
54. Posidonius
55. Littrow
56. Maraldi
57. Vitruvius
58. Mt. Argæus
59. Macrobius
60. Proclus
61. Plinius
62. Ross
63. Arago
64. Ritter
65. Sabine
66. Jansen
67. Maskelyne
68. Mt. Hæmus

69. Promontorium Acherusia	108. Pallas	148. Aristarchus
	109. Ukert	149. Herodotus
70. Menelaus	110. Eratosthenes	150. Wollaston
71. Sulpicius Gallus	111. Stadius	151. Lichtenberg
72. Taquet	112. Copernicus	152. Harding
73. Bessel	113. Gambart	153. Lohrmann
74. Linné	114. Reinhold	154. Hevel
75. Mt. Caucasus	115. Mt. Carpathus	155. Cavalerius
76. Calippus	116. Gay Lussac	156. Galileo
77. Eudoxus	117. Tobias Mayer	157. Cardanus
78. Aristoteles	118. Milichius	158. Krafft
79. Egede	119. Hortensius	159. Olbers
80. Alps	120. Archimedes	160. Vasco da Gama
81. Cassini	121. Timocharis	161. Hercynian Mts.
82. Theætetus	122. Lambert	162. Seleucus
83. Aristillus	123. La Hire	163. Briggs
84. Autolycus	124. Pytheas	164. Ulugh Beigh
85. Apennines	125. Euler	165. Lavoisier
86. Aratus	126. Diophantus	166. Gérard
87. Mt. Hadley	127. Delisle	167. Repsold
88. Conon	128. Carlini	168. Anaxagoras
89. Mt. Bradley	129. Helicon	169. Epigenes
90. Mt. Huygens	130. Kirch	170. Timæus
91. Marco Polo	131. Pico	171. Fontenelle
92. Mt. Wolf	132. Plato	172. Philolaus
93. Hyginus	133. Harpalus	173. Anaximenes
94. Triesnecker	134. Laplace	174. Anaximander
95. Manilius	135. Heraclides	175. Horrebow
96. Julius Cæsar	136. Maupertuis	176. Pythagoras
97. Sosigenes	137. Condamine	177. Œnopides
98. Boscovich	138. Bianchini	178. Xenophanes
99. Dionysius	139. Sharp	179. Cleostratus
100. Ariadæus	140. Mairan	180. Tycho
101. Silberschlag	141. Louville	181. Pictet
102. Agrippa	142. Bouguer	182. Street
103. Godin	143. Encke	183. Sasserides
104. Rhæticus	144. Kepler	184. Hell
105. Sömmering	145. Bessarion	185. Gauricus
106. Schröter	146. Reiner	186. Pitatus
107. Bode	147. Marius	187. Hesiodus

307. Tacitus
308. Geber
309. Azophi
310. Abenezra
311. Pontanus
312. Sacrobosco
313. Pons
314. Fermat
315. Altai Mts.
316. Polybius
317. Hypatia
318. Torricelli
319. Theophilus
320. Cyrillus
321. Catharina
322. Beaumont
323. Isidorus
324. Capella
325. Censorinus
326. Taruntius
327. Messier
328. Goclenius
329. Biot
330. Guttemberg
331. Pyrenees
332. Bohnenberger
333. Colombo
334. Magelhaens
335. Cook
336. Santbech
337. Borda
338. Langrenus
339. Vendelinus
340. Petavius
341. Palitzsch
342. Hase
343. Snellius
344. Stevinus
345. Furnerius
346. Maclaurin

347. Kästner
348. Lapeyrouse
349. Ansgarius
350. Behaim
351. Hecatæus
352. Wilhelm Humboldt
353. Legendre
354. Stöfler
355. Licetus
356. Cuvier
357. Clairaut
358. Maurolycus
359. Barocius
360. Bacon
361. Buch
362. Büsching
363. Gemma Frisius
364. Poisson
365. Nonius
366. Fernelius
367. Riccius
368. Rabbi Levi
369. Zagut
370. Lindenau
371. Piccolomini
372. Fracastorius
373. Neander
374. Stiborius
375. Reichenbach
376. Rheita
377. Fraunhofer
378. Vega
379. Marinus
380. Oken
381. Pontécoulant
382. Hanno
383. Fabricius
384. Metius
385. Steinheil

386. Pitiscus
387. Hommel
388. Vlacq
389. Rosenberger
390. Nearchus
391. Hagecius
392. Biela
393. Nicolai
394. Lilius
395. Jacobi
396. Zach
397. Schomberger
398. Boguslawsky
399. Boussingault
400. Mutus
401. Manzinus
402. Pentland
403. Simpelius
404. Curtius
405. Kinau
406. Pingré
407. Chevallier
408. Moigno
409. Peters
410. Teneriffe Mts.
411. Smyth, Piazzi
412. Herschel, J. F. W.
413. Robinson
414. South
415. Babbage
416. Clausius
417. Rosse
418. Cauchy
419. Crozier
420. McClure
421. Bellot
422. Wrottesley
423. Phillips
424. Lubbock

ALPHABETICAL TABLE OF LUNAR NOMENCLATURE.

(The Roman Numerals indicate the Quadrant.)

Abenezra, 310. iv.
Abulfeda, 305. iv.
Adams, 437. iv.
Agatharchides, 233. iii.
Agrippa, 102. i.
Airy, 291. iv.
Albategnius, 289. iv.
Alexander, 472. i.
Alfraganus, 300. iv.
Alhazen, 2. i.
Aliacensis, 296. iv.
Almamon, 306. iv.
Alpetragius, 205. iii.
Alphonsus, 207. iii.
Alps, 80. i
Altai Mts., 315. iv.
Anaxagoras, 168. ii.
Anaximander, 174. ii.
Anaximenes, 173. ii.
Ansgarius, 349. iv.
Apennines, 85. i.-ii.
Apianus, 294. iv.
Apollonius, 8. i.
Arago, 63. i.
Aratus, 86. i.
Archimedes, 120. ii.
Archytas, 46. i.
Argæus, Mt., 58. i.
Argelander, 467. iv.
Ariadæus, 100. i.
Aristarchus, 148. ii.
Aristillus, 83. i.

Aristoteles, 78. i.
Arnold, 39. i.
Arzachel, 204. iii.
Atlas, 28. i.
Autolycus, 84. i.
Azophi, 309. iv.
Azout, 6. i.

Babbage, 415. ii.
Bacon, 360. iv.
Bailly, 245. iii.
Baily, 49. i.
Ball, 464. iii.
Barocius, 359. iv.
Barrow, 45. i.
Bayer, 235. iii.
Beaumont, 322. iv.
Beer, 446. ii.
Behaim, 350. iv.
Bellot, 421. iv.
Bernouilli, 21. i.
Berosus, 18. i.
Berzelius, 33. i.
Bessarion, 145. ii.
Bessel, 73. i.
Bettinus, 251. iii.
Bianchini, 138. ii.
Biela, 392. iv.
Billy, 266. iii.
Biot, 329. iv.
Birmingham, 463. ii.
Birt, 451. iii.
Blancanus, 260. iii.

Blanchinus, 468. iv.
Bode, 107. ii.
Boguslawsky, 398. iv.
Bohnenberger, 332. iv.
Bond, G. P., 439. i.
Bond, W. C., 465. i.-ii.
Bonpland, 218. iii.
Borda, 337. iv.
Boscovich, 98. i.
Bouguer, 142. ii.
Boussingault, 399. iv.
Bouvard, 283. iii.
Bradley, Mt., 89. i.
Brayley, 479. ii.
Briggs, 163. ii.
Buch, 361. iv.
Bullialdus, 213. iii.
Burckhardt, 19. i.
Burg, 50. i.
Büsching, 362. iv.
Byrgius, 279. iii.

Cabeus, 257. iii.
Calippus, 76. i.
Campanus, 226. iii.
Capella, 324. iv.
Capuanus, 238. iii.
Cardanus, 157. ii.
Carlini, 128. ii.
Carpathus, Mt., 115. ii
Carrington, 447. i.
Casatus, 254. iii.
Cassini, 81. i.

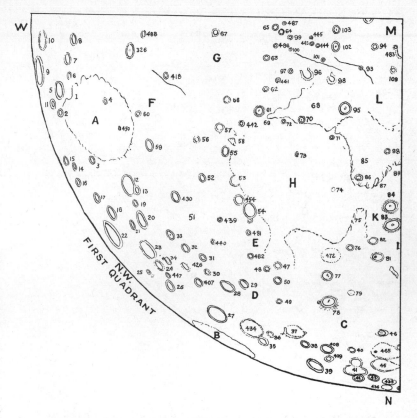

Index Map of the Moon by W. Goodacre, F.R.A.S. First Quadrant.
See page 104.

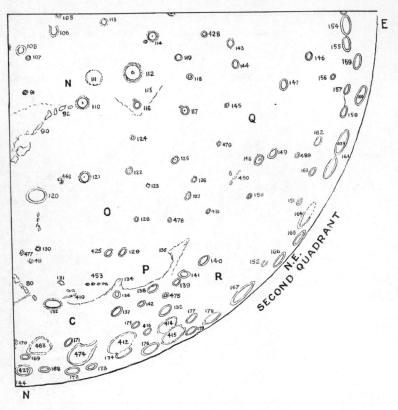

Index Map of the Moon by W. Goodacre, F.R.A.S. Second Quadrant.
See page 119.

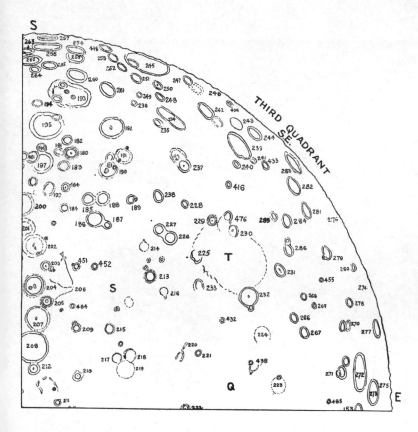

Index Map of the Moon by W. Goodacre, F.R.A.S.   Third Quadrant.
See page 130.

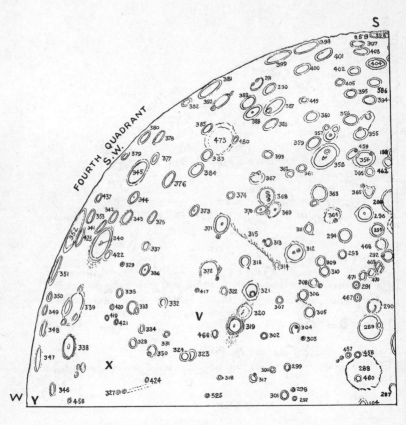

Index Map of the Moon by W. Goodacre, F.R.A.S.   Fourth Quadrant.
See page 141.

APPENDIX.

By Walter Goodacre, F.R.A.S.

MARE CRISIUM. FIRST QUADRANT.

A. The statement that " central hills seldom occur in craters here," is hardly correct, as Picard, Peirce, and Peirce A contain central peaks, and there are several ruined rings near the eastern margin which show the remains of central elevations. The suspected cleft across the centre of **A** has not yet been confirmed. Between Picard and the margin of **A**, a little SE., Molesworth has found two short clefts, these, so far, are the only objects of this nature discovered on the surface of **A**.

The white spot two diameters W. of Picard is a depression. This spot has been found to decrease in size as sunset approaches; at its centre is a small crater, seen by Gaudibert (1874) and others, this spot is apparently of the same nature as that surrounding Linné.

CLEOMEDES (12). The interior contains several conspicuous craters and four or five clefts. On the summit of the central mountain mass Schmidt shows two craterlets. Neison mentions a pass in the W. wall, which I have not been able to find; my large map shows a number of details hitherto unrecorded.

BURCKHARDT (19). Has curious ear-shaped enclosures attached to its E. and W. walls.

ENDYMION (27). Madler says the floor contains neither craterlet nor elevation. Schmidt, however, shows some mounds near the centre. Major Molesworth (1894) has found in addition some narrow bright longitudinal streaks, and a conspicuous white spot just S. of the centre, and near the N. end a row of three small craters, the centre one having a companion on its SE. side, all very delicate.

ATLAS (28). There are two dark spots on the interior at opposite ends of the floor; these have been found variable by Elger, A. S. Williams, and Prof. W. H. Pickering—the latter has detected a delicate craterlet at the centre of each spot, and a number of fine dark lines in connection with them, which he describes as " river-beds." There is a fine drawing of Atlas, by Major Molesworth, in the fourth repors of the Lunar Section of the B.A.A., showing several clefts and the dark spots. I have seen near sunset a light brown shade extending from the crest of the wall halfway across the floor.

HERCULES (29). At the centre is a pair of minute craters and a low curved ridge, the latter being possibly the remains of a central peaked noted by Schmidt.

DEMOCRITUS (38). Contains a central peak. To the SW. is Gärtner, whose S. wall has been destroyed. To the SE. is another ruined formation nearly as large, whose seaward wall has disappeared.

POSIDONIUS (54). To the W. of the central crater (A) is a group of four or five isolated hills arranged in a semicircle, which strongly suggest that they are the remains of a once complete ring. There is a break in the E. wall where the ground drops steeply on the outside, and appearances seems to indicate that it was through this break that lava flowed and spread itself on the plain beyond.

VITRUVIUS (57). Contains a central peak; there is a pass in the W. wall.

PROCLUS (60). In comparison with the walls the floor is dark. From the NE. wall runs a bright streak, which has been seen by R. Parry and others to vary in shape, sometimes being seen straight and at other times curved.

PLINIUS (61). I have seen the central mountain bearing the appearance of a double crater. The broad cleft referred to is situated on a sloping bank, this bank indicates that the M. Tranquilitatis is higher than the M. Serenitatis at this spot. The middle cleft is a delicate object, and lies at the foot of the slope.

MENELAUS (70). There are several mountain masses on the floor. On the plain to the W. is a delicate cleft running from TAQUET (72) to SULPICIUS GALLUS (71).

LINNÉ (74). The white spot on which Linné stands varies in size, it decreases with the increase in the sun's altitude, and increases as sunset approaches. The present appearance of Linné is well shown in a drawing by H. Corder, in the fifth report of the Lunar Section of the B.A.A.

GREAT VALLEY OF ALPS. The NW. end does not debouch on the plain, its exit being blocked. Prof. W. H. Pickering has found a delicate cleft running down the centre of the valley, visible only in the largest telescopes.

CASSINI (81). Unaccountably missed from the maps of Hevel and Riccioli; it disappears in full. The walls though low are very broad. The interior contains two large craters, and another large object W.

of the centre, often seen as an incomplete ring, and in addition a number of craterlets and hills seen by Brenner, Kreiger, and Molesworth.

THEATUS (82). The existence of a central peak is suspected.

ARISTILLUS (83). Is the centre of a bright ray system; some of the rays reach nearly to Plato. On the outside of the E. wall is a large mountain mass shown only on my map.

AUTOLYCUS (84). The interior is crossed by a chain of craters running N. to S.

CLEFT OF HYGINUS. The large dark spot on the SW. side contains two small bright points, probably hills or craterlets, to which I called attention some years ago. The western branch extends as far as the W. wall of Agrippa, where it ends in a little crater.

CLEFT OF ARIADÆUS. Unlike the Hyginus cleft, disappears at full.

CLEFTS NEAR TRIESNECKER. This system connects with that of Hyginus. It is curious that no clefts are known to exist on the E. side of Triesnecker.

JULIUS CÆSAR (96). The N. end is darker than the S. end. There is a low central elevation sometimes seen as a crater ring.

BOSCOVITCH (98). Is crossed by a cleft running NW. to SE.

AGRIPPA (102) and GODIN (103). Both have central peaks, and Agrippa has a cleft on each side of its central mountain.

RHÆTICUS (104). Is crossed E. to W. by a cleft, which reaches as far as Réaumur. On the crest of its eastern wall is a long chain of craterlets.

SECOND QUADRANT.

SCHRÖTER (106). Contains a minute crater. There is also a pass in the N. wall. The S. wall has partially disappeared. Pickering (1891–97) gives drawings of a probable eruption of steam from Schröter.

SINUS ÆSTUUM. There are at least twenty craterlets on this area.

ERATOSTHENES (110). The central mountain shows curious alterations in appearance according to the angle of illumination; sometimes it appears to consist of three peaks. I have seen it as an imperfect crater-ring. Weinek draws it as a shallow complete crater-ring. Prof. W. H. Pickering found a large bright oval marking on the inner slope of the E. wall, and a number of other details which he says are subject to regular changes each lunation (*Harvard Observatory Annals*, No. 4, vol. 53).

COPERNICUS (112). The central mountain mass consists of several isolated peaks; between these and the S. wall the surface is covered with small hills; on the opposite side the surface is remarkably smooth. It is curious that no craterlets have been found on the interior. One diameter to the S. is a fine double crater A.; the wall separating these is very low, and only visible for a short time.

CARLINI (128). Contains a central peak and a small crater close to the wall on the NW. side.

HELICON (129). There is a small central peak as well as the crater referred to; the interior is also traversed by a ridge which extends some distance beyond the wall on the N. side. There is also a craterlet on the floor S. of the central peak.

PICO (131) is the principal of several mountain masses which are all that is now left of a once complete ring as large as Plato, and to which it once in all probability formed a fitting companion.

PLATO (132). Prof. W. H. Pickering has brought up the number of recorded spots from 36 to 71. He finds many are crater pits, and has measured the diameters of the five largest as follows; 7200 ft., 4200 ft., 4200 ft., 3000 ft., 3000 ft. (*Annals Harvard College Observatory*, vol. 32, pt. ii.). J. Adams (*Eng. Mech.*, No. 2374) noted on two occasions near sunrise, when the interior was filled with shadow, that two beams of light traversed two-thirds of the floor from the W. wall resembling searchlights; they were parallel and well-defined, and had the appearance of passing through a slight vapour resting on the surface. The Rev. W. R. Waugh has seen the interior speckled over with minute points of light as if reflected from flocculent clouds lying on the surface. R. Hodge, at Highgate, London, observing Plato near sunset, 1904, Oct. 2, at 13ʰ, could detect no craters on the floor which had been visible two days earlier under a higher light. I was observing Plato on the same date, but about 3 hours later, with a 12-in. reflector, when sunset was rapidly approaching, but could detect no detail on the floor, which was apparently hidden by a low-lying mist.

MARIUS (147). In the fourth report of the Lunar Section of the B.A.A. is a sketch by Major Molesworth, which shows the crater referred to, and seven other objects. I have also found two minute craters close outside the wall, one on NE. and the other on SE. There is also a long winding cleft on the plain to the N.; this may be the one referred to in the text, but erroneously said to be to the south.

ARISTARCHUS (148). I have seen on several occasions a faint bluish tint on the inner slope of the NE. wall soon after sunrise.

Molesworth, when the crater was filled with shadow and the inner E. and W. terraces should have been invisible, saw them as faint, knotted glimmering streaks, and the central peak was also dimly discernible; he suggests phosphorescence as an explanation. The inner side of the E. wall is crossed by several dark fan-shaped streaks radiating from the centre, these were first seen by me 1896, Mar. 6, and do not appear to have been previously recorded.

SOUTH (414). A larger shallow depression on the margin of the Mare, NE. of Harpalus, with low and broken walls, containing some craters; on the floor is a large crater near the centre. In my map I have also shown three smaller ones; at the NW. end is a rugged plateau, on this Dr. W. H. Maw saw on 1913, June 15, when the plateau was on the terminator, a distinct small reddish spot, which became diffused into a patch as the terminator advanced.

LE VERRIER (425). Has also a central peak, and several minute craters are to be found near the outside of the ring.

THIRD QUADRANT.

CICHUS (189). On the floor Dennett and Simms have recorded three or four low hills which I have also seen; there is in addition a low central mountain.

CLAVIUS (193). The interior contains much detail which has not yet been adequately mapped; curiously no cleft has yet been found on its floor, a peculiarity which applies to nearly all the large ring-plains in the southern hemisphere of the moon.

MAGINUS (195). The interior contains a large amount of detail. Some of the rings on the floor are in a state of ruin, showing only fragments of the original ramparts.

WALTER (200). On the floor is a group of five conspicuous craters, the largest of which is seven miles in diameter; there are many other objects also. The floor, however, is very free from ridges, and no clefts have been found.

PURBACH (202). On the interior are a number of curved ridges, evidently the remains of once complete rings. There are also a number of minute craters, and just W. of the centre a shallow crater, which shows as a dark spot under a low sun.

THE STRAIGHT WALL is apparently highest at its N. end, as shown by the width of the shadow at sunrise, unless the plain is lower at that part. I have found a curved shallow valley, which reaches the wall on its W. side, about one-fifth of its length measuring from the N. end. The well-known cleft to the E. of the wall runs N. to S., passing close to the E. wall of Birt; the portion which lies N. of Birt is coarse, and a fairly easy object, but the southern portion is much narrower and most difficult to trace.

ALPHONSUS (207). I have seen a crater-like depression on the summit of the central peak. Three well-known dark spots are found on the interior, two on the W. side, and one on the E. side, all close to the wall, and each contains a crater pit; there is also another small dark spot halfway between the central peak and the E. wall. The NE. rampart is cut by several parallel valleys, which I have traced across the floor to the SE. wall; they are delicate objects, best seen near sunrise.

PTOLEMÆUS (208). The floor contains a number of shallow saucer-like depressions with very low walls, and only visible for a short time at sunrise or sunset. The interior has been studied by a number of observers, and much detail recorded. The late S. A. Saunder, M.A., F.R.A.S., devoted much time to this formation, and measured the positions of nearly one hundred objects. The record of this work is to be found in the fifth and sixth reports of the Lunar Section of the B.A.A. A cleft has been suspected close to the foot of the W. wall.

MOESTING (211) contains a small central peak, and S. of it a ridge crossing the floor E. to W. On the plain close to the NW. are a number of detached hills and ridges arranged in a circle, which appear to be the remains of a once complete ring. There are many examples of ruined ring-plains round the margin of the Sinus Medii, of which Réaumur, Somering, Schroeter, and Murchison may be mentioned.

BULLIALDUS (213) is very similar in appearance and character to Copernicus, and evidently formed by the same forces. From the central peak runs a chain of small hills to the SW. wall. Half a diameter of Bullialdus to the S., and midway between it and a crater marked C on my map, is a distinct crater pit without walls. There are others more minute, about one diameter of Bullialdus to the W., these Prof. W. H. Pickering describes as lava pits, and finds corresponding terrestrial objects in the Hawaiian Islands. A little more than one diameter of Bullialdus to the SW. is a complete ring, about 15 miles in diameter, the walls of which though continuous are now mere banks, and can only be seen near the terminator; it has a minute crater on the inner side of its W. wall. Pickering sees in this object a similar formation to Wargentin, and Molesworth considers the floor raised above the plain.

FLAMSTEED (223). Within the ancient ring on which this object stands. I have recorded one crater (D) on my map, and fifteen other objects, hills or craterlets.

CAMPANUS (226). In addition I show two small hills on the interior. Between Campanus and MERCATOR (227) commences a delicate cleft, which ruus as far as RAMSDEN (228).

VITELLO (229). The inner rampart is evidently an ancient ring now in ruins. In the N. wall is a broad pass.

MERSENIUS (231). There is a chain of craters running down the centre. Two craterlets under the W. wall and a cleft. My map shows on the E. side of the floor three small hills, and outside the W. wall three parallel clefts running N. past GASSENDI (232).

SCHICKARD (239). The interior contains several large craters, also a number of smaller ones, and two long clefts on the E. side.

WARGENTIN (243). Running down the centre is a curious low curved ridge, the floor also contains four craterlets. Pickering notes that here is one of the few well-marked cases of a lava stream. It overflows the crater at the NE.

KLAPROTH (255). The level interior contains several craterlets. The southern boundary has been destroyed by the intrusion of the rampart of CASATUS (254).

MORETUS (262). There are some hills between the central peak and the S. wall.

SIRSALIS CLEFT. Some observers have seen a prolongation as far as the W. side of BYRGIUS (279).

GRIMALDI (272) contains a large amount of detail which has never been properly mapped. It should be observed whilst it is bisected by the terminator, as a few hours later the details on the floor become invisible.

RICCIOLI (273). Rev. H. Wadsworth has found a cleft running from the NW. wall, almost as far as LOHRMANN (153), having a branch from it about midway in its length to the S. My map shows a cleft from the NW. wall, which runs NW. across the floor of HEVEL (154).

LASSELL (484). To the E. is a curious ridge, with a crater on its E. flank, and a double crater on its W. side. A little further E. is a bright spot with a crater pit on its southern margin.

FOURTH QUADRANT.

HIPPARCHUS (288). On the interior are several interesting examples of ruined rings. On the SW. quadrant are some parallel ridges running SW. to NE. It also contains the large crater ring

HORROCKS (460); from the SW. wall of this formation a very delicate cleft runs as far as the western rampart of Hipparchus.

ALBATEGNIUS (289). On the interior are a number of shallow saucer-like depressions first noted by Molesworth. I have not found them difficult if looked for close to the terminator; though similar in character they are smaller than those on the interior of Ptolemæus. The great similarity of Albategnius and Ptolemæus is very striking, and suggests they were both formed at the same epoch.

THEOPHILUS (319), CYRILLUS (320), CATHERINA (321). There is a fine photograph of these three large ring plains in the fifth report of the Lunar Section of the B.A.A. Theophilus would appear to have been formed at a later period than its two neighbours.

CAPELLA (324) contains a large central mountain joined to the SW. and NE. walls by a high ridge.

MESSIER (327) and MESSIER A. From a critical examination of the text of Beer and Mädler's description, Prof. W. H Pickering concludes that their observations were directed to the examination of the "comets' tails," and that there is no evidence that they compared the two craters many times or even more than once. Prof. Pickering has devoted much time to the observation of these objects, and the results of his work are to be found in the fifth report of the Lunar Section of the B.A.A.

GUTTEMBERG (330) is traversed by a cleft from SW. to NE., which also extends some distance on the plain in the latter direction. There are in addition three clefts to the NW., which originate in GOCLENIUS (328).

COLOMBO (333). At the centre I have found four small hills arranged in a circle, suggesting that they are the remains of a considerable mountain mass. These may constitute the central hill seen once only by Schmidt.

LANGRENUS (338). Between the central peak and the W. wall are two ancient rings with low walls.

PETAVIUS (340). The cleft running from the central peak to the SE. wall is a very coarse and easy object; but on the opposite side of this peak is a much more delicate cleft, it crosses the floor and penetrates the NW. wall. There is also a curved cleft on the W. side of the floor running N. to S. The large well-known cleft on the SE. side is in turn crossed by a delicate cleft near its centre, which runs from the SE. wall to a point in the NE. wall opposite Wrottesley (422). Another very narrow cleft runs from the S. wall to the central peak. The central mountain mass consists of several detached peaks, and it suggests the idea that it was rent asunder by some violent explosion, which also caused the clefts on the floor which radiate from it.

FURNERIUS (345). The cleft referred to also crosses the N. wall and traverses the plain for some distance; under certain angles of illumination Furnerius presents an oblong appearance.

MAUROLYCUS (358). Elger gives the diameter as 150 miles, but measuring the distance from the E. to W. crests on a photograph the diameter would appear to be only about 75 miles. There are evidences of great landslips on the inner side of the rampart; near the centre there is a complex mountain mass from which curved ridges run to NE. wall, enclosing a circular space of about 25 miles in diameter, evidently an ancient ring.

Between Maurolycus and Stöfler I see a short cleft, a very unusual object in this portion of the moon's surface. The S. wall of Maurolycus has encroached on the interior of a more ancient ring.

STÖFLER (354). Its symmetry has been destroyed by the intrusion of the ring of Faraday. On the floor at the foot of the NE. slope Elger has found a triangular dark spot, like those in Alphonsus. Stöfler disappears at full.

BACON (369) contains a central peak; there is a crater row running from the NE. wall as far as BAROCIUS (359), it curves round the E. wall of the fine crater BAROCIUS A.

LINDENAU (370) contains a complex central mountain, between two peaks of which is a minute crater.

PICCOLOMINI (371). I have noted two little hills E. of the central mountain, otherwise the floor shows no detail.

FRACASTORIUS (372). The interior has been carefully examined by a number of observers from time to time, and the details fully recorded. The fine drawing by Kreiger in his Mond Atlas gives more details than found elsewhere. I have often looked for the continuity of the N. wall, but have never seen it; all that now exists of that wall are some low detached banks seen with difficulty. The northern half of the floor is darker than the southern, and is the same tint as the plain; this seems to suggest that when the latter was in a liquid state it destroyed the N. wall, and its material flowed half way across the interior of Fracastorius.

BOUSSINGAULT (399) is a very fine ring plain close to the S. limb, remarkable from the fact that the ring is double, the inner being separated by a considerable distance from the outer ring. When seen in profile the cliff-like appearance of the inner side of the rampart presents a remarkable and unique spectacle.

Curtius (404) has a distinct crater at its centre, otherwise the floor is bare of detail.

Webb (456). This ring contains a small central peak, and a crater A outside its NE. wall. From the N. wall runs a long curved ridge terminating in an unnamed ring larger than Webb, and marked P in my maps.

Halley (458). There is a considerable pass in the NE. wall.

— •◦• —

MARS.

(Abbreviations, additional.—D., *Dawes*; ♅, *Herschel I.*; H., *Herschel II.*; La., *Lassell*; Se., *Secchi*; Schi., *Schiaparelli.*)

This planet, with a diameter of 4210 miles, only about twice the size of the Moon, and not much more than half as large as our own globe, is yet peculiarly interesting to us, as presenting the most intelligible features of any object within our reach. In overtaking him about once in two years we find, as he turns to us his broad round face, that this supposed malignant aspect is changed into that of a miniature Earth, which we might, without much extravagance, imagine to be habitable by man. Not every *opposition*, however, as it is called, admits of an equally near prospect. The orbits of the Earth and Mars are both elliptical, and not fixed with respect to each other, and no two following oppositions happen in the same part of either orbit,[1] so that the most favourable possible juncture, when the earth is furthest from the Sun and Mars nearest, occurs ordinarily but once in 15 or 17 years, when the diameter of Mars, only 13″ in reversed circumstances, may expand to nearly 30″.[2]

---

[1] Pickering makes the mean opposition magnitude—2·25; that is 3·25 magnitudes brighter than a standard first mag. star, such as α Aquilæ.

[2] The best opposition is in 1924.

Every opposition, however, should set the telescope to work; and we will proceed to describe what we may expect to see.

1. The *Phases.* These are not remarkable : in opposition, a full moon rising through ruddy haze, and, with sufficient power, larger than our Moon to the naked eye: in other situations a dull gibbosity, never sinking to quadrature. M. stated at one time, as Schr. had previously done, that this phasis is always narrower than it should be by calculation ; but in a subsequent publication the remark is not repeated. Pastorff thought he saw a phosphorescence on the dark part; but this could hardly have been other than a deception.[1]

2. The *Dark Spots.* The disc, when well seen, is usually mapped out in a way which gives at once the impression of land and water, the outlines, under the most favourable circumstances, being extremely sharp : [2] the bright part is orange,—according to Se., sometimes dotted with red, brown, and greenish points; sometimes found by Schi. filled with a complete network of thin lines and minute interspaces: the darker regions, which vary greatly in depth of tone, are in places brownish, but more generally of a grey-green,[3] or according to Se., bluish tint, possessing the aspect of a fluid absorbent of the solar rays. If so,[4] the proportion of land

[1] On two occasions Schr. observed a partial flattening of the limb, as on Venus. Schwabe also has seen it. Zöllner makes the 'albedo' of Mars 0·27, so that a little more than ¼ of the sun's light falling on the planet is reflected back.

[2] Se.'s illustration is strikingly expressed: 'è tutto variegato come una carta geografica.'

[3] H. refers this colour to contrast. Jacob does not detect it. I have seen it with a 9-in. mirror, beautifully blue. The accurate Humboldt has puzzled himself about these colours. (*Cosmos,* iv. 503.)

[4] On one occasion of very fine definition, Burton, with 900 on 3-ft. Parsonstown refl., found a dusky space composed entirely of

to water is considerably greater on Mars than on the Earth ;
so that the habitable area may possibly be much more alike
than the diameter of the planets. The water, however, if
such it be, is everywhere in communication, and long connecting straits are more common than on the Earth. Schi.
(1877-8) especially claims to be the discoverer of a multi-
plicity of dark narrow channels, splitting up the continents
into islands : they appear to have been partially seen by
others as far back as Dawes ; but the observation is of
peculiar difficulty, and Green considers some of them to be
merely the edges of faint tones, and of very questionable
permanency.[1] The dark spots were early seen, and a long

exceedingly minute dark dots ; Klein has seen something of the same
nature, and Pratt has remarked this *stippled* character, and seen
glimpses of a structure too complicated and delicate to be reproduced.
Frequently 'a broad hazy streak has been, by patient watching for
the best moments, resolved into several separate masses of shading
enclosing lighter portions full of very delicate markings,' occasionally
almost white.

[1] During the last few years, many of Schi.'s discoveries have been
confirmed by other observers, particularly the numerous narrow dark
streaks usually known by the name of ' Canals.' In 1881-2 Schi.
discovered that many of these canals were double, that is, consisting
of two narrow parallel streaks lying close together. This remarkable
peculiarity has now been disproved by more recent observations.
Indeed, many of the narrow canals, apart from their duplication, have
been disputed, but there is no doubt that there are a number of dusky
streaks, presenting a distant resemblance to canals, visible on the
surface of the planet and particularly in his northern hemisphere.
But they are not much like the hard, straight lines depicted by some
observers, being rather under the form of delicate bands of shading
with dusky condensations. Antoniadi has recently investigated this
subject thoroughly, and with the great refractor at Meudon, Paris,
has shown that the supposed doubling of the canals must have
resulted from an optical illusion, and that many of the drawings
giving a network of abundant canals are not true to nature.—(D.)

It is necessary to bear in mind that the terms ' canal,' ' lake,' and series of drawings is extant, from Hooke, Cassini, and Campani, in 1666,[1] to a great number of the first observers of the present day, with some general correspondence,[2] but much difference of detail; which seems due in part to differences of telescopes, eyes, climates, and skill in delineation; in part to altered perspective owing to the inclination of the axis,[3] showing us sometimes more of N., sometimes of S. hemisphere; and in part also to changes in the planet's atmosphere. The older observers thought the spots variable:[4] ♃ perhaps took the lead in supposing them to be permanent—an idea which Kunowsky, as late as 1822, fancied was due to himself. Schr.'s work on Mars, the

'sea,' are merely convenient names by which to distinguish the different features, and do not necessarily imply the existence of water. Linsser, and more recently Schæberle, have supposed, indeed, that the dark markings represent the continents rather than the oceans. The latter observer states that, seen from the summit of Mount Hamilton in California, the water of San Francisco Bay always appear lighter than the neighbouring land surface.

[1] Humboldt, following Delambre, says that Cassini does not seem to have discovered the rotation of the spots till after 1670. He must have overlooked the figures in *Phil. Trans.*, No. 14. Kaiser has shown, from the MS. Journal of Huygens, that the latter discovered the rotation in 1659.

[2] ♃'s combined figure in *Phil. Trans.*, 1784, if *reversed*, as it may have been in engraving, will be not unlike B. and M.'s polar projections.

[3] Lowell, from observations 1901-1909, gives 23° 3′; Schiaparelli and Lohse, 1887-1894, made it 23° 9′.—(Es.)

[4] Some of the markings certainly show decided changes in tone, and apparently in form also. In May, 1903, Dumarq noticed an apparently luminous veil, partially overlying the Syrtis Major, and the same effect was remarked at several other stations. In recent years striking changes and developments have taken place in the region marked by the Lacus Moeris and the Nepenthes and Thoth 'canals.' There are also variations of colour and intensity, which are obviously of a seasonal character.—(D. and P.)

'Areographische Fragmente,' which was to have contained
224 figures, left in MS. at his death in 1816, has been
recently examined by Dr. Terby, of Louvain, to whom the
accurate study of this planet is especially indebted. He
finds that Schr. considered the dark spots to be clouds,
among which he saw many rapid variations.[1] B. and M.
took up the subject with great spirit at the peculiarly
favourable opposition in 1830, recovered some of Kunowsky's
spots, and from their further observations in 1832, 1834, and
1837, though the same hemisphere was not always equally
visible, inferred their permanence. M., a little shaken as to
this in 1839, retrogrades still further at Dorpat in 1841 :
the drawings, however, of later observers exhibit substantially
many of the same forms, and, notwithstanding numerous
discrepancies, there can be no reasonable doubt that the
dark spots are really part of the surface. The distant view
of the Earth, indeed, might be much of this nature; its
features at one time distinct, at another confused or dis-
torted by clouds: besides, one affirmative—the reappearance of a spot—proves more, where widespread atmospheric
obscuration seems to be frequent, than can be disproved by
many negatives. The existing maps of Mars, of which
there are several, can only be considered as approximations ;

---

[1] Schr.'s complete work was published in 1881, under the editorship of Bakhuyzen. A most complete monograph on the physical
aspect and condition of Mars has been published by Flammarion in
the form of a large octavo volume of over 600 pages, and illustrated
by reproductions of 571 drawings and maps of the planet, besides
many other illustrations bearing on the subject. The work gives a
complete account and discussion of all the observations that have
ever been made on Mars since the invention of the telescope. It is
published at a price very moderate for the size of the volume, and
should be in the hands of every student of the planet conversant with
the French language.

nor shall we ever know the N. so well as the S. hemisphere, as it is turned towards us in the planet's aphelion;—even were its markings equally defined, which B. and M. deny. Under favourable circumstances the dusky spots are not difficult objects; I have repeatedly been able to draw them with my $5\frac{1}{2}$-ft. achromatic;[1] a much smaller instrument will sometimes show the darker ones plainly; while at other times, and on other parts of the globe, they are feeble even in large telescopes, and for delicate purposes require a long and steady gaze. The presence of haze, or the use of a light screen-glass, may be advantageous with a large aperture in reducing the glare. The motion of the spots will soon be evident, and as the rotation is completed, according to Proctor, in 24^h 37^m 22·735^s,[2] they will not vary greatly from night to night at the same hour.

The nomenclature is at present in a state of confusion, and can only be accepted as provisional, as well as to some extent the representations to which it is applied. The old one of B. and M. was soon found inapplicable, and was superseded by others, based on the names of observers. Of these the most received is that of Proctor, enlarged by Green; but this in turn has been laid aside by Schi. for one

---

[1] A number of small dark spots have been seen by W. H. Pickering, and have been called Oases. He believes them to be craters, and the 'canals' are cracks radiating from them, as in the case of some in the moon. Carbonic acid escaping from them might cause a low form of vegetation on either side of them, and so render them visible. It is worthy of note that the last remains of volcanic agency take the form of the emission of carbonic acid.—(Es.)

[2] This period is, however, too long. Prof. Lowell asserts that the rough drawings by Hooke, Huyghens, and others in the seventeenth century were not sufficiently exact to be employed in computing the exact rotation period. He finds from the more accurate observations of recent years that the rotation period is 24^h 37^m 22·58^s.—(D.)

founded on ancient geography.[1]   The land is designated by
letters, the water by numbers.   The expansion of the polar
regions, inseparable from Mercator's projection, must be
mentally corrected ; and in comparing the portrait with
the original the perspective of a sphere must be carefully
borne in mind, where the foreshortening is much greater
than we are frequently aware of, the eye being probably
early biassed by maps of the terrestrial hemisphere, in
which it is artificially removed.

3. The *Polar Snows.*   A spot surrounding either pole is
so white and luminous as to have occasionally remained
visible when a cloud obscured the planet : and frequently
to seem, from irradiation, to project beyond the limb, as I
have myself noticed.   These zones were figured by Maraldi
in 1704, who says they had been occasionally seen for 50
years ;[2] in fact, they could not long escape the telescope.
They were thought to resemble snow before Ħ's time ;
he gave consistency to the idea by ascertaining that they
decreased during the summer, and increased during the
winter of Mars, and B. and M. have fully confirmed it, with
the addition that the S. polar spot has a greater variety of
extent, corresponding with its greater variety of climate from
the excentricity of the orbit.[3]   Each pole comes alternately

---

[1] The map in the present edition is that of Antoniadi, which
appeared in the Mars Report of the B.A.A., 1905, and which the
Council of the B.A.A. have kindly allowed to be reproduced.
Observers are strongly recommended to consult their ' Memoirs ' on the
Sun and Planets and other Celestial Objects.   The observing sections
of the society do most valuable work, and the amateur cannot do
better than join them.—(Es.)

[2] B. and M. erroneously make him the discoverer in 1716.   A
figure by Huygens, in 1656, may be meant as a rude representation
of them.

[3] But Flammarion finds from a discussion of all available material
that both polar spots vary to nearly the same extent, and that the

into sight, and both are sometimes visible on the edge at once, when the opposition of Mars concurs with his equinox. H̱ found they were not (or not always) opposite each other, both being sometimes in or out of the disc at the same time. M., and Se. with the admirable achromatic at Rome, of $9\frac{6}{10}$-in. aperture and 15-ft. focus, bearing ordinarily a power of 1000, found the N. zone concentric with the axis, but the S. considerably excentric; according to Schi., always 5° or 6° from the pole. It has been suggested by B. and M. that the poles of cold, like those on the Earth, may not coincide with the poles of rotation;—still, one would expect that they might have been diametrically opposite; but in this case, as Schi. remarks, the climate may be affected by the position of the neighbouring land. B. and M. found in 1837 the N. pole surrounded by a conspicuous dark zone,[1] the only well-marked spot in sight, which they thought might possibly be a marsh at the edge of the melting snow: in 1839 M. perceived it had decreased; in 1841 it was no longer visible. About the opposition in 1856 I had interesting

excentricity of the orbit appears to cause no visible difference in the climates of the two hemispheres.

[1] A narrow dark zone was seen by several observers surrounding the S. polar spot in 1892, and so dark in parts as to appear nearly black. In the same year the changes attending the melting and breaking up of the southern icecap were very great and complicated, and the process of dissolution took place with great rapidity. Photographs of Mars, taken on two successive nights in 1890, by W. H. Pickering in California, show a large increase in the size of the S. polar spot in the course of only 24 hours. The increase is said to affect an area of 2,500,000 square miles (somewhat less than the area of the United States), and the cause is ascribed to a fall of snow. In 1888 a dark line was seen extending across the N. polar cap by Perrotin, Schi. and Terby, dividing it into two parts. A similar rift was seen in the S. cap by a number of observers in 1909.—(P.) Antoniadi and Dr. Johnstone Stoney both doubt the reality of the dark band round the Polar Snows.—(Es.)

views of these zones, which did not seem exactly opposite to each other: the S. was surrounded by a very dark region, never seen by B. and M.; on the intervening limbs were occasionally luminous spaces, so bright by contrast as to give the impression of *four* patches of snow, as in one of Cassini's figures in 1666: these were also seen by Se. at the same time. April 4, 1871, Crossley and Gledhill saw a very bright spot on SW. limb, not far from, and closely resembling, the polar snow. In 1845 Mitchel with an achromatic in America noticed a very dark spot in the centre of the snow, which disappeared the next night: [1] at another time he saw some movements in a small bright spot at the edge of the snow. Such luminous spots have been seen, though fixed in position, near the pole, by Green. Se. in 1858 found the appearances at the poles irreconcilable with the idea of circular caps, and was forced to adopt the supposition of complicated and lobate forms. Schi. alludes to the possibility of a mass of floating ice.

4. The *Atmosphere.* Such an appendage is implied in the formation of snow, the varying outline or distinctness of the dark spots, their usual disappearance towards the limb, while they can be more readily traced to the terminator, and their greater clearness noticed by B. and M., and Lockyer, in the summer than the winter of Mars. Maraldi saw and delineated a dusky belt for a considerable time in 1704;

---

[1] D. saw (1847, Nov. 9) a minute black point near the middle of the disc, perhaps the Schiaparelli Lake. Ward has seen (1879, Nov. 22) one of the dark lakes (Solis Lacus) as black and defined as the shadow of a satellite on Jupiter, though the general definition on the planet was very bad. A small lake called Juventæ Fons, connected with Auroræ Sinus by a narrow 'canal,' is often intensely dark, almost like a spot of ink. It is only visible, however, in comparatively large instruments, and under good conditions, owing to its minuteness.—(P.)

possibly, however, only a bad view of some of the 'seas;' something like it also appears in the designs of Schr., who from movements in these belts, inferred winds as rapid as our own. Some of ♅'s figures show white belts, and he says that besides the permanent spots he often noticed occasional changes of partial bright belts, and once a darkish one; we should, however, perhaps, have expected that clouds, viewed from without, would always reflect a brighter light than land or water. Some of the principal continents are occasionally bordered with white, as though snow or clouds were lying on lofty ground; and Helas has been seen by Schi. nearly as brilliant as the pole. D. has at times noticed changeable white spots: one of these, in the Erytræum Mare, seen by him 1865, Jan. 21, 22, 23, but invisible 1864, Nov. 10, 12, and looking ' precisely like a large mass of snow,' has been called ' Dawes's Ice Island,' but appears as 'Hall Island' in the map of Green. The same, or more probably a similar one, was seen by me with 9-in. refl. 1871, April 4.[1] Browning frequently noticed in 1867 the transit

---

[1] 1842, Feb. 3, A.M., rain fell over nearly every part of the United States, from the Gulf of Mexico to beyond Lake Superior, and from the Mississippi to far out in the Atlantic. The upper side of this vast cloud must have appeared as a great white spot if seen at the distance of Mars. In 1892 W. H. Pickering saw a small conspicuous white spot in the region just to the N. of the Solis Lacus, which had disappeared two days later. A similar spot was seen on one night by Barnard in the same year in longitude 219° and latitude 30° or 40° N., which could not be recovered on subsequent nights.—A very curious feature was observed in 1890 by Holden, Keeler, and Schæberle, with the Lick 36-in. refractor, in the form of a narrow bright streak or arm projecting beyond the line of the terminator, and curving round to meet another smaller arm about 2″ further south. The planet at the time shewed considerable phase, like the gibbous moon, and at one time there was a nearly complete semicircle of light projecting beyond the terminator. W. H. Pickering observed somewhat similar projections in 1892. He ascribes them to clouds, and states

of faint white spots, becoming, as they neared the limb,
almost as brilliant as the polar snows; similar changes
were observed by Schi. in 1877. The bright 'menisci' or
crescents which some observers have seen illuminating the
E. and W. borders of the disc may have had an atmospheric
cause, as well as numerous patches of yellowish and bluish
light upon the limb described by M., at Dorpat in 1841,
and a bright green patch seen by myself on the E. limb,
1862, Oct. 11.[1] The atmosphere, according to D., is only
of moderate density; and seems not to be the cause of the
ruddy tinge, as this is most decided in the centre of the
disc, while in 1864 he noticed patches of greenish light
near the limb. Huggins has also found the planet reddest
when its atmosphere was clearest, and remarks that the
colour does not effect the snow. His spectroscope showed
a vaporous envelope similar to, but probably not identical
with, our own: Janssen's, Vogel's, and Maunder's indicate
aqueous vapour.[2] Cassini, and in this century Tralles,
exceeded all bounds in supposing that the atmosphere could
obscure small stars at some distance; this effect, resulting
from the contraction of the pupil in a bright light, was

that some of them attained an altitude of at least 20 miles above the
surface of the planet. Apparent projections were also recorded by
Phillips in 1901, Jan. 2, and by Molesworth on March 7 in the same
year.

[1] Molesworth, in 1903, on three nights saw a curious bluish light
along the terminator. Lau, in 1914, found a variation in the light of
Mars of 0·17 mag., arising from the actual aspect of the planet, the
maximum being beyond longitude 120°, and the minimum at 300°.—
(Es.)

[2] Slipher at the Lowell observatory found faint traces of water
vapour, other observers, however, have failed to confirm this result,
and Stoney has shown that water vapour cannot be held by a body
whose mass is less than one-quarter the mass of the Earth.—The
mass of Mars is only $\frac{1}{9}$.—(Es.)

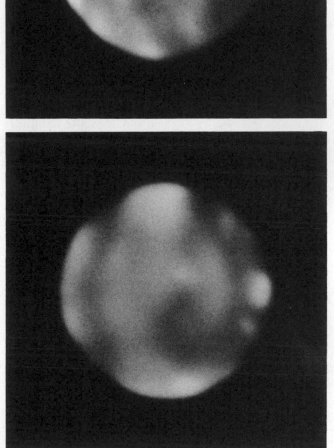

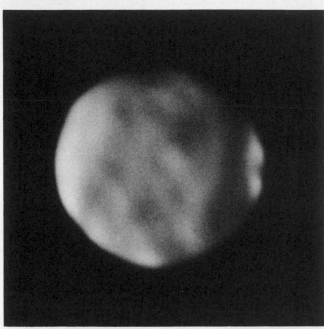

(*Photographs from the Mount Wilson and Palomar Observatories*)

Mars, two views in blue light.   200-inch photographs.

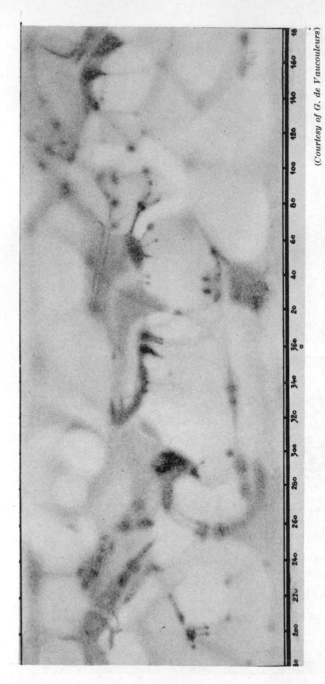

Mars. From visual and photographic observations made in 1939.

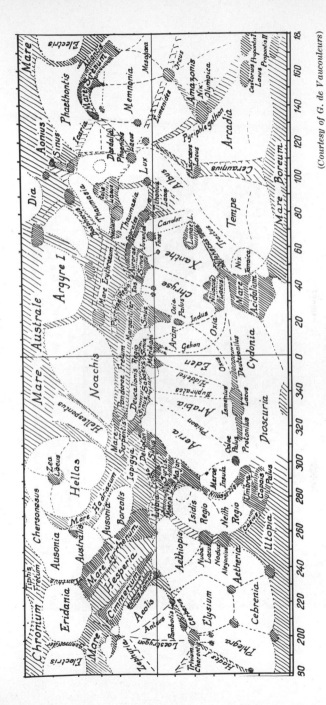

Chart of Mars. Named features from visual and photographic observations made in 1939.

(Courtesy of G. de Vaucouleurs)

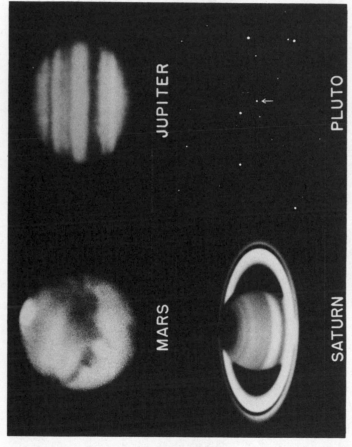

MARS

JUPITER

SATURN

PLUTO

(*Photographs from the Mount Wilson and Palomar Observatories*)

Mars, Jupiter, Saturn, and Pluto. First three photographed with 100-inch telescope. Pluto with 200-inch telescope.

imperceptible in the great telescopes of ♅, and the idea has been overthrown by the experience of South, who has seen one contact and two occultations of stars without change : in the last, his achromatic (now at the Dublin observatory), $11\frac{7}{8}$-in. aperture and nearly 19-ft. focus, actually showed the star neatly dichotomised in emerging. This is not surprising, for the atmosphere, if in proportion to ours, would not extend $0''\cdot4$ beyond the limb when nearest to the Earth.—♅ ascribed a great ellipticity ($\frac{1}{16}$) to this planetary globe; D. could detect none; Schr. made it less than $\frac{1}{81}$; Hartwig gives it $\frac{1}{250}$.[1]

5. The *Satellites*, one of the most unexpected of modern announcements, are not so utterly out of place in a work like the present as might be supposed from their tardy discovery. Deimos, the outermost, has been seen by Pratt, with an $8\frac{1}{7}$-in. 'With' refl. Erck has seen it with $7\frac{1}{3}$-in. achr., and Common believes that whoever sees Enceladus may catch both by hiding the planet; of course at or near their elongations : moonlight being no disadvantage. At Harvard Observatory Deimos is thought to be brightening, especially E. of Mars. Its diameter is supposed to be 6, that of Phobos 7 miles.[2]

The MINOR PLANETS [3] hardly come within the design of these pages, though the more conspicuous of them may some-

[1] W. H. Pickering found a distinct polar flattening in 1892, amounting to at least $\frac{1}{70}$. He considers that the differences found by different observers may have really existed, and were due perhaps to an equatorial cloud formation.

[2] Aitken estimated Pholos as 2 mags. brighter than Deimos in 1909. Barnard, however, on Oct. 5 of the same year, makes Phobos 12·0 mag. and Deimos 12·3 mag.—(Es.)

[3] Now numbering some 800, the majority of which have been detected by photography. The most interesting of them is Eros, discovered by Herr Witt in 1898, and which has a period of 643·1 days.—(Es.)

times be found by the 'Nautical Almanac' with little trouble, and Vesta, when nearest to us, is visible to the naked eye. But any investigation respecting the discs, supposed nebulous envelopes, and variable light of a few of these extremely minute bodies, belongs only to first-rate instruments.

—•◇•—

JUPITER.

THIS magnificent planet is an excellent object, in view for months together, and for some part of every year, shining with a brilliancy which near opposition casts shadows in a darkened room, and in the Earl of Rosse's reflector has been compared to that of a coach-lamp;[1] ♃ is attended, too, by a most interesting retinue. In the latter even a very moderate telescope will show one of the most diversified scenes in the heavens. Not only from night to night, but often from hour to hour, incessant changes will catch the eye; and since the

[1] Bond II. has often seen it with the naked eye in high and clear sunshine: so Denning occasionally; and it is recorded of Horrocks and Humbolt. ♃ visible to naked eye in sunshine every 12 years, when opposition occurs in October, e.g., 1904, 1916, etc.

Zöllner's photometric experiments make the reflective power of Jupiter very great. According to these as much as 63 per cent. of the incident light is reflected.

The Rev. S. J. Johnson, M.A., speaks of the window-frame of a room being distinctly illuminated during the apparition of 1891. Pickering mean opposition Magnitude −2·52.

The question of inherent light has recently engaged the attention of Jovian students, and the very probable high temperature of the body, and the dense atmosphere would sanction a state of semi-incandescence. Capt. W. Noble, writing in '92 of the chocolate colour of the shadow of Sat. II. when in transit, says, 'The only feasible explanation of this appearance which occurred to me was, that the portion of the planet's disc from which all sunlight was shut off was in a red-hot or glowing condition.'

orbits of all the satellites lie nearly edgeways with respect to the Earth, the retreating and advancing motions appear to intersect one another, and these miniature planets are seen overtaking, passing, meeting, hiding, and receding from one another in most beautiful and endless mazes. We begin with the features of the globe.

1. The *Ellipticity.* No heavenly body (except at times Venus) shows a disc so readily as Jupiter; a very low power will bring out his noble face, 87,900 miles in diameter, or 11 times larger than our Earth; [1] and with higher magnifiers we shall soon perceive that it is not circular, but a little flattened N. and S.[2] Obvious as this is, it was doubted at one time by Cassini, and missed by Hooke, though he drew the spots of Mars, and directed particular attention to the polar flattening of the Earth. Astronomers differ as to its amount; from many comparisons and observations Main

fixed it at a little more than $\frac{1}{17}$ of the equatorial diameter; Se. gives $\frac{1}{16}$; Engelmann, from a mean of 11 observers, $\frac{1}{15\cdot82}$. Once noticed, it is so evident that a correct eye will not tolerate the circular figures too often used to represent this planet; and the student who wishes to draw the belts should prepare oval discs beforehand, which may be done thus.

[1] ♃ would contain 1389 Earths.
Such is the great size of Jupiter that, mass for mass, he is larger than all the other planets of the Solar system put together.
[2] The beginner may be reminded that the points of the celestial

Make a rectangle 15 high, 16 wide, on any convenient scale
of equal parts; find its centre by intersecting diagonals;
from this describe a circle touching the top and bottom, and
then *pull out* as it were the sides of the circle to touch the
ends of the rectangle, altering the curves by eye and hand
till a tolerable ellipsis is produced : if many discs are wanted,
cut one out neatly in card, and draw the others by means
of its edge. The accompanying diagram may assist the
process.

On one occasion Schr. perceived a local flattening near
the S. pole, which was confirmed by other eyes and instruments, but never returned; an appearance similar to what he
noted in Mars and Venus. Birmingham and myself have
seen the limb deceptively flattened by the close proximity
of a satellite.

2. The *Phasis.* The orbit of Jupiter is so far external
to that of the Earth that there can be but little defalcation
of light—ordinary books say *none :* a diminished breadth is,
however, measurable, if not visible, in our best instruments,
and a moderate telescope will show the *approach* of the
gibbous form about the time of Jupiter's quadrature, in a
slight shade along the limb furthest from the Sun. This
was recorded by myself as far back as 1838, May 30, but I
believe I had seen it previously, as often since, with the
$5\frac{1}{2}$-ft. achromatic : more recently, De la Rue, Se., and others
have mentioned it. I have thought it plainer in twilight
than darkness; a fact in accordance with many similar
observations by eminent astronomers.[1] At Adelaide (S.

compass only stand straight when the object is on the meridian ; but
at all times they may be verified by recollecting that the motion
through the field is always from E. to W.

[1] The most perfect telescopic vision is sometimes attained under
unlikely circumstances—such as fog, twilight, and moonlight; every

Australia), II and III have been seen with an 8-in. achr. to emerge, in consequence of phasis, at a sensible distance from the limb.[1]

3. The *Belts and Spots.* Grey streaks across the disc, unnoticed by Galileo, perhaps from their occasional faintness, were soon detected by Torricelli, and by Zucchi in 1630; and it would be found that, though always lying in one equatorial direction, they were not permanent in position, but subject to sometimes very gradual, sometimes very rapid changes, which, when we bear in mind the size of the planet, must often be on an enormous scale. The equator is frequently luminous, having on each side of it a broad dusky streak, beyond which a series of apparently narrower stripes extend to either pole. Here, however, perspective must be taken into account. The planet appears so like a flat disc that we easily become unmindful of the spherical foreshortening in every direction, counterbalanced, indeed, in its effect near the equator by rotation, but irremediable towards either pole, where large tracts must ever remain almost unknown. Inattention to this material point would be, and probably has been, the cause of much unsatisfactory delineation. We can easily perceive, however, that the visible arrangement of details is very uncertain in all respects except that of a general E. and W. direction; oblique,[2] curved, or ragged

object is best seen under certain proportions of light and power and contrast, which are matter of experience; and in such experience lies much of the observer's skill. Under certain atmospheric conditions, not fully understood, a light mist certainly improves the definition of Jovian markings similar to reducing the aperture by stops, thus cutting off an excess of light.

[1] With the larger instruments now in use such observations are not now uncommon.

[2] The change of inclination in one of these oblique belts in 1860 was very remarkable, and might be supposed to indicate that the

streaks are sometimes seen, and dark spots of various sizes; and the belts are often interrupted, as well as varied by notched or wavy outlines : but Green remarks that the masses of dark and light,[1] large or small, usually balance one another on the whole. Occasionally the belts [2] throw out dusky loops or festoons, whose elliptical interiors, arranged lengthways, and sometimes with great regularity, have the aspect of a girdle of luminous egg-shaped clouds surrounding the globe. These oval forms, which were very conspicuous in the equatorial zone (as the interval of the belts may be termed) in 1869–70, have been seen in other regions of the planet, and are probably of frequent recurrence.[3] Their outlines were seen jagged in the great achr.

atmosphere revolved faster at the equator than at some distance of N. latitude (*Monthly Notices*, xx. 243).

[1] It is the opinion of Green that the light spots are higher in the Jovian atmosphere than the darker ones. He speaks of them as lying across and obscuring those of darker tint. His memoir published by the R. A. S. contains some very beautiful drawings, and with the accompanying descriptions gives a most interesting account of these markings.

[2] The belts or bands on the disc of Jupiter are usually denominated as follows. North and South Equatorial—North and South Temperate—North North and South South Temperate. The equatorial band, whose latitude is very near the Jovian equator, being faint, requires a large aperture, and good atmospheric conditions to see it. It is sometimes much broken up, and sometimes partially obscured by masses of dark or light matter. The North and South Polar regions are the other chief divisions of the planet's disc. Both these regions are frequently though lightly banded, the bands being frequently broken in parts. White and dark spots are often seen in these regions, and sometimes the bands in the S. polar region are curved toward the pole. Light spots are very common on the equatorial zone, and are often seemingly related to one or other of the equatorial belts. Sometimes they partly lie over the belt and produce the appearance of bays or rifts.—(P.)

[3] They were very conspicuous along the S. edge of the N. equatorial belt in 1913.—(P.)

at Bothkamp. The earliest distinct representation of them is said to be that by G. in 1838, followed by Lassell, 1850, and D., 1851, March 8; but they are perhaps indicated in drawings of the last century. It is by no means easy to assign a reason for this prevalent configuration, which sometimes shows itself in a solitary ellipse (Gledhill and Mayer, 1869–70; Gledhill again, 1871). Schwabe has observed the whole disc traversed by minute parallel dark lines, most distinct in the dusky belts, where also they have been recognised by the Earl of Rosse, Jacob, and Burton. According to Schwabe the belts fade off by the formation of longish white spots, or bays, and return by a similar process; [1] and in either case the two principal streaks frequently show corresponding patches. The edges nearest the equator are usually the darkest and most permanent parts. The larger belts, especially, have at times a brownish, coppery, or purple hue: Se. (1860) calls the principal belt red, with other alternate bands of green and white; but the more luminous equator sometimes exhibits a remarkable ruddy, yellow, or brown tint: this, which had formerly been noticed by ♄ (1790) and probably by G. (1834?), was seen by Professor Herschel in 1860, Carpenter in 1861–2, and has been frequently remarked since 1869. In 1870 Lord Rosse found it so conspicuous as to affect the whole colour to the naked eye. Burton could not trace it, however, in 1873. Airy and Browning suspect a periodical return. [2] Generally

---

[1] New belts are formed by the outbreak of dark spots, the material of which gradually distends itself in a longitudinal direction. In 1860, Feb. to May, a new belt was produced in about 63 days, and in 1880 Oct. to 1881 Jan. a new belt was formed in 93 days.—(D.)

[2] For colour of large belts see a remarkable paper by A. Stanley Williams, M.N., LIX. No. 7, p. 376, who finds periodic variation in

speaking, there is often 'something rich and strange' in the
colouring of the disc. Lord Rosse describes yellow, brick-
red, bluish, and even full-blue markings; Hirst, a belt
edged with crimson lake; Miss Hirst, a small sea-green
patch near one of the poles: and the great red spot[1] was
conspicuous from 1873 to 1881. Such spots are not
uncommon, though seldom of so decided a hue. They are
occasionally luminous, more frequently very dark: one of
the latter, seen by Hooke in 1664, and Cassini in 1665,
was unusually permanent, having been observed, with many
interruptions, till 1715; it even seems to have reappeared
as late as 1834,[2] always with the S. equatorial belt, though
the belt had often been seen without it. G. once (1822) saw
and drew a small elliptical black speck close to the limb
near the S. pole. An observation by South affords a beautiful illustration of the evanescent nature of some of these

the N. and S. Equatorial belts in P. 12·08 years, when one is at a
max. the other is at a min. His epochs are :—

Max. N. belt 1867·65 + 12·08
S. belt 1872·71 + 12·08.—(Es.)

[1] The Great Red Spot has been very carefully observed by many,
pre-eminently by Messrs. Denning, Williams, Phillips, and Green in
England. Of late years the spot has been only rarely visible from
extreme faintness, but on nights when the atmosphere permits very
successful views to be obtained, its outlines can still be detected in a
good instrument. This marking is situated partly within a bay on
the .S. side of the S. equatorial belt, and this feature conspicuously
guides the eye to the exact position of the red spot. This bay or
hollow in the belt has certainly been visible since 1831 September,
when Schwabe, at Dessau, delineated it, and his drawings in subsequent years contain many representations of the same object.—(D.)

[2] According to Hind, however, these spots were on opposite sides
of the equator. The spot, or rather spots, of 1834 had been seen by
Schwabe in 1828, and by myself with a fluid achromatic in 1831 and
1832. D. observed a very large black spot in 1843. Two were visible
at the close of 1858.

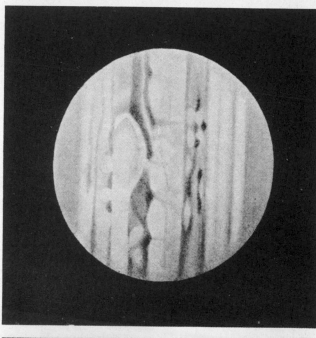

(Courtesy of the Royal Astronomical Society)

Jupiter, drawn by Rev. Theo. E. R. Phillips, with
12¼ reflector, on Feb. 27, 1908.

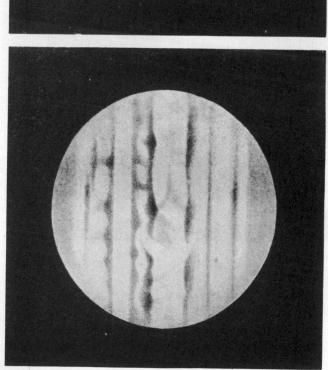

(Courtesy of the Royal Astronomical Society)

Jupiter, drawn by Rev. Theo. E. R. Phillips, with
12¼ reflector, on Jan. 11, 1908.

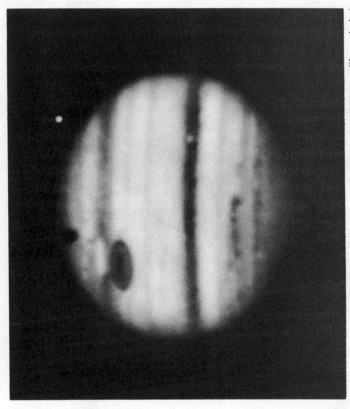

Jupiter, in blue light, showing large red spot, satellite Ganymede and shadow above. 200-inch photograph.

objects. 'On June 3, 1839, at $13^h 45^m$ (sidereal time) I saw with my large achromatic, immediately below the lowest [? edge] of the principal belt of Jupiter, a spot larger than I had seen before : it was of a dark colour, but certainly not absolutely black. I estimated it at a fourth of the planet's equatorial diameter. I showed it to some gentlemen who were present : its enormous extent was such that on my wishing to have a portrait of it, one of the gentlemen, who was a good draftsman, kindly undertook to draw me one : whilst I, on the other hand, extremely desirous that its actual magnitude should not rest on estimation, proposed, on account of the scandalous unsteadiness of the large instrument, to measure it tricometrically (*sic*) with my 5-ft. equatorial. Having obtained for my companion the necessary drawing instruments, I went to work, he preparing himself to commence his ; on my looking, however, into the telescope of the 5-ft. equatorial, at $13^h 45^m$ (*sic*), I was astonished to find that the large dark spot, except at its eastern and western extremities, had become much whiter than any of the other parts of the planet, and at $14^h 19^m$ these miserable scraps were the only remains of a spot which, but a few minutes before, had extended over at least 22,000 miles.' The speedy resolution of a spot [1] into minute points was once noticed by Schwabe, who also found that the large spots were composed of smaller masses, surrounded in one case by a general penumbra, like a sun-spot. A very different kind of spots has recently been observed—minute white roundish specks, about the size of satellites, on the dark S.

---

[1] On 1903 Dec. 17 Molesworth observed an apparently sudden development of a white spot at the S. edge of the S. equatorial belt, which in a few minutes formed a deep rift or indentation in the belt, and almost joined a white spot at the end of a rift extending into the belt from the N. side.—(P.)

belts. D. first saw them in 1849, Lassell in 1850, with his
Newtonian reflector, of 2-ft. aperture, 20-ft. focus. D. has
since given several striking drawings of them in the 'Monthly
Notices of the Astronomical Society,' and they have been
subsequently seen by many observers. They are evidently
not permanent. Common telescopes will have little chance
with them, or with the similar traces which Lassell has
detected (1858) on the bright belts. All these phenomena
prove the existence of an envelope like that of the Earth in
instability,[1] without, however, necessarily inferring (as has
been done) perturbation by tempestuous winds: even in our
own atmosphere, when near the 'dew point,' or limit of
saturation with moisture, surprising changes sometimes occur
very quietly; a cloud-bank observed by H., 1827, April 19,
was precipitated so rapidly that it crossed the whole sky
from E. to W. at the rate of at least 300 miles per hour;
and alterations far more sudden are conceivable where everything is on a gigantic scale. The ancient astronomers soon
recognised the signs of an atmosphere, and Huygens speaks
of clouds and winds on Jupiter; but they seem to have
looked upon the dark as the cloudy belts, forgetting that to
an eye placed *above them*, vapours in sunshine would appear
whiter than the globe beneath. Schr. made the same mistake,
and ♅ for a time, though subsequently he perceived the

[1] The spectroscopes of Huggins, Buckingham, Le Sueur, and
Vogel indicate an atmosphere similar to, but not identical with, our
own. Water could not exist there in a state of fluid or vapour, except
on the supposition of internal heat. The current opinion of later date
is that the atmosphere of ♃ is not analogous to our own, but consists
very largely of metallic vapours, that its analogy to the Sun is closer
than to the earth; such condition rendering habitability very improbable except by creatures differently constituted to any with which
we are familiar. The recent observations with large apertures, such
as the 36-in. Lick telescope, conjoined with spectroscopic researches,
corroborate this opinion.

probability that the dusky belts may be the real body of the planet. This is supposed to be established by the invisibility of the darkest spots when near the limbs, and the fading away of the grey streaks towards their ends; but the argument is not conclusive: in the former case sufficient allowance may not have been made for foreshortening; and the great red spot is seen on the limb: the latter phenomenon is less evident than has been sometimes stated; it is not mentioned by ♅, though described and represented by his son: greatly exaggerated in the clumsy figures of B. and M., it does not appear in the elaborate design of De la Rue: it comes out in Lohse's drawings at Bothkamp with the $11\frac{1}{2}$-in. achr.; in fine air it is questionable with my $9\frac{1}{3}$-in. mirror. Burton with 12-in. finds the darker belts enfeebled only, the faint stripes effaced near the limb. However, it may be admitted as the likelier alternative that what we call clouds are the more reflective portion of the disc. That the atmosphere does not extend far enough beyond the limb to affect the brightness or motion of the satellites in passing behind the disc, was proved by D. with his 'solar eye-piece,' and theory demands great thinness for an envelope exposed to such powerful central attraction;[1] but we have very little knowledge of the true constitution of the apparent surface. Terrestrial analogies will be found feeble in proportion as they are pressed. Vapours like our own would reflect no such variety of colour; and the very inferior density of the planet, only $\frac{1}{4}$ that of the Earth, may well lead us to anticipate startling discrepancies. The

[1] Cooke observed 1911, Aug. 13, the occultation of a star by Jupiter, and was convinced that the light diminished 7 or 8 seconds before disappearance, and similarly increased at reappearance. Chevalier, observing the same occultation directly and by photography, found the disappearance and reappearance instantaneous.—(Es.)

equatorial direction of the streaks, and the swift rotation of
the globe, appear to be connected, though in what manner it
is not easy to explain, as the analogy of our trade-winds will
be found insufficient; but the general aspect cannot be mistaken; and Piazzi Smyth, in his charming book 'Teneriffe,'
has described in the most graphic manner the appearance
of 'a windy sky' and the shapes of drifting and changing
vapours, 'most picturesque clouds,' seen with a $7\frac{1}{4}$-in. achr.
on 'the peak of Teyde,' and beautifully delineated in his
more scientific ' Report.' The great dark spots possess more
stability, as though some portions of the surface cleared the
sky above them for a considerable time; yet these, or rather
the vapours around them, are liable to displacement, and do
not always give the same period of rotation. This, however,
appears to be very nearly $9^{h} 55^{m} 27\cdot48^{s}$ for day and night; [1]
so that the equator of this huge globe is flying 28,000 miles
an hour, or between 7 and 8 miles every second! and a few
minutes show the movement of the spots, but puzzle the
draftsman.[2]   We must now proceed to

[1] The rotation period, derived by Denning from the motion of the
great red spot during the 68 years from 1831 to 1899, was $9^{h} 55^{m} 36\cdot4^{s}$
(60,074 rotations).   Since 1901 the motion of the spot has been
accelerated by the action of a large dark marking in the same latitude,
which moving more rapidly overtakes it at intervals.   In 1901 the
rotation period of the red spot was $9^{h} 55^{m} 41\cdot7^{s}$, but in 1913 had
decreased to $9^{h} 55^{m} 35\cdot9^{s}$.

[2] Spots on or near the equator move much more rapidly than
others towards the poles except in special cases.   Between 1877 and
1913 the rate of rotation calculated from equatorial spots varied from
$9^{h} 50^{m}$ to $9^{h} 50^{m} 35^{s}$ (in 1913 it was $9^{h} 50^{m} 10^{s}$), averaging about
$5^{m} 20^{s}$ less than the great red spot.   This implies a rapid westerly
motion of the equatorial current amounting to 260 miles per hour
relatively to the red spot, situated in about lat. 20° S.

    In 1880, Oct., a group of small dark spots appeared on a belt in
lat. 25° N. which travelled with great celerity, and gave a rotation
period of $9^{h} 48^{m}$ only.—(D.)

The Satellites.

Are these little moons visible to the naked eye? The question has been usually negatived, as, though I (*i.e.* the first, or nearest) is about as far from Jupiter's surface as our Moon from the Earth, they are very minute, and over-powered by the planet's rays. Yet there have been exceptions. Benzenberg speaks of 16 correct observations by 3 independent observers. A tailor, named Schön, at Breslau, who died in 1837, is said to have perceived I and III, when sufficiently distant from Jupiter. The Marquis of Ormonde is said to have seen them in the sky of Etna; Jacob and another have made out III at Madras: the missionary Stoddart at Oroomiah, in Persia, states that he could detect some of them in twilight, before the glare of the planet came out; and under the same circumstances two were seen by Levander and two of his pupils at Devizes 1859, April 21.[1] The keen eye of Heis could occasionally see two when close together. Once (1832, Sept. 1), III and IV being on the same side, and far from Jupiter, I saw them, though not separately, through the concave eye-glass which corrects my near sight: so Denning, separate, 1874; officers of the 'Ajax,' II and III, 1860. Banks has seen I and II as one; III often, and once a glimpse of IV. II and III were seen separately by Boyd, 1860; I, II, IV as one by Todd (U.S.A.), 1874. Mason saw III, 1863. Buffham has frequently detected it.[2] To try this experiment, the planet had better be just hid behind some object, though I did not

---

[1] This occurred about 20m before a remarkable crimson aurora, 1859, April 21. Compare the observation of Venus, p. 72. ♃ found no perceptible effect on stars from auroral light.

[2] Jacob saw it, 1856, at Madras, Brook in 1896, Porter and Parson 1903, Mr. and Miss Kitching at York, 1910.

find it necessary.[1] Any small telescope will bring them out, and a powerful instrument shows them even in the day-time.[2] Like Galileo, we may not at first perceive all 4, as some are often invisible before or behind Jupiter, or in his shadow; and this happened to them all, 1681, Nov. 2; 1802, May 23; 1826, April 15; 1843, Sept. 27; but we shall soon recognise the whole train, and must attend to the following particulars.

1. Their *Identification*, a matter of some importance. III, if well situated, is usually brightest at first sight. IV goes much further than the others; but the best way is to consult the daily configurations in the ' Nautical Almanac,' attending to the explanation of the symbols.[3]

2. Their *Magnitudes*. Even a small instrument will show that their light is steadier than that of stars; this arises from their possessing real discs, which will soon be ' raised ' or drawn out, with increase of aperture and power; and beautiful miniature full moons they will be found to be, by no means, however, of one size. Engelmann, as a mean from various observers, gives I, $1''{\cdot}081$; II, $0''{\cdot}910$; III, $1''{\cdot}537$; IV, $1''{\cdot}282$,[4] corresponding respectively to about

---

[1] Pickering finds their stellar magnitude $5{\cdot}28$; $5{\cdot}31$; $4{\cdot}88$; $5{\cdot}98$ respectively.

[2] Grover has seen III, 45^m before sunset, with only 2-in.

[3] Their identification becomes easy to those familiar with observing them. III is unmistakable from its superior size and rosy orange colour; IV from its steel-grey colour; II from its smallness compared with the others, and its whiteness; and I from its straw-colour, and rapid motion. References to the N.A. are rarely needed for identity to those who are constantly observing their phenomena. A kind of intuition born of practice is a great aid.

[4] Se. made them $0''{\cdot}985$, $1''{\cdot}054$, $1''{\cdot}609$, $1''{\cdot}496$; but the first two measures were due to a single day: this anomaly will be again mentioned. With the Chicago $18\frac{1}{2}$-in. achr. they have been measured $1''{\cdot}114$, $0''{\cdot}980$, $1''{\cdot}778$, $1''{\cdot}457$. The measures and the magnitudes

2500, 2100, 3550, and 2960 miles. This accounts in part for their different brightness, but a difference of reflective power (*albedo*) must be combined with it in the general effect; and the individual light of each varies at different times. From many comparisons ♅ and Schr. considered that, like our Moon, they always turn the same side to their primary, and consequently different faces—some of which may be darkened by spots—to us : this has been confirmed by B. and M., but is still an inadequate explanation : its results are not always uniform, and singular anomalies occur, especially with IV.[1] As far back as 1707 Maraldi noticed that, though usually faintest, it was sometimes brightest (a variation which he ascribes to all the satellites), as Klein has seen it at the present day ; in 1711 Bianchini and another once saw it for more than 1ʰ so feeble that it could hardly be perceived ; 1849, June 13, La. made a similar observation with far superior means ; Key once found it very small and obscure for at least 48ʰ, and T. T. Smith and Denning have noticed extraordinary faintness. III is more consistent, usually taking the lead, yet Maraldi and Bond have sometimes observed the contrary : and many years ago, when I paid some attention to this subject, I have seen it repeatedly surpassed by IV. Engelmann thinks that, as a mean, II is relatively the most, IV the least, luminous. In studying these changes we should hide the planet behind a narrow bar in the field, made by placing a thick wire, or strip of metal, or wood, or card, across the opening in the diaphragm

deduced from them will all be a little too large from the effect of irradiation. These tiny discs are easily seen with a 4-in. aperture, and their differences of diameter perceived by the practised observer. A sharp definition of these discs is a good test for atmospheric and optical excellence.

[1] During the apparition of 1892, IV was much brighter than its average.

between the lenses of a Huygenian eye-piece; it is also advantageous to throw the satellites a little out of focus, in order to *eliminate*, as mathematicians say, or get rid of, the impression of size, which might mislead the eye. Ħ used a convenient mode of expressing differences of light by stops of different value; thus III : I = II, IV would signify that III was very much brighter than I and II, and both these again a very little brighter than IV. Employing this notation, Dennett, from a long series of observations in 1879, gives the mean reflective brightness III; I, II, IV : reflective power II, I, III; IV : variability IV; II = I, III. He thinks III is growing much darker and more variable, IV slowly brighter. The distances from Jupiter must be estimated in diameters of his disc, and the direction of each satellite's motion noted, to avoid confusing the near and remote halves of its orbit. The approximate periods here given will be of use—I, 1^d 18^h 28^m; II, 3^d 13^h 15^m; III, 7^d 3^h 43^m; IV, 16^d 16^h 32^m. Spots, as we shall presently see, may easily cause this variable light: but a stranger anomaly has been perceived; the discs themselves do not always appear of the same size or form. Ħ noticed the former fact and inferred the latter; and both have been since confirmed by others. B. and M., La., Se., and Buffham have sometimes seen the disc of II larger than I, and La., Se. and his assistant, and Burton have distinctly seen that of III irregular and elliptical; and according to the Roman observers, the ellipse does not always lie the same way;[1] Mitchel also, with 11-in. achr., has observed this disc irregular and hazy. Buffham has often found IV the smallest

[1] The irregularities in the form of III have been repeatedly observed in recent years. Innes has sometimes found III of a cottage-loaf shape, and on 1911, May 24, saw the shadow when near mid transit of the same shape.—(P.)

of all, and irregular-looking. Phenomena so minute hardly find a suitable place in these pages, but they seem too singular to be omitted; and in some cases possibly small instruments may indicate them; at least, with an inferior fluid achr. reduced to 3-in. aperture I have sometimes noticed differences in the size of the discs which I thought were not imaginary.

3. Their *Colours*. Different eyes and instruments have here given different results. Ḥ makes I and III white, II bluish or ash-coloured, IV dusky and ruddy. B. and M. call I rather bluish, II and III yellowish, IV always bluish. Se. finds III sometimes whitish, generally red. Engelmann states that III is intensely yellow with low powers, and IV in achromatics a distinct dusky blue: but D. considered IV ruddy, as I have often thought; especially with 9-in. mirror.[1] One unfavourable night of very thin white haze (1832, Oct. 8) I found with $3\frac{7}{10}$-in. the colours of II, III, and IV unusually contrasted, though the discs were not well seen. Many times, both with the fluid and the $5\frac{1}{2}$-ft. achr., I used to fancy IV, when distant from Jupiter, and especially when viewed obliquely, encompassed with a little scattered nebulous light: but I have been unable to confirm this with better instruments. It certainly is very unlike III when they are near together; but the difference perhaps arises from colour. The spectroscope of Vogel gives indications of atmospheres.

4. Their *Eclipses*. The fading away or breaking forth of these little attendants as they pass into or out of the great cone of shade which their monarch casts behind him for half a hundred millions of miles, is always interesting, and, when not too near the primary, within the reach of moderate instruments. The time being taken from the

[1] Sa. sees I yelsh. wh., II yel., III ruddy yel., IV decided bl.

almanac, long enough beforehand to be quietly prepared with the most suitable eye-piece, a sharp look-out must be kept, as the diminution or increase of light, though not instantaneous, is speedy, especially with I and II. The planet had better be concealed behind a bar. Both Immersion and Emersion may be seen of III and IV, if not too near opposition; this can seldom be done with II (four instances only are on record), never with I, as the disc of the primary interferes. As the planes of their orbits pass so nearly through the Sun and our eyes, it seems remarkable that though respective occultations have been seen, there is only one recorded instance of the eclipse of one satellite by the shadow of another.

5. Their *Occultations* by the globe of Jupiter : frequent, but not usually of much interest, as they show no effect of the planet's atmosphere. Occasionally, however, singular appearances have been noticed. Schumacher once saw a satellite hang on the limb, and seem to recede again, or make an indentation in it; Gorton, 1863, April 26, found that II appeared and disappeared several times before occultation, perhaps from unsteady air ; but at the same time Wray, with an 8-in. object-glass, saw it projected distinctly within the limb for nearly 20^s. 1857, Jan. 3, Hodgson saw I projected on the disc for nearly 1^m with clear space round it. Carlisle, at Stonyhurst, saw II within the limb for about 45^s after last contact in occultation, 1878, Sept. 20 ; and in the same year Todd and Ringwood at Adelaide observed, with an 8-in. achr. and splendid definition, 3 certain and 2 doubtful cases of projection of I and II, as though seen ' through the edge of the disc.' We are at once reminded of the projection of stars on the Moon; but all such anomalies are worth recording. Todd says that the satellites are visible through the dusky, hidden by the bright, parts of the limb ;

but this might result from projection on a different back-ground. Ne. is of opinion that they are seen through a spurious limb produced by irradiation, and extending perhaps $0''·5$ beyond the true.[1] A very singular occurrence was observed at Melbourne, 1879, Sept. 14 :—the occultation of the star 64 *Aquarii*, which in the great reflector occupied about 35^s in disappearing, and could still be traced for 10^s longer ' as a speck of light seen through ground glass; this also disappeared gradually;' it may be a question whether through the irradiation-limb or the atmosphere.

6. Their *Transits.* The most beautiful phenomena of this beautiful system; often recurring, and not too difficult for a moderate telescope : the first known instance having been seen as early as 1658, with one of the old unwieldy refractors, by its skilful maker Campani, and my fluid achr. of 3-in. aperture having often given me a pleasing view of the scene. When a satellite is seen rapidly approaching Jupiter, on the f side (that is, the side *following* as the object passes through the field), a transit is inevitable ; the satellite will glide on to the disc like a brilliant bead, and remain visible from its greater brightness for some distance—according to South, $\frac{1}{6}$ or $\frac{1}{8}$ of Jupiter's diameter—till it is lost in the luminous background, to reappear after a time, and pass off in the same manner : or, if it traverses a dark belt, it may be perceptible throughout. But this is not all. An astronomer on Venus might witness a similar transit of our Moon across the Earth at the time of one of our solar eclipses, but he could scarcely if at all perceive the black dot of shade which our attendant casts upon us, as, from our

[1] It is the current opinion of practised observers that the disappearance is gradual, each satellite having been seen dichotomised on the edge of the primary—when observing circumstances have been highly favourable.

comparative nearness to the Sun and the breadth of his disc, the cone of lunar shadow tapers so rapidly that its end falls short of the Earth in annular eclipses, and in total ones covers so small a spot on the surface that it would be invisible at any considerable distance,[1] notwithstanding the expansion due to the 'penumbra' or border of fainter shade extending over the region where the Sun's disc would be deeply but not entirely obscured. But Jupiter is so much further from the Sun that the shadows of his satellites form much longer cones, and falling little diminished upon his disc, traverse it as singular and conspicuous objects, perfectly round and as black as ink, at varying distances p or f (that is, preceding or following the satellites), according to the relative positions of the Sun, Earth, and Jupiter. At opposition I has been seen projected on its shadow, which, enlarged by penumbra, appeared as a dark ring.[2] The sharpness

---

[1] The greater axis of the elliptical dark spot (neglecting the penumbra) which traversed England (very nearly in the course of the annular eclipse of 1858) during the last total eclipse, 1715, April 22, is given at 150 miles, from Dartford to Oswestry, in a curious 'Description' or map of its path, by Halley, formerly in my possession, now in that of the Royal Astronomical Society. It is accompanied by the following characteristic notice:—'The like Eclipse having not for many Ages been seen in the Southern Parts of Great Britain, I thought it not improper to give the Publick an Account thereof, that the suddain darkness, wherein the Starrs will be visible about the Sun, may give no surprize to the People, who would if unadvertized, be apt to look upon it as Ominous, and to interpret it as portending evill to our Sovereign Lord King George and his Government, which God preserve. Hereby they will see that there is nothing in it more than Natural, and no more than the necessary result of the Motions of the Sun and Moon; and how well those are understood will appear by this Eclipse.'

[2] On 1905, Nov. 23, II was seen by Denning in transit, projected on the S. part of its shadow, which looked like a dark crescent. A partial occultation of its shadow by II was also observed by Nangle on

with which the entrance of the shadow can be traced has been pointed out by Klein as a good test of defining power in a telescope. When not near opposition, the shadow, especially of III or IV, may be far within the disc, while the satellite shines out in the dark sky. Occasionally two of these total solar eclipses may be seen at once on Jupiter, and it will be interesting to mark their unequal velocities and distances from the satellites to which they belong.—Such is the regular mode of transit. But remarkable exceptions are not uncommon, owing to the variable brightness of the satellites, which sometimes cross the disc as dusky or even black specks; when deepest, almost like their shadows. This seems to have been first noticed by Cassini in 1665, but was more fully described by Maraldi in 1707, and referred to rotating or variable spots. After a long interval Schr. and Harding reobserved the phenomenon in 1796,[1] and perceived that the spots were sometimes only partial. More recently the great telescopes of La., Bond, D., and Se. have shown that these little moons[2] are liable to the formation of spots, just dark enough to be imperceptible in front of the fainter limb of Jupiter, but to start out rapidly in advancing upon the greater brightness of his centre, where they are generally dusky, irregular, and smaller than the

1910, March 31. Bolton saw the shadow of II partly occulted by I on 1907, Feb. 21. Allison, 1915, Sept. 16, saw I superimposed on its shadow, only a small segment of a circle showing beneath the bright satellite.—(D. P. Es.)

[1] In 1785 and 1786 Schr. repeatedly saw round black spots traversing Jupiter rapidly, like shadows of satellites, which M. says could not have been *dark transits*. It is quite unaccountable that Ψ, and B. and M. in their *Beiträge* should have passed by these transits in silence.—De Gasparis is said to have seen (1864, July 22) a black point on the disc, which passed off it in 15ᵐ.

[2] With the exception of II, which D. finds always bright: the brightest of all for its size.

shadow.   I have sometimes seen them thus readily with my
5½-ft. telescope. South, who once found, with his large achr.,
two satellites of a light chocolate colour and their shadows
on the disc at once (which must have been, what he calls it,
'a glorious view'), says he never saw one black : but at
Cambridge, U.S., 1848, Jan. 28, when the shadows of I and
III were both in transit, III itself 'was seen with the great
refractor'[1] (Bond's) 'under very beautiful definition, as a
black spot between the two shadows, and not to be distinguished from them except by the place it occupied.   It was
smaller than its shadow in the proportion of 3 to 5, not
duskish simply, but quite black like the shadows.' Tebbutt
saw several dark transits of III in 1873.   That of IV,
March 26 in that year, remarkable for its absolute blackness,
was seen by many observers in England ; among them the
late much-regretted Key, who noticed its very small appearance afterwards.[2] Sometimes these spots have been so
marked on III as actually to be visible to D., La., Se.
Burton and Sadler, when it was shining freely on a dark
sky ; the former has given the following figures, of which

the 1st represents what was seen both on and off the planet,
1860, Jan. 24, 31 : and the 2nd the appearance during
transit, 1849, Feb. 11 ; so as to imply in each instance an

----

[1]   22⅔-ft. focus, 14·95-in. aperture, by Merz, Fraunhofer's successor.
[2]   Innes, 1909, March 13, saw IV in transit as a large dark spot, its
shadow being darker and larger.—(Es.)

unchanged position of the satellite towards the Earth.[1]
1867, Aug. 1, when Jupiter was without visible satellites
outside the disc, three being in transit at once, he again
saw the double spot,[2] but on the opposite or SW. side. The
3rd fig. represents IV as he has sometimes observed it, with
portions near the edge almost invisible from small reflective
power. Burton, too, has seen it polygonal. Se., who found
III reddish, and like the spotted face of Mars in a small glass,
made designs during 1855, some of which are copied here,
and from which he would infer a swift axial rotation;[3] if so,
these satellites must differ essentially from our Moon : that
they do so to some extent is clear from the ephemeral nature

Aug. 26. 19h 20m.   Aug. 26. 12h 10m.   Aug. 27.   Sept. 9.

of their obscurations, the same satellite often passing across
Jupiter bright and dark at the interval of a single revolution
in its orbit. An extract from my own observations, of a
date long anterior to those of La. and Se., may be permitted as an encouragement to the possessors of ordinary
instruments. '1835, Jan. 26, 10h 30m, 250 [power of 5½-ft.
achr.]. The 4th [a little past inferior conjunction] was very
pale, and rather ruddy ; its disc not only smaller than that

----

[1] G. says that on two occasions he has seen the light of this
satellite reduced to a mere ring. Ingall, with a 5½-in. dialyte, saw
it (1870, Feb. 17) like a double star in contact.

[2] Barneby also, who ascribes to it a ginger colour.

[3] Innes has given drawings of the shape of this satellite in M.N.
LXIX. and LXX., and believes that it rotates and revolves round
Jupiter in the same time.—(Es.)

of the 1st or 2nd, but apparently imperfect as if spotted. Had the night been more favourable, this might have been a very interesting observation.'

From this change in the aspect of a satellite in dark transit—than which, as D. observes, no more delicate photometer could be applied to the different parts of the disc—we must infer a far greater difference of brightness between the centre and circumference of Jupiter than could have been suspected: a white disc would not be converted into a black one from mere contrast, unless the light of the background varied in a corresponding manner: and it is very strange that this variation is so little otherwise apparent to the eye. Browning, however, has detected it, as I have since done, by means of a graduated darkening glass. On optical grounds we should hence deduce a very smooth surface for Jupiter, and one not covered with vapour, since this, as we see in the dense white clouds of our own sky, would not grow less bright towards the edge. One of the apparent anomalies of this system has been recently explained. The unexpected magnitude of the shadows, especially of IV, in transit, which had been noticed ever since Maraldi's time, has been shown independently by Proctor and Buffham to be due to enlargement from penumbra, into which, in consequence of its distance from the primary, nearly the whole shadow of IV is resolved, III being considerably affected by it, throwing a smaller and blacker shadow from a larger disc, and even I not exempt; these diffused borders, the visible extent of which will vary with the optical power employed, have actually been detected on several occasions by La. Buffham, Gorton, and others. An elliptical form which has been seen by Burton in the shadows is not fully explicable as the result of oblique projection, and seems rather to indicate penetration through an imperfectly transparent and

not very shallow medium. Other appearances not easily
accounted for are on record.[1] Cassini once failed in finding
the shadow of I when it should have been on the disc.
Gorton saw it grey on one occasion. The shadow of II has
been seen especially indistinct by Buffham, Birt, and Grover;
Terby and Flammarion found it grey, 1874, March 25, when
that of III, very near it, was black. I saw it abnormally
small with $9\frac{1}{3}$-in. mirror, at the same time. The Melbourne
observers have seen the shadow of III flattened at its poles,
in mid-transit, in a high N. Lat. ; and Grover has recorded
two somewhat similar observations of the same shadow.
South, many years ago, published in one of the public
journals a most interesting observation, which I greatly
regret that I cannot recover, but I am confident as to its
tenor, which was, that in his great achr. he perceived each
of two shadows of satellites on Jupiter to be attended by a
faint duplicate by its side ; traces of which could be just
detected with a smaller telescope (I believe) 5 ft.[2] But the
most surprising is a phenomenon which requires, and
possesses, the highest attestation. 1828, June 26, II,
having fairly entered on Jupiter, was found 12 or 13^m afterwards *outside the limb*, where it remained visible for at least
4^m, and then suddenly vanished. The authority of such an

---

[1] Some time since it was authoritatively announced that Messrs.
Burnham and Barnard had seen Sat. I duplex. Full verification was
not forthcoming. There was much conjecture among astronomers
as to the cause of this appearance—such as close conjunction with
spots in transit, markings on the surface of the satellite, optical
reflection due to special atmospheric conditions, etc. The above
eminent observers have indicated their belief that the form of the
satellite in question is elliptical, which would to some extent account
for apparent duplicity. *Vide* Burton's observation on page 178.

[2] Trouvelot saw the shadow of 1st satellite double on April 24,
1887; and Sadler, May, 1874.

observer as Smyth would alone have established this wonderful fact; but it was recorded by two other very competent witnesses, and (what is especially remarkable) at considerable distances, Maclear at 12 miles and Pearson at 35 miles from Smyth at Bedford. Explanation is here set at defiance; demonstrably neither in the atmosphere of the Earth nor Jupiter, where, and what could have been the cause? At present we can get no answer.[1]

---•◇•---

SATURN.

FORTUNATELY for the student, a common telescope will exhibit some part of the wonders of this superb planet, unparalleled in our own system, invisible elsewhere; and they whose expectations have not been unduly raised by designs made with the best telescopes will be delighted with the

---

[1] Gambart says that, at the immersion of I, 1823, Oct. 19, 'le satellite a disparu et reparu plusieurs fois;' but in this case qu. as to the state of the air, or the eye? Observations by Se. and Main, in which the limb alternately approached and receded from a satellite for 4 or 5^m, were obviously due to unsteady air. Grover on one occasion saw the advance of II towards occultation entirely arrested for 1^m when 3 or 4 of its own diameters from the limb: definition splendid, and observation very certain.

One of the most important Jovian discoveries of recent years was that by Professor Barnard, who, on the night of Sept. 9, 1892, detected a fifth satellite revolving in a period of 11^h 57^m 23·06^s. The distance from Jupiter is about 67,000 miles, and its velocity per second 16·4 miles. The VI and VII Satellites, with periods of 251 and 265 days, were detected in 1905–06 by Perrine at the Lick Observatory by Photography, and the VIII two years later, by Melothe, at Greenwich. The VIII takes about 2 years and 2 months to complete its circuit, and the motion is retrograde. The IX by Nicholson, in 1914, at the Lick Observatory.—(Es.)

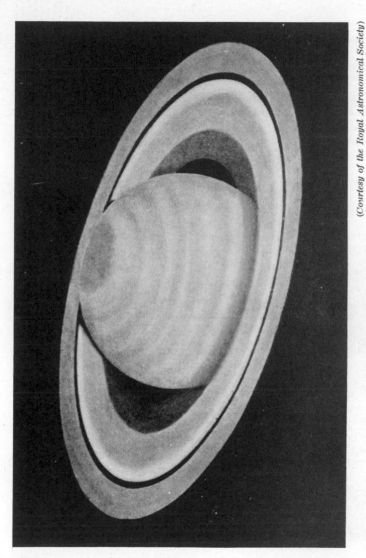

Saturn, drawn by Professor Barnard, 1908.

(*Photograph from the Mount Wilson and Palomar Observatories*)

Saturn and ring system photographed with 100-inch telescope.

scene in their own.   The minuter details require in general
great optical perfection ; but some of them may now and
then be reached, though with a feeble grasp, by ordinary
instruments, and our readers may have occasional access to
more powerful means ; it seems best, therefore, to be circum-
stantial.   We shall describe the Globe, the Rings, and the
Satellites, in succession.

The *Globe.*   Though about 69,200 m.[1] in equatorial
diameter, second only to Jupiter, and about 9 times larger
than the Earth, this noble ball has so little density that it
would float like oak on water, which is actually heavier, and
therefore, if any were found there, would sink to its centre;
while on the probable supposition that the density of the
globe decreases outwards, its surface-material must be lighter
still, and the conditions of existence there so unlike our own
as to render conjecture hopeless.   Seidel has shown that its
reflective power is only $\frac{1}{5}$ of that of Venus, Mars, or Jupiter.[2]
Day and night, summer and winter,[3] and possibly clouds and
winds, the only steps in the analogy, leave an immense distance to be overpassed ; and the tenfold nearer approach of
modern astronomers has not bridged over the chasm which
foiled the inquiries of Huygens, and kept him still in ignorance of the wonders beyond it.[4]

1. *Ellipticity.*   There is no doubt of this compression,

[1] Measurements differ a little ; this is the value given by Ne. as
freed from irradiation.

[2] The mean opposition mag. is − 0·93 according to Pickering.

[3] The inclination of Saturn's equator to his orbit is found by
Mr. A. Marth to be 26° 43′ 23″.   The inclination of the orbit to the
ecliptic was 20° 29′ 34″, in 1892.

[4] 'Ad longinqua Saturni regna propius nunc quam antehac quis-
quam adivi, et usque eo progressus sum, ut vasti adeo itineris pars
una centesima tantummodo reliqua fuerit : quam si quo pacto superare
potuissem, quot, qualiaque . . . narranda haberem !'

but much uncertainty as to its amount : the inclination of
the axis, corresponding with that of the ring, causes some
difficulty; the intersecting outlines of the ring occasion more
by deceiving the eye : and this has been the reason generally
assigned why ♅ and others in 1805 considered that the ball
was doubly flattened, at the equator as well as at the poles.[1]
As, however, the great observer confirmed the appearance,
with several instruments, by comparison with Jupiter, and
by actual measurement, the suspicion may recur that something is not altogether explained. The same peculiar outline
presented itself to G. in 1844. Others, especially Bond II.,
have thought the two hemispheres not precisely alike in
flattening. The best values of the compression vary between
a little less than $\frac{1}{9}$ and a little less than $\frac{1}{12}$: at any rate it is
very considerable. It is of course best seen during the dis-
appearance of the ring.[2]

2. *Excentricity.* Schwabe, though anticipated by Gallet,
1684, in perceiving that the globe is not accurately central
in the ring, first drew general attention to the fact, observed
by him in 1827 with a $3\frac{1}{2}$-ft. achr. It has been doubted, but
seems established by measures which give the dark opening
a very little smaller on W. than E. side :[3] the Roman

---

[1] Proctor has shown very ingeniously that remarkable illusions

are caused by the juxtaposition of lines
of different character. This will be
apparent from a diagram (taken from
his in *Intellectual Observer*, x. 33) in
which the two chords, though apparently curved, to most eyes at any
rate, are really straight lines.

[2] J. A. C. Oudemans obtains an apparent equatorial diameter of
$17''\cdot3$, and a polar diameter of $15''\cdot4$, at the mean distance of Saturn
from the Sun, with a resulting compression of $\frac{1}{9}$.

[3] Gallet reverses this position; while no certain excentricity either
way is shown by the measures of Hall (1884-7) and Barnard (1894).
—(P.)

observers as well as Schwabe considered it very evident, but
rapidly variable, in 1842 and 1843 : and I have sometimes
fancied it visible with the 5½-ft. achr.   It has been thought
theoretically essential to the stability of the ring.

3. *Belts* and *Spots*.   The globe is diversified by darker
and lighter bands, changeable, but usually parallel to the
equator, though ♄ noticed occasional deviation.   His 'quintuple belt' of alternate light and shade is now seldom to
be seen : [1] usually there is a strong central whitish band, the
brightest part of the ball ; on each side of it a broad brown
or somewhat ruddy zone, with many streaks and markings,
generally parallel, and, according to some authorities, reaching to the limb ; to the principal of which the Washington
achr. gives wavy edges : then a similar greenish or bluish
grey region extending to the poles, which are capped by a
darker patch of the same tint, with sometimes a pale central
space.   ♄ found the brightness of the polar regions variable.
Browning describes the colours in 1868, with a 12¼-in.
mirror, as light cinnamon and bright azure blue.   Strange
to say, B. and M. missed these belts, which Huygens discovered with his old refractor, and Grover has often seen
with only 2 in. of aperture.—Spots or streaks are uncommon,
and the instances easily enumerated : Cassini and Fatio, two
bright streaks, 1683 : ♄, 1780,[2] 1806 ; Schr. and Harding,
1796, 1797 ; Schwabe, 1847 ; Busch and Luther, a round
bright spot near S. limb, 1848.   Bond I., in 1848 and 1854,
and De la Rue in 1856, figure some darker patches.   La.

---

[1] Seen by A. S. Williams and Rev. A. Freeman in March, 1892,
on the N. part of the ball.

[2] The object figured by ♄ in *Phil. Trans.*, 1790, is called 'a strong,
dark spot near the margin of the disk,' where even Bond's great achr.
fails to trace the belts, and where, on Jupiter, the darkest spots are
usually said to be imperceptible through his atmosphere.

and Jacob, 1852; Coolidge and Bond II., 1856; D. and La.,
1858; Se., 1861. From the unequal strength of parts of
his quintuple belt ♄ found the rotation 10^h 16^m 0.44^s.
Schr., from various spots, 11^h 51^m, 11^h 40^m 30^s, and rather
more than 12^h. A more modern determination is that of
Hall, who, 1876, Dec. 7, observed with the great Washington
telescope, a well-defined white spot of $2''$ to $3''$ which was
seen at four other places, and continued for some weeks,
extending itself ultimately on one side into a streak. This
gave a period of 10^h 14^m 23.8^s.[1] An appearance which indicated an atmosphere to ♄—the hanging of the satellites on
the limb previous to passing behind it—is as yet uncon-
firmed. The spectroscope of Huggins shows the existence
of an atmosphere of similar quality to that of Jupiter;
Janssen's indicates aqueous vapour in both. Vogel's shows
more atmospheric bands on the ball than the ring. From
the transit of Titan Chacornac found the reverse of Jupiter
in Saturn as to reflective power, the edges being brighter
than the centre.[2]

The *System of Rings*, so far as has been ascertained, is
unique; the only level surface, or rather collection of level
surfaces, that we know. From the combination of its
inclined position, its parallelism with itself, and the planet's

[1] In 1903 there occurred an extensive outbreak of white spots in
the planets N. temperate zone. The principal of these watched
during the last six months of the year named, had a rotation period
of 10^h 37^m 56.4^s according to Denning.

The latter period, exceeding Herschel and Hall's about 25^m, was
corroborated by the independent observations of other observers, and
sufficiently proves that in different latitudes of Saturn there are
currents of various velocities, as in the case of Jupiter.—(D.)

[2] But on March 11, 1892, Titan entered bright upon the SSE.
limb of N., and became dark as it neared the central meridian, as
seen by Dr. Terby, Rev. A. Freeman, J. Guillaume, and others.

revolution round the sun, it will alternately show each side to a distant spectator, and in two opposite points of the orbit come into an edgeways position and disappear. The whole revolution occupying nearly 29½ years, all the phenomena of increasing and decreasing breadth will be gone through in something less than 15 years for each side of the ring. To a spectator in the Sun, the ring would vanish but once as it changed sides to him, being invisible, or nearly so, from its thinness; on the Earth, being neither in the centre of Saturn's orbit, nor at rest, we may find it disappear in 4 positions—either edgeways to Sun and Earth —edgeways to Sun but not to Earth, when it will be too faint, each side having only a very little horizontal light— edgeways to Earth but not to Sun, when, though enlightened, it will be too narrow to be visible—or edgeways to neither, but having its dark side towards Earth : the motion of Saturn, however, carries it before very long through all these points, and the previously hidden side comes definitely into view. We must now consider it as it was in 1914·7, with the ring at its greatest width projecting beyond each pole of the globe : in this position it is brought out by a very small power—(I have seen it with about 20 on only 1⅓-in. aperture)—the dark sky being visible on each side through the 'ansæ' (or *handles*), as the semi-ovals of light are termed into which the ring is projected. Galileo's telescope, though it magnified upwards of 30 times, could not define it thus, and he imagined that he saw a large globe between two smaller ones : then followed a number of queer-shaped misrepresentations by various hands, till in 1659 Christian Huygens made for himself a refractor of 23-ft. focus and 2⅓-in. aperture, which, bearing the power of 100, solved the mystery. His exulting father celebrated the discovery by a copy of verses, closed by a passage

worthy of preservation, in which he thus anticipates for his
son a fame as lasting as the firmament :

Gloria sideribus quam convenit esse coævam,
Et tantum cœlo commoriente mori.

The telescope now improved rapidly, and the cumbrous
and troublesome refractor of those days was often exceedingly good for the kind of thing. The principal division
in the ring was discovered by Cassini in 1675, one of whose
refractors, 20 ft. long, with not quite 2½-in. aperture, bore a
power of 90. A much lower power would not show it all
round, as Cassini seems to have seen it, even in a modern
achromatic. But we must proceed to details, adopting
Otto Struve's designation of the three principal rings, by
the letters, A, B, C.

1. The *Outermost Ring* (A), about 154,500 miles outside
measure,[1] was perceived by Cassini, as early as 1675, to be
considerably fainter than the outer part of its neighbour; a
small telescope will readily show the difference. There
seems reason to believe that its structure is either always,
or temporarily, multiple.[2] Short in the last, Kater in this

[1] According to J. A. C. Oudemans, a discussion of all the best
measures gave the following results for the apparent diameters of the
ring system, if seen from the mean distance of Saturn, namely,
9˙53885 times the radius of the Earth's orbit: outer ring, exterior,
39‴·5; inner ring, interior, 27‴·5; dusky ring, interior, 21″·8. To
which we may add the following measures of A. Hall: inner edge of
outer ring 34‴·95, outer edge of inner ring 34‴·11.
Outer edge of ring A to inner edge of B—

	Barnard (1894–5)	Phillips (1912–3)
	7‴·269	6‴·727
Inner edge B to limb „	3″·924	4‴·397
Outer diameter of A „	40″·186	40‴·037

For a discussion of the proportionate dimensions of the planet and
his rings see a paper by Hepburn, M.N., 1914, June.

[2] Three divisions in ring A, and also in ring B, have been seen
by Lowell.—(Es.)

century saw, on rare occasions, several concentric fine lines upon its surface. The strongest of these, named after Encke, who first drew attention to it in 1837, is perceived from time to time rather outside the middle of the ring. Jacob saw it constantly at Madras, and P. Smyth found it very distinct in the pure sky of the Peak of Teneriffe; La. and Se. find only a dusky mark like a pencil line, D. and De la Rue consider it a black division.[1] Immediately within it, the latter observer represents a brighter streak in the exquisite drawings taken in 1852 and 1856 with his reflector of 13-in. aperture, now at the observatory of Oxford. Se. has perceived another most minute line interior to the first. With has seen several hair-lines upon A at once with one of his own specula. D. and Coolidge (Bond's assistant) have remarked a greater brightness at the inner edge, La. (at Malta) at both edges of this ring. Common telescopes of course break down here, yet I have once or twice suspected a streaky aspect with the $5\frac{1}{2}$ ft. achr.: but it is very strange that these markings have escaped many of the best telescopes, especially directed to Saturn,—those of the two Herschels,[2] Schr., Struve at Dorpat, and Mitchel at Cincinnati. Possibly they may be subject to obscuration or change. Trouvelot has seen with the $26\frac{1}{2}$-in achr. at

[1] In 1851 and 1852 D. saw this line when Bond, Struve, and La., with three of the finest telescopes in existence, missed it. It was subsequently seen dusky in Bond's. 1858, April 17, during an unusual display of Saturn, La. could only detect a very slight shade. Burton has recently seen it even across the ball, in the present imperfectly opened condition of the ring (Aug. 1880), which Trouvelot failed to do with the great Washington achr. in a much more favourable position. I caught the *line*, 1880, Oct. 14, with $9\frac{1}{2}$-in. refl. Maggini, in 1910, found it in general more perceptible on the left side.

[2] In an admirably perfect view of Saturn by H., 1830, April 4, with his 20-ft. reflector, $18\frac{3}{4}$-in. aperture, no subdivision could be traced ' with all possible attention and with all powers and apertures.

Washington minute notches in the inner edge at each apparent extremity.

2. The *Ring* B begins from its very sharp outer border with a luminous region, sometimes the brightest part of the whole system, though according to Schr. and Schwabe variable—a circumstance which I have also noticed, finding it more conspicuous in 1853 and 1855 than in 1856 and 1857 : the inner edge is very obscure; Schumacher and D. have seen it much better defined on one side of the ball. From one rim to the other there is an increasing shade, formerly considered regular, but found by La., D., and Se. to consist of 4 or 5 concentric and deepening bands, compared by La. to the steps of an amphitheatre ; each may be a separate ring, since fine black lines were at times traced here by Encke, De-Vico, and Coolidge,[1] and Bond's telescope showed markings like narrow waves of light and darkness. De la Rue and D., in another year, have seen a lighter central band. The innermost edge is sometimes brightened up—in other seasons it fades. I saw it in 1853 without any previous knowledge, on one ansa, with only $3\frac{7}{10}$-in. aperture : in 1856 it was less visible, and went beyond my range in 1857.[2]

3. The *Ring* C, the crape or gauze veil, is one of the greatest marvels of our day. How it could have escaped so long, while far minuter details were commonly seen, is a mystery. Schr., in 1796, with his great reflector, 26 English ft. focus, 19-in. aperture, particularly examined the space on each side of the ball, and found it uniformly dark; if

---

[1] I saw such a line in June 1780, for a few days on one ansa only. De-Vico's observations are not always satisfactory.

[2] In November, 1903, Denning remarked a large bright spot on this ring, and reobserved it on several evenings. Its approximate rotation period was 14^h 32^m.

anything, darker than the sky.[1] Our great observers the two
Herschels never perceived it.   Struve measured Saturn
repeatedly in 1826 with the superb Dorpat achromatic, 14-ft.
focus, $9\frac{6}{10}$-in. aperture, but missed it, though he saw the
inner edge of B very feebly defined.   In 1828 a fine Cauchoix
achromatic of $6\frac{1}{3}$-in. aperture having been placed in the
Roman observatory, it was seen, as an old assistant informed
Se., both in the ansæ and across the ball, yet, strange to say,
and little to the credit of Roman Science at that time, *no
notice whatever was taken of it.*   Ten years later, in 1838,
the matter fell into worthier hands ;—Galle of Berlin, with
a glass the counterpart of that at Dorpat, detected and
measured it very accurately, and published his observations ;
yet they somehow went on the shelf till, in Nov. 1850, Bond
in America, and our own D., had each the honour of an independent and original discovery ; and now everybody may
find it with a sufficient aperture : it has been well seen with
$3\frac{3}{8}$-in. achr. by Ross ; I saw faint traces of it with my $3\frac{7}{10}$-in. ;
anything larger, if good, is sure to bring it out.—Where was
it for so many years ?   Probably some change may have
rendered the part projected on the sky more luminous ; but
it is not a new formation, for where it crosses the ball it has
been seen ever since Campani's time, 1664 : and it was even
repeatedly noticed that its outline did not suit the perspective of a belt on Saturn, as it was supposed to be, or that of
a shadow thrown by the ring : on this bright background
it is so easy that Grover has seen it with a 2-in. aperture.
It reaches halfway or rather more from the edge of B to
Saturn : at its first discovery D., and Otto Struve at
Poulkova (the Czar's observatory), with the superlative achr.
by Merz, $22\frac{1}{3}$-ft. focus, $14\frac{9}{10}$-in. aperture, considered it to be

---

[1] Bond's telescope shows the same appearance between C and the
ball.   It has been seen also by Whitley, 1870.

divided in two by a dark line; but this has not been seen
since; nor is it certain whether there is a division between
it and B, or whether it is fainter towards its inner edge.
Its general slaty hue has been at times found different on
the two sides of the planet, reddish and bluish; and a repeated interchange of these tints, noticed by La. and D.,
might indicate rotation; its width and brightness in the two
ansæ have been occasionally seen different; its narrowness
in front of the ball has induced an idea that it is not in the
same plane with the rings A and B; and, in 1861–2, some
nebulous light attending the edge-view of the ring, on each
side of the globe, as observed by Struve II. and Wray,
might perhaps be the result of its perceptible thickness:
1863, Mar. 26, Carpenter at Greenwich found it almost as
bright as B, for part of which it might easily have been
mistaken. D., Jacob, and La. have concurred as to the very
curious fact of its partial transparency, permitting the limbs
of Saturn to be traced through it.[1] Trouvelot, with the
26½-in. achr., and Common, with his noble 36½-in. mirror,
have thought it speckled, as though consisting of separate particles. Possibly a similar material may fill Cassini's division,
as this has been sometimes seen not quite black, and Jacob
has even followed the shadow of Saturn across it. Many
slight variations lead to the inquiry whether this grand
system is really permanent in its detail. Se. thought the
bright rings might be clouds in an imperfectly transparent
atmosphere,[2] which is visible in the rings C and Cassini's

[1] Perceived by Whitley (1870) with a 6½-in. silvered mirror.
Bond saw it transparent throughout; but Trouvelot, in 1876, distinctly
found, with the Washington achr., the transparency gradually diminish
from the inner edge, till halfway across it disappeared.

[2] The ring was suspected to have an atmosphere by ♅ from the
apparent threading of the minutest satellites upon it when reduced
to extreme thinness.

division; and the American mathematician Pierce considers it demonstrable that the ring is not solid, but may be a stream or streams of a fluid rather denser than water, adding, in the spirit of a true philosopher, 'Man's speculations should be subdued from all rashness and extravagance in the immediate presence of the creator.' An idea suggested by Cassini II., that it may consist of a multitude of satellites,[1] has been earnestly advocated by Proctor, but would not be applicable to C, excepting on Burton's ingenious suggestion, that the separate particles, though brighter than the sky, may be less luminous than the ball; corresponding with the 'dark transits' of the satellites of Jupiter. The passage of the rings over a considerable star might give us some further information; but such events are very infrequent.[2] Whiston states that Dr. Samuel Clarke and his father, about 1707 or 1708, saw a star with a 17-ft. refractor between the ring and Saturn, but nothing of the kind has been since recorded. D. alone has seen, but under unfavourable circumstances, a star between 8 and 9 m^g. pass behind the outer edge of A. In such a case, all attention should be given to the visibility of the star through at least Cassini's division, and the dark ring. The shadow [3] of the planet upon the rings is readily

[1] This idea was also that of Thomas Wright of Durham (1750). In 1857 Clerk Maxwell proved mathematically that the rings must consist of fine particles revolving independently with periods determined by their distances. Keeler, in 1895, with the spectroscope, showed that the outer travelled more slowly than the inner ring.—(Es.)

[2] The passage of the outer satellite Iapetus through the shadow of the crape ring was observed by E. E. Barnard with the 36-in. Lick refractor. Iapetus continued visible during the whole of its passage through this shadow, but the absorption of sunlight became more and more pronounced, until finally the satellite entered the shadow of the bright inner ring, 1889, Nov. 1, and then was eclipsed.

[3] In April and May, 1892, the shadow of the outer ring upon the ball was noticed to be *concave* to the south pole, though south of the

seen, except near the opposition, cutting off one of the four arms of the ansæ from apparent contact with the ball: Grover has perceived it with a 2-in. aperture. The outline of this shadow has often been found curved the wrong way for its perspective, or deviating on ring A from its line on B;[1] something of this kind has been noticed ever since Cassini's time, and I have seen traces of it with the 5½-ft. achr.; the shadow of the ring on the ball has also been observed notched by Schr., La., De la Rue, and Jacob.[2] Hence an uneven surface would be inferred, and Se. finds that a reversed curvature would result from a slight convexity in the ring; but in each case we are at once confronted by its total or nearly total disappearance when viewed edgeways, seeming to demonstrate absolute flatness: it cannot however be quite symmetrical, for not only do the opened ansæ sometimes show an unequal breadth of some or all of their lines and markings E. and W., but about the time of their vanishing or reappearance they have been repeatedly seen, ever since 1671, variable and unlike in length and thickness and

ring, which was, of course, convex to the same pole, by Rev. A. Freeman and H. MacEwen. This is a geometrical necessity when the ring is nearly edgewise to the earth.

[1] Bond II. and Coolidge, in 1856–7, saw it strangely flattened with a deep notch, like the eaves of a roof, and it was unequal in depth of shade: it was also visible on each side of the ball at once, and exhibited corners in crossing Cassini's division; several of these strange anomalies have been confirmed by D., La., Se., Jacob, and Trouvelot, and have been carefully studied by several observers in recent years. It seems probable that both the "false shadow" sometimes seen where a shadow is geometrically impossible, and the corner formed by the true shadow at the Cassini division arise from some sort of illusion.—(P.) Grover has several times seen very distinctly a penumbra to the shadow of the ball, as in the frontispiece to *Kitchiner on the Telescope*.

[2] See also T. G. Elger's observations in 1888 (M.N. of R.A.S. xlviii. pp. 368–9).

continuity. When the light of the ring has been reduced to a thread, knots of greater brightness have often been noticed upon it. From the supposed motion of some of these in 1789, ♄ deduced a rotation in $10^h 32^m 15^s$, which an examination of the original observations will show to be without foundation. Schr. and Harding (1802, 1803), Schwabe (1833, 1848), Schm. and Bond (1848), and Se. (1862), found them all immovable.[1] Schr. supposed that they were mountains; Olbers, more probably, that they were the perspective aspect of such parts of the ring as show the greatest breadth of light. Bond finds this insufficient, as they are not lost when the dark side is turned to us, and he thinks that they may be explained by the reflection of light from the interior edges, seen through the openings of the rings. Yet many observations indicate too much irregularity to be so readily accounted for. When it stands edgeways, or turns its dark side to us slightly, the whole system totally vanishes in ordinary instruments. ♄ seems to have kept hold of it, probably in parts, and Bond did not quite lose it in 1848, though it was seldom continuous: in 1862 Se. kept the thread in sight, and the Greenwich equatorial showed an interrupted line.[2] The thinness of this enormous plane is literally matter of astonishment; H. estimated it at 250 miles; Bond allowed it but $0''\cdot01$, or 40 miles—about $\frac{1}{4000}$ of its diameter! In 1848 and 1862 D. saw traces of the dark side when turned to us, of a deep coppery tinge;— Huggins, 1862, dark blue. The reappearance in 1891 was watched with especial interest; and the possessors

[1] Projections were measured by Aitken with the Lick 36-in. in 1907. De-Vico saw on several consecutive nights in 1840, and once in 1842, a fixed bright point attached to the open ansa. This, with the instrument and eye of his successor Se. would alone have negatived a rotation.

[2] Aitken, 1907, found it narrower than the micrometer wire.—(Es.)

of ordinary instruments need not be disheartened; the slender line of light is a beautiful spectacle; and my fluid achromatic of 4-in. aperture, but of which much of the light went the wrong way, lost it in 1833 only one day sooner than Smyth's achr. of nearly 6-in., and but four days sooner than H.'s 18-in. reflector.[1] Saturn at such times shows usually a dark and very visible streak across his face, which D., Schm., and Wray have divided lengthways,—the unenlightened side of the ring, and its shadow: the latter has sometimes been invisible when it ought to have been seen; D. thinks from an atmosphere. Schwabe and other observers have thought the belts not exactly parallel to the ring in this position.

The *Satellites*. The very confused way in which the members of this numerous retinue were formerly designated, by numbers counted in two different directions, has been superseded by H.'s ingenious nomenclature, in which the names reckoned towards Saturn are easily remembered in a Latin pentameter and a half—

> Iapetus, Titan, Rhea, Dione, Tethys,
> Enceladus, Mimas.[2]

This arrangement has been since disturbed by the simultaneous discovery in 1848 by La. and Bond of an 8th, Hyperion, extremely faint, between Iapetus and Titan.—The

---

[1] Lardner says, H. did *not* lose it: not a solitary instance of inaccuracy.

[2] The exact order of all the satellites, together with their classical quantities, is indicated by the two hexameters—

> Ecce Mimas nitet, Enceladus, Tethysque, Dione,
> Inde Rhea, et Titan, Hyperion, Iapetusque.

Tethys and Dione have been found to be variable to the extent of 0·25 mag. at the Lowell Observatory, and Mimas and Enceladus also to an extent of 0·43 and 0·33 respectively, and it has been inferred that their period of revolution and rotation are synchronous.—(Es.)

lesser of them belong only to the highest instruments : the innermost has never been seen certainly with anything smaller than a $6\frac{1}{3}$-in. object-glass, and with that only in the purer skies of Paris, Rome, and Madras. Kitchiner and Wray have seen it with a 7-in. in England. The next, though easier, is still very minute ; Ward, however, has detected it with a $4\frac{3}{10}$-in. achr., Franks with 5-in. do. ; Perry with a $6\frac{6}{10}$-in., I with a $9\frac{1}{3}$-in. mirror. But Titan, the leader, is very conspicuous, being equal to an 8·5 m^g. star, so that it was discovered by Huygens in 1655, in which year it was also seen, though not suspected to be a satellite, in England, by Sir Paul Neil and Sir Christopher Wren. In fact, this little point of light, which may be seen with 1-in. aperture, has in large telescopes a disc of about 0″·75,[1] and probably ranks in size between Mercury and Mars. Its shadow was watched by ♅ in 1789 in transit across the disc of Saturn; G. saw it in 1833 ; in 1862 it was observed by D.[2] and several others, including myself ; it was seen twice

[1] W. H. Pickering's micrometric measures of Titan and Rhea in 1892, combined with the photometric measures of all the Satellites, supposed all to have the same reflective power, give the following dimensions at the mean distance of Saturn :—

Satellite.			Miles.	Diameter.	Magnitude.
Mimas	...	...	600	0″·15	12·5
Enceladus	...	...	800	·18	12·3
Tethys	...	...	1200	·28	11·4
Dione	...	...	1100	·27	11·5
Rhea	...	...	1600	·35	10·8
Titan	...	...	3000	·70	9·4
Hyperion	...	...	400	·10	13·7
Iapetus (maximum)		...	1200	0″·28	11·4

[2] This observer also witnessed the immersion of Titan in the planet's shadow. In 1892, January 4, an eclipse of Rhea was seen with $6\frac{1}{2}$-in. refractor by Rev. A. Freeman. The close conjunctions of pairs of the satellites are very pretty objects when the ring is nearly edgewise; sometimes one is then occulted by another.

at Dun Echt in 1877, and once by Hunt in 1878. Gledhill, Ward, and Bazley have also witnessed this curious but not difficult phenomenon, which Banks saw with $2\frac{7}{8}$-in. as easily as the shadow of I on Jupiter.[1]—Iapetus is not small, though probably, from a spotted surface and rotation like our Moon, not always equally visible, being much brightest at his W. elongation.[2]—Rhea, Dione, and Tethys are more minute.[3] D. considers Tethys superior to Dione.[4] Kitchiner states, from a friend, that, by hiding the planet, they have been seen with $2\frac{7}{10}$-in. aperture; Capron has seen them with $3\frac{1}{4}$-in.; Banks has seen four with $2\frac{7}{8}$-in.; Grover two, with only 2-in.; $3\frac{3}{4}$ or 4 in. may be expected to show all five. The three smaller are easier when further from the planet, but they only depart from it respectively 9·6, 6·9, and 5·4 of its radii. ♁ could follow all then known up to the disc. Schr. found them variable, like Iapetus, but brightest towards E. instead of W. ♁ has seen 7 brighter than 6. The inclination of the orbits, nearly similar to that of the ring, by spreading them over the sky, increases the difficulty of distinguishing them from small stars in one night's

---

[1] The shadows of *every* satellite, except Hyperion and Iapetus, were observed several times each by Rev. A. Freeman and A. S. Williams in 1892 with refractor and reflector of equal apertures, $6\frac{1}{2}$-in.

[2] The change, according to ♁, is equivalent to that from 2 to 5 m^g. Cassini had found it uncertain. So Banks, 1866.—A confusion exists in some writers as to the relative size and variable light of this satellite and Titan. Pickering gives 11·4 and 12·7 as the max. and min. m^g. of Iapetus.

[3] That Cassini with his inferior means should have not only discovered them, but traced their periods, reflects great credit upon his ability: it is gratifying to be able to subjoin the striking encomium of his Éloge:—'Les cieux qui racontent la gloire de leur Créateur n'en avoient jamais plus parlé à personne qu'à lui, et n'avoient jamais mieux persuadé.'

[4] Occasionally, though rarely, Dione is as bright as Tethys.

observation; and hence, probably, many mistakes have been made. To a spectator placed on Mimas, revolving in less than 23^h at a distance of only 32,000 miles from the edge of A, the whole system of rings and the included globe would float before the eye in such a spectacle of grandeur and beauty as the imagination is wholly unequal to conceive.[1]

URANUS AND NEPTUNE.

THESE planets may be reached, but to no great purpose, with ordinary means. URANUS, being visible in clear weather to the naked eye, will be easily caught up in the finder by the help of the almanac, and will be large and planetary-looking in the telescope; its disc indeed subtends less than 4″, but I never found the light of $3\frac{7}{10}$-in. sufficient to define it perfectly; $5\frac{1}{2}$-in. dealt far better with it : with Lawson's 7-in. object-glass, bequeathed to the Greenwich Naval School, I have seen it beautifully, as a little Moon : no one has made out much more : M. has seen it elliptical, and measured the flattening : La. with his 2-ft. speculum, and in the sky of Malta, once thought it possible there might be a spot : Buffham (1870–1) considered that he succeeded in detecting, with a 9-in. With mirror, white spots, portions probably of a discontinuous belt, from which a rotation from N. to S. might be imagined. The $26\frac{1}{2}$-in. Washington achr. finds nothing, but the Bothkamp $11\frac{1}{2}$-in. achr. has shown a lighter speck on the N. limb of the sharp sea-green disc.[2] The two rings

[1] Two additional satellites were discovered by W. H. Pickering in the year 1898 and 1905, viz. Phœbe, which has retrograde motion, revolving 550^d 10^h 34^m, and Themis, revolving in about 20^d 20^h 24^m. —(D.)

[2] Young, with 23-in. achr. at Princetown, and Perrotin with the

suspected by H̬ have long been abandoned, and La. has reduced the satellites to 4, which even the $5\frac{9}{10}$-in. object-glass of Smyth was incapable of reaching. Ward, however, has glimpsed the two outer ones, Oberon and Titania, with a $4\frac{3}{10}$-in. Wray achr., as Huggins has with 8-in. achr., and Sadler with a $6\frac{1}{2}$-in. mirror. My less acute eye has just caught one with $9\frac{1}{3}$-in. speculum. Marth has found their visibility not affected by moonlight. Huggins and Se. differ as to the details of its spectrum, but it is unquestionably a very extraordinary one, crossed by 6 broad absorption-bands,[1] one corresponding with hydrogen, the rest of unknown character.

NEPTUNE may be found in the same way, but will hardly repay the search : I have several times seen him with my $5\frac{1}{2}$-in. achr., but dull and ill-defined ; neither indeed would the great instruments of Se. or Vogel give him a sharp contour.[2] His satellite, supposed by some to be the largest of its class, and held by D. with 8-in. achr., no common telescope of course would touch ; though Ward has glimpsed it with a $4\frac{3}{10}$-in. achr. But who can say how grand a spectacle this inconspicuous globe might present on a nearer approach ? or what mysteries might be developed in a spectrum much resembling, according to Se., that of Uranus ? or that he is

30-in. at Nice, have seen belts. Henderson has seen a bright equatorial zone with $10\frac{1}{2}$-in. reflector.

[1] Spectroscopically Slipher finds that Uranus differs from Saturn and Jupiter in the increased strength of bands at λ 543 and λ 577. Neptune shows many strong absorption bands, which are so pronounced between F. and D. as to leave the solar spectrum unrecognizable. There are also new bands not observed in the other planets. He believes that free hydrogen is present in the atmospheres of both Uranus and Neptune.—(Es.)

[2] Maxwell Hall, from observations in the variation of light (7·1 to 7·7), finds period of rotation 7^h 50^m 6^s.—(Es.)

the most distant planet that obeys our central Sun ? or what
unexplored wonders may lie in still remoter space ? ' Quis
unquam exhaustas dixerit cœli copias ? ' [1]   The advance of
optical power may be expected either to open up fresh
marvels, or prove to us that, as far as the dominion of our
own Sun is concerned, we have reached the boundary of
our knowledge.

COMETS.[2]

> ' Thou wondrous orb, that o'er the northern sky
> Hold'st thy unwonted course with awful blaze !
> Unlike those heavenly lamps, whose steady light
> Has cheered the sons of earth from age to age,
> Thou, stranger, bursting from the realms of space
> In radiant glory, through the silent night,
> Thy tresses streaming like the golden hair
> Of Atalanta, or that beauteous maid
> Pursued by Phœbus, upward shalt invite
> Many a dull brow unus'd on heav'n to turn,
> And many a bosom read with deep alarm.
>
> Where is thy track throughout the vast expanse ?
> Still onward hast thou urged thy bold career,
> From that first hour when the Creator's hand
> Impell'd thy fire along the fields of light,
> Nor ever yet arriv'd within the verge
> Of mortal ken, nor drank the distant beams
> Of our inferior sun, unask'd by thee
> To guide thee harmless on thy rapid way.'
>
> REV. JOHN WEBB (1811).

WHEN Kepler stated his belief, not merely that comets in-
habited the æther as fishes the ocean, but that the ocean

---

[1] Bianchini.

[2] The new matter and the chapter on Meteorites is by Mr.
Denning.

was not fuller of fishes than the æther of comets,[1] his con-
temporaries probably amused themselves with his luxuriant
fancy. Yet Kepler was not so far wrong as regards number ;
for it is now believed that upwards of 10,000[2] have approached
the Sun within the orbit of Mars during the Christian era.[3]
A twelvemonth seldom passes by, in these days of telescopic
activity, without the announcement of several; 1858 produced
8, and sometimes 3 and even 4 (as in Feb. 1845) have been
in sight at once :[4] but conspicuous ones are far from
common. The generality are faint, and so much alike, at
least in ordinary telescopes, that they offer little attraction
beyond the curiosity of watching their progress. But larger
comets are often equally imposing to the naked eye and
marvellous in the telescope; of which we had a splendid
instance in 'the Donati,' or, in astronomical language,
Comet VI, 1858—that is, the 6th in order of that year—
and again in the less beautiful, but in some respects more
impressive, Comet II, 1861 : while Comets III, 1860, and
II, 1862, were not less worthy of notice for peculiarity of

[1] 'Nec minus ætherem cometis refertum esse puto, quam oceanum
piscibus. Quod autem rari apparent nobis, ingens ætheris vastitas in
causâ est.'

[2] Of late years new comets have been discovered at the rate of
nearly 5 annually. It is clear, therefore, that if we make an allowance for those which have escaped observation, the rate per century
has been at least 600, and the aggregate number of comets during
1893 years, considerably upwards of 10,000.

[3] The probable number of comets, if we suppose the perihelia of
these bodies to be equally dispersed within the orbit of Neptune, has
been calculated as 17,558,424 An investigation by the late J. Kleiber
as to the mean number of comets always present in the solar system
gives the figures 5934! See Ast. Nach., No. 3104.

[4] During the last week in November, 1892, no less than 7 were
visible ! In 1911 12 comets were under observation, but not all at
the same time.

structure; and the 'Coggia' of 1874, by the brilliancy of its star-like nucleus, and the complexity of its intersecting envelopes, distinguished itself above its congeners through many previous and successive years.[1] It would lead us into too wide a field, as well as one already cultivated by abler hands,[2] were we to describe separately the more remarkable of these bodies; it will be better, therefore, to sketch a general outline, which may serve to direct our expectations in future. First, however, we will give directions for finding them, when invisible to the naked eye.

If a comet is too faint to be readily perceived by moving about, over the proper quarter of the sky, a hand telescope with a large field (an opera glass may answer well), we must take our larger instrument and 'sweep' for it thus: ascertain its probable position—not, of course, at the date of discovery, but at the time of the search, if the announcement gives a clue to it; put in the lowest eye-piece, point the telescope some

---

[1] More recently Comet III, 1881, presented a fine effect in the N. sky during the summer months of that year, and in the autumnal mornings of 1882 a large comet, with a beaded nucleus and a tail of 22°, formed an object of intense interest. At perihelion the latter comet may be said to have grazed the sun's surface (like the bright comets of 1680, 1843, and 1880), and actually made a transit across the solar disc on Sept. 16, but it was quite invisible in that position, hence Pastorff's observation of 1819 is disproved.

A fine comet, with a long-spreading tail, was visible in January and February, 1910, situated near Venus in the twilight of the evening sky. It suddenly became visible near the sun, and was known as the 'daylight comet.'—(D.)

[2] See Hind's excellent treatise, *The Comets* (1852), and Bond's *Account of Donati's Comet*, Cambridge, U.S., 1858; but especially his admirable Memoir in *Annals of Observatory of Harvard College*, iii. Pingré consulted 616 authors for his Cométographie (1783); and there were, in 1841, 382 works on the subject in the Poulkova library. See also Chambers' *Story of the Comets*, 1909.

distance below, and on one side of, the supposed place of the comet, and gently move it horizontally right or left, as the case may be, till it points about as much on the other side. When your first 'sweep' has been thus completed, raise the telescope vertically half the breadth of the field, or not much more (as a faint object too near the top or bottom might be missed), and sweep back again the same distance the reverse way, ending pretty nearly where you began but of course half a field higher ; raise again another half-field, and sweep on, till either the comet sails across the field, or you are evidently pointing much too high for it : in which case you may conclude that it is too faint for you, or has gone away so far as to make further search useless. The movement may, of course, as well be begun above as below the supposed place of the comet. This process of sweeping is equally available for finding Mercury or Venus in the daytime,[1] or minute stars or nebulæ at night ; the chief difficulty lies in so proportioning the vertical movement that the object shall not escape between the sweeps ; this is easy with rackwork, as the breadth of the field, and the suitable number of turns of the handle, may be previously ascertained by trial on a terrestrial object ; with a plain stand there is little trouble in it where stars occur frequently to guide the displacement of the field ; but by day, or in twilight, or in barren tracts of sky, sweeping without rackwork is less certain, and may require to be repeated.

The light of most comets is too faint for high powers, and demands a contrast with the dark sky which small fields do not admit : to get the whole extent of head or tail the lowest

[1] Denning made many observations of Jupiter in daylight, and found that with a refl. telescope of 10-in. aperture, mounted on a simple altazimuth stand, the average time occupied in sweeping up the planet was only two minutes.

power should be chosen, and for the tail the naked eye will be more effective than any glass, except the appropriate instrument called a comet-finder : [1] high powers may be used for the details of the nucleus, but the contraction of the field and the want of contrast must always be allowed for. Small comets are frequently nothing but luminous mists without trains, sometimes without central condensation;— as we ascend in the scale, nuclei, trains, envelopes, and various anomalous appearances succeed, depending probably upon diversities in the constitution of the comets themselves, as well as on their degree of approach to the Sun;—even Venus was thought to have influenced the aspect of 'the Donati,' as it passed near her. In common language, a comet consists of *head* and *tail;* but we have to make a telescopic analysis, and shall begin with—

1. The *Nucleus :* the most luminous part, occupying in a general sense the centre of the head. It is sometimes absent in telescopic comets, which are mere fogs, permitting the minutest stars, even such as would be effaced by the slightest terrestrial mist, to be seen through the very centre ;—thus H. saw a group of 16 and 17 m^g. stars through the heart of the comet of Biela in 1832 : from this diffused state they present every stage of condensation, including sometimes a sparkling or granulated appearance, up to the aspect of a star, which has occasionally, as in 1744, equalled Venus in brightness, and been visible to the naked eye in broad noonday, or, as in 1843, blazed out yet more splendidly like a bright white cloud, close to the glowing meridian Sun.[2]

---

[1] An opera-glass is also strongly recommended for these observations.

[2] Other comets visible by day (omitting some questionable ones):—A.C. 43, the star of 'the mightiest Julius,' which appeared during the games held soon after his assassination, and gave rise

High powers, however, usually dissolve any apparent solidity, and different instruments may give very different sizes to what looks like a planetary disc, throwing much doubt upon its reality : sometimes a very minute point (as ♅ found in 1807 and 1811) holds out against any magnifying ; and such was the case again in 1862, when it remained a point at Poulkova, under a power of 1458 ; and this—like broader nuclei—is not always central in the head. In some comets (1618, 1652, 1661, 1707, Winnecke's 1869, III, 1882, etc.) the nucleus seems to have been composed of separate masses, —a marvellous structure ;[1] would that we could often study it with modern advantages ! Had 'the Donati's' nucleus passed about 20′ further N., it would have gone right over Arcturus—and we might have obtained some negative information at any rate as to its composition. Miss Mitchell alone seems to have caught what seemed the central transit of a comet (1847) over a 5 m^g. star, which shone through it unchanged. Still, were the nucleus a mere point, it might have been only a very close appulse ; and some minor examples are less conclusive.[2] Hirst, however, at Sydney,

to the star on the forehead in his coins and statues ;—1106, 1402, 1577 (Tycho's great comet), 1618. That of Feb. 1847 was seen by Hind, and that of Aug. 1853 by Hartnup and Schmidt very near the Sun ; but in each case with the telescope, in which they showed planetary discs. Donati's comet was not visible, except with very powerful instruments, by day. In 1882 two comets were observed when close to the Sun. Comet Wells (I, 1882) was seen by Schmidt on June 10, when only 2°·8 from the Sun's limb, and the great comet of the following autumn was watched until it entered upon the Sun's disc on Sep. 16. In these cases telescopes were necessarily used.

[1] There is a strange story of visible internal movement among these subordinate nuclei in 1618—as if of coals stirred in a fire. This seems like a bad telescope or an alarmed observer—yet where all is mystery, neither credulity nor its opposite is the part of wisdom.

[2] Donati saw a 7 m^g. star enlarged so as to show a sensible disc,

witnessed what appeared a good instance, when Encke's comet passed directly over one of two neighbouring 10 m^g. stars, affording an excellent criterion of absolutely unchanged light. Were a defined phasis to show itself, a certain amount of density might be inferred; but if we except 'the Donati' as seen by D. in daylight, Oct. 8, this has never been satisfactorily the case, as the retroverted form often assumed by luminous sectors throws a doubt upon the observations. The darkness close behind the nucleus in 1858, if not real shadow, seemed at least to prove that the nucleus was not permeable to the solar energy, in whatever way exerted, and that it had no rotation upon an axis. The arrival of the next great comet will be a season of absorbing interest, as we shall be much better prepared for its reception. The spectrum analysis, first of Donati, subsequently of Huggins, Se., and several others, has shown not only the native light of the comets which have appeared since its employment, but what had been little anticipated, their gaseous character, and the close resemblance of the majority of their spectra to those of some of the compounds of carbon.

when the nucleus of Comet III, 1860, passed very near it. Stars are said to have started, or become tremulous, during occultation by comets. Birmingham observed the comet of Encke illuminated by a star over which it passed, 1868, Aug. 23; and Klein in 1861 remarked an exceptional twinkling in 5 m^g. stars involved in the tail.

On July 23, 1890, Denning watched a small comet, which he had discovered on previous night, pass over a star of about 8 m^g. The comet apparently disappeared, but the star suffered no diminution of light. Wolf's periodic comet, at its first return in 1891, passed over one of the stars in the Pleiades early in Sept. of the year named, and was invisible during the transit, but the star was not sensibly dimmed.—Esclangon observed an occultation of a 10·5 m^g. star by Comet Brooks (1911 c.). At the least distance it was impossible to separate the star and the nucleus. The star's light remained constant when in the nebulosity, but sensibly diminished when the nucleus and star were inseparable.

There can now be little doubt that such is the general constitution of these bodies : but probably with much variety in composition, as the acknowledged difference in colour makes sufficiently evident ; and the nature of the nucleus is still incomprehensible.

2. The *Coma* is the sphere of mist around the nucleus, forming in popular language the *head* : this is sometimes of considerable extent—2° 40', or 5 times the Moon's diameter, in 1770, when the nearest recorded approach of a comet to the Earth took place, of 1½ million of miles. The coma fades away into the surrounding sky, with an outline, including that of the commencing tail, usually considered parabolic; Bond, however, found in 1858 that its section approached much more nearly to a catenary curve. Its denser part, if distinguishable by any set-off or outline, is called—

3. The *Envelope*. This is an interior and brighter layer of mist, suspended as an atmosphere around the nucleus, at least where exposed to the sun : in Donati's comet some observers (amongst them myself) carried it a good way round the back of the nucleus; but usually it turns straight off on each side to form the commencement of the tail : within it is sometimes a darker narrow band, separating it from another interior and brighter envelope.[1] In 1858 no fewer than four such dark spaces at once were sometimes shown by the great achromatic at Cambridge, U.S., indicating the consecutive rising of five shining waves, which had spread themselves in succession outwards from the nucleus ; the latter seeming to diminish in size and brightness after each of these emissions of luminosity. M. at Dorpat noticed an actual increase of

---

[1] Huggins has made the important remark that these non-luminous spaces may correspond to a condition of the vapour too cool to emit light, and yet not condensed so as to reflect it.

one of these envelopes from 18″ to 27″ in 2ʰ. Occasionally, as in 1861 and the 'Coggia,' the nucleus appears not to occupy the axis of some of these veils, which consequently seem to cross one another in front of it. In 1811 the whole coma and envelope were raised in one parabolic mass from the nucleus, which was surrounded by clear dark sky on every side: when the extreme diameter of the luminous cloud amounted, according to Schr., to 947,000 miles, considerably exceeding the bulk of the Sun, and almost doubling the Moon's orbit. As this comet receded, the dark space became indistinct, and the envelope sank finally down upon the nucleus. Envelopes sometimes contain dark spots and streaks (1858), and more frequently brushes or fans of light, where the shining matter seems to stream out from circumscribed portions of the nucleus; these are rapidly variable, and in Halley's comet at its return in 1835 showed such a libration from side to side, traceable from hour to hour, that Bessel inferred some powerful polar force unconnected with gravity. Such a swinging was less distinctly recognised in 1858. In Comet II, 1862, in which these sectors or aigrettes were very striking, Se. and Chacornac perceived, otherwise than Schm. no motion of this kind, but thought that the jets proceeded alternately from different parts of the nucleus. The last observer found the light of the nucleus variable inversely as the breadth of the sector in 2·7 d., and that the luminous matter ascended towards the Sun with a velocity of nearly 2200 miles in a second. In Coggia's comet With saw an evident oscillation one evening. The envelope and coma together form the origin of—

4. The *Tail*. This, when not greatly foreshortened, appears as a long cylinder or more usually cone, widening in general as it advances, and showing a hollow structure by an interior darkness. There seems, however, a doubt of

the adequateness of the explanation;[1] since the perspective of 1858 required a very different proportion either of the *breadth* or the *intensity* of the dark space : some other cause may possibly be combined with vacancy to produce the effect. This interval in the Donati was very dark close behind the nucleus ; Schwabe found it darker than the twilight sky, and D. and Hartnup considered it a *real shadow :* in 1811, however, such a vacancy surrounded the nucleus on every side. The division into two streams effected by it was seen with the naked eye in the great comet of 1577, which astonished Tycho at his fishpond before sunset, and it has been frequently noticed since the discovery of the telescope ; in 1843 it was absent; and a brighter ray filled the middle when Halley's comet [2] in 1835 was withdrawing from the Sun. The preceding stream according to the comet's motion is usually brighter and sharper defined, as well as curved backwards. Kepler noticed this in 1618, and compared it in his own graphic way to the appearance of a heap of corn swept over by the wind in the threshing-floor : and no one will forget it who

[1] It appears probable, in the light of certain modern researches, that the tail is due to electrical action.

[2] This comet returned to perihelion in 1910, April 19, and was visible for some months. Discovered by Wolf in September, 1909, it remained distinguishable on large instruments until May, 1911. In England it proved a disappointing object in the evenings of May and June, 1910, but in S. Africa and certain other parts it was splendidly presented at a high altitude in pellucid skies, and exhibited a tail more than 100 degrees in length. The Earth passed through a section of the tail on May 18, but no appreciable effect was produced either in the sky or on our globe. A few shooting stars were seen early in May, 1910–12, at Bristoe and a few other places, and they were directed from the comet's radiant point in Aquarius. But no brilliant shower took place, though the identity of Halley's comet and this meteoric system is supported by the recent observations.—(D.)

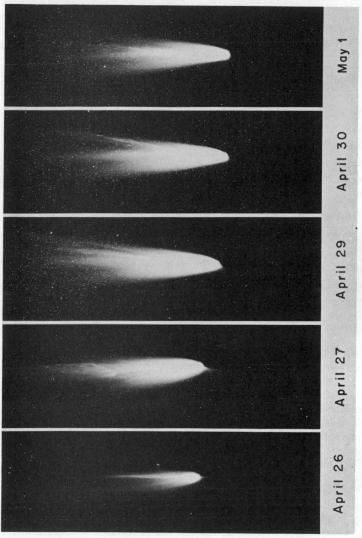

April 26   April 27   April 29   April 30   May 1

(*Photographs from the Mount Wilson and Palomar Observatories*)

Arend-Roland Comet, 1957. Five views taken with 48-inch schmidt telescope.

(Photo by Charles Cuevas of the Observing Group, Amateur Astronomers Association of New York)

Comet Arend-Roland, May 3, 1957.

saw the form of the Donati.[1] It has been usually referred to motion through a resisting medium : but Pape, from an elaborate investigation, finds that the curvature may be explained by the combination of the comet's motion with a repellant power in the Sun. The axis of the tail was calculated by him to differ 6° 18' from exact opposition to the Sun, being left a little behind—a deviation of which there have been previous examples.[2] The length of the tail is sometimes enormous. According to Boguslawski, that of the wonderful comet which in 1843 nearly grazed the surface of the Sun, and, as Se. expresses it, issued from it like a dart of light, was cast away to the almost incredible extent of 581 millions of miles[3]—more than 6 times the distance of the Earth from the Sun, and crossing the orbit of Jupiter ; and this astounding stream, the longest object, as far as our senses can reach, in all space, must have been shot out with an equally inconceivable velocity after passing the perihelion ; for, but a short time before, the head was on the other side of the Sun, half round which it had been whirled in $1\frac{1}{2}^{h}$ or 2^{h}, and under such circumstances the whole direction of the same tail could not be supposed to have been reversed. Even should the length be considered to be overstated, we certainly have before us here one of the greatest marvels in the universe.[4] Minor trains are occasionally seen ; in some

[1] Towards the close of its appearance, the American observers noticed a reversal of the brightness and definition of the sides of this comet's tail. They also found, contrary to the common opinion, that the plane of its curvature was not identical with that of its motion : how this can be reconciled with Pape's theory does not appear.

[2] According to Schi., the tail of Comet III, 1862, was forced out in a direction very different from that of the *radius vector*. The very long train in 1769 was stated to have shown a double curvature towards its end.

[3] According to the then received solar parallax.

[4] Photography has recently played a very important part in

cases (1769, 1811) the prolongations of an outer envelope; in others apparently separate branches (1806, 1843); according to Chéseaux, six of them, each hollow, formed a glorious fan in 1744. A straight, long, narrow, and very faint ray of this kind, directly opposite to the Sun, was seen by several observers steadily preceding the great curved tail in 1858. The grand visitor of 1861 had a straight and a curved tail, the latter of which probably swept over our globe, or, according to Liais, buried it to a depth of 110,000 leagues. From certain periodical returns of lateral streams, Dunlop in 1825 inferred a rotation of the tail[1] in $20\frac{1}{2}^{h}$, and similar appearances were noticed in 1769, 1811, and 1862; but the explanation is perhaps precarious, from the immense velocity required. An additional stream has sometimes, though rarely, been directed *towards* the Sun; this extraordinary phenomenon, called an *anomalous tail*, was noticed in 1824, when it was longer and brighter, though narrower and more tapering, than the usual one; subsequently it was found recorded that the grand comet of 1680—Newton's comet—had left a similar glowing wake upon the æther; and it has since been noticed in 1845, 1848 (Encke's,— perhaps again in 1871), 1850, and 1851.[2] The principal tail in 1858 was seen by the Americans crossed obliquely by a number of brighter bands like auroral streamers, diverging from a point between the nucleus and the Sun.

showing the structure and rapid variations of the tails of comets. Morehouse's comet of 1908 exhibited knots and bends of conspicuous character, and these changed quickly from night to night. It became evident that clouds of luminous material were driven from the nucleus along the tail at surprising velocities.—(D.)

[1] The details shown in Barnard's photographs of Swift's comet (1892) appear to suggest that there was a rotation of the tail upon an axis through the nucleus in a comparatively short period.

[2] One of the three short rays, besides the tail, seen in 1577, may possibly have been of this character.

A few other details should be noticed. *Coruscations* or flashings have been often remarked in the tail : that of 1556 was said to waver like the flame of a torch in the wind ; and numerous other instances might be given, before and since the use of telescopes. The accurate Hook took many pre-cautions before he satisfied himself of their reality in 1680 and 1682, and Schr. stoutly maintained their existence in 1807, referring them to electricity or some analogous cause; others negative them as too rapid for the progressive motion of the light by which we should see them—an objection, however, applying only to foreshortened tails—and treat them as illusions depending on our own atmosphere, or the uncertainty of weary sight. Polarization experiments concur with spectrum-analysis in discrediting their reality, by showing that the denser portion of the tails, as well as comæ, shines in part by reflected light, owing probably, as Huggins suggests, to the cooling of the incandescent material of the nucleus. It would have added greatly to the interest of the present pages, could they have embodied more satisfactory results of spectroscopic research. But we are waiting for favourable opportunities.[1] There seems no doubt, as we

---

[1] These opportunities were afforded by the bright comets III, 1881, IV, 1881 (Schæberle), I, 1882 (Wells), III, 1882, I, 1887, etc., and we proceed to quote, chiefly from Mr. Plummer's reports, a few results of spectrum analysis as given in the *Monthly Notices* and other publica-tions :—' The spectrum of comet III, 1881, appeared to be continuous with 3 bright bands in the yellow, green, and blue. Dr. Huggins succeeded in photographing the spectrum of the comet which showed 2 groups of bright bands in the violet and a continuous spectrum. IV, 1881, exhibited a spectrum consisting of 3 bright bands approxi-mately coincident with the 3 brightest bands of the spectrum of the Bunsen flame and a faint continuous spectrum. I, 1882, showed a remarkable departure from the normal characteristic. Ever since 1864, when Donati first submitted a comet to this kind of examination, the spectra of these bodies had revealed the bands of hydrocarbon,

have said, that the materials of the smaller comets are of a gaseous nature, generally, though not invariably, affording spectra analogous to those of compounds of carbon. This is sufficiently marvellous; but the still more curious inquiry

but in this instance there was a striking deviation from the ordinary type. This was indeed so marked on April 21 that the cometary nature of the object would scarcely have been identified by its spectrum. At the close of May a bright sodium line in the nucleus and envelope was detected at Dun Echt. Early in June, when the comet was at its brightest, this line under adequate dispersion was seen to be double, and the behaviour of the more refrangible line indicated to Professor Vogel that the density of the incandescent gas was very great. III, 1882. It is curious to notice that while the spectrum of I, 1882, was continuously observed as the comet approached the Sun, and illustrated the effects of great and increasing excitement, the spectrum of III, 1882, could only be observed as it receded from perihelion, and consequently the phenomena that were observed in regard to I, 1882, might be expected to repeat themselves in III, 1882, but in the reversed order, and this to a great extent actually occurred. When first examined on Sept. 18 the sodium lines were at once seen to be distinctly double, both in the nucleus and outlying material, while a number of other bright lines, coinciding with the more prominent iron lines were visible. There was no indication of the usual banded spectrum. When the comet had reached the Earth's distance from the Sun, all trace of the sodium lines had vanished, and the 3 bands of hydrocarbon were distinctly present. The full explanation of the phenomena witnessed cannot be found in the simple increase or decrease of temperature depending on the interval separating the comet from the Sun, but a satisfactory solution may be found if we suppose that cometary light is to some extent due to electric discharges The spectrum of Holmes's comet on Nov. 18, 1892, did not show the ordinary bands, but appeared to be continuous through a considerable portion of the green, and this would seem to indicate that the comet shines by reflected sunlight only. Slipher points out that spectroscopically comets Brooks 1911, Gale 1912, Zlatinsky 1914, were similar, and form apparently the usual type. Comet Halley and Daniel 1907 had a less common type, while that of Morehouse 1908 was exceptional. Fowler has identified some of the bands in this comet with those of low pressure and high pressure carbon monoxide.

into the nature of the nuclei in the grander specimens remains unsolved. The chief instance, that of the 'Coggia,' to which it has as yet been applicable, has only increased the mystery. The spectrum of this resplendent stellar point was so far continuous as to prove unborrowed light; so far interrupted, especially at the red end, as to indicate emission or absorption by materials wholly unknown. Possibly some more intelligible disclosures may be in store for us. But even should we be permitted to lift partially in some special instance the veil, we are still confronted by those differences of colour which appear to indicate a difference of constitution. 'Omnia incerta ratione, et in naturæ majestate abdita.' [1]

As regards *colour*, a wide margin must no doubt be left for the superstition of the ancients, who dreaded the herald of disaster, 'terris mutantem regna cometen,' [2] and held it as a malignant genius that—

—— 'from his horrid hair
Shakes pestilence and war.'

Those who noticed the fiery hue of the sabre-like comet that passed to the E. at the commencement of the Crimean war will understand with what feelings our fathers would have gazed upon it, like the astonished spectators of the comet of the Norman Conquest,[3] represented in the Bayeux tapestry with the inscription 'Isti mirantur stellam:' nor will the exaggeration of those beautiful lines seem unnatural,

—— 'Liquida si quando nocte cometæ
Sanguinei lugubre rubent.' [4]

---

[1] Seneca.

[2] Lucan. The 'comet-dollars' still existing in Germany are a curious evidence of this feeling as late as 1664. See *Illustr. Lond. News*, July 20, 1861.

[3] An apparition of Halley's comet.

[4] Virgil.

It is however certain, both from the Chinese and modern observations, that there is much difference in respect to colour:[1] ⟨ even found the nucleus of the same comet (1811) pale ruddy, the envelope greenish or bluish-green : and a similar contrast was noticed by Struve in Halley's comet in 1835, and by Winnecke in 1862. That the Sun induces in them a polar force superior to that of gravitation—the hypothesis, in the main, of Olbers—is most probable from the form of the envelope and tail, as if repelled alike from the nucleus and Sun : and that a certain portion of the rarer material must be dissipated during the perihelion passage is evident from the very aspect of a tail such as that of 1858, whose restoration to the rapidly advancing nucleus is, to our apprehension, an impossibility. And in this, and in the resistance which comets which traverse the solar corona may be presumed to suffer, we find sufficient indications that our system was not made to be eternal. The perfect balance of its construction might at first lead to another impression, and seem to countenance the old objection, that 'all things continue as they were from the beginning of the creation.' But here is evidence to the contrary—slight, but decisive symptoms that—' they all shall wax old as doth a garment ; ' that they ' shall be changed.' The traces of dissolution may be perceived in the comet of Biela, whose separation into two parts is one of the marvels of modern astronomy.[2] Single

---

[1] This comes out well chemically. The ' Donati ' was photographed : with Comet II, 1861, it was found impossible even by De la Rue. Several recent comets have been very successfully photographed. Jansen and Draper obtained some excellent photo-views of III, 1881, which exhibited many interesting features in the structure of the envelope and tail. Some beautiful photographs of Swift's comet of 1892, by Barnard, are reproduced in *Knowledge* for December of that year.

[2] Liais at Olinda saw a second smaller and fainter nebulosity on

in all previous observed returns (those of 1772, 1805, 1826, 1832), in 1846 it became elongated, and then threw off a portion which increased till it rivalled and even for a short time surpassed its parent, each having at one period a starry nucleus and short tail, while they were connected by faint streams of light : and thus they continued in sight for more than 3 months, keeping a distance of something more than 150,000 miles, the companion being the first to vanish. When next seen by Se., in 1852, the distance was more than 8 times greater, being 2^m in R.A , and 30′ in Declination, as though they were becoming independent bodies : their next favourable return (1866) was looked for with no common interest; but they were not seen, and probably will never again be seen by mortal eye.[1] Nor has the larger comet of De Vico, discovered by him in 1844, with an apparent period of 5½ years, ever shown itself again—it has

—— 'wandered away alone,
No man knows whither.'

Comet seeking forms an attractive field of labour, though not always productive unless the observer perseveres. Moreover, it is a branch specially suitable for amateurs,

several nights by the side of Comet I, 1860, previous to its disappearance. Several cometary fragments were observed (by Schmidt, Brooks, and others) near the great comet of 1882, from which they were no doubt evolved by a process of disintegration operating on the parent mass. But the most remarkable instance of a divided comet was that of Brooks' (V. 1889), which Barnard saw separated into five parts on August 1, 1889. One of the minor fragments existed for several months. Mellish's comet (1915) had four nuclei, which slowly receded from the main body, indicating the probable break-up of the comet.

[1] We have doubtless seen the comet in another form, for the brilliant meteor showers of November 27, 1872 and 1885, and November 23, 1898, represented a wholesale expenditure of its material by collision with our atmosphere.

some of whom, such as Swift, Barnard, and Brooks, in America, have distinguished themselves in it before entering upon a professional career. A Kellner eye-piece, or, in its absence, an ordinary eye-piece with a low power and large field, is necessary, and the telescope should not have a smaller aperture than 4 inches. The observer will require the New General Catalogue of nebulæ, published by the Royal Astronomical Society in 1888, and the subsidiary lists of Dreyer, and some reliable star maps; for during the progress of sweeping, he will be sure to encounter numbers of nebulæ which it will be necessary to identify. Should a suspicious object be found, it must be watched for traces of motion, and should this become apparent, its direction and daily rate will have to be determined. The position of the object should also be fixed as accurately as the observer's means allow, and, if it agrees with no known comet, details of the discovery should be telegraphed to the Astronomer Royal, who will take means to confirm it and distribute the information.

METEORS.

Their Cometary Relations.—These phenomena have acquired a special interest in recent years, and their astronomical origin and associations have been placed beyond doubt. The identity of several well-known meteor-systems with periodical comets was shown by the researches of Newton, Schiaparelli, and others, about a quarter of a century ago, and the singular behaviour of Biela's comet, and its resultant meteor stream of Andromedes on November 27, 1872 and 1885, and November 23, 1892, form an interesting chapter in the history of the subject. Four of the most brilliant of the known meteor showers display a similarity of orbit with the same number of well-observed comets, thus the April Lyrids match with Comet I, 1861, the August Perseids with III, 1862, the November Leonids with I, 1866, and the November Andromedes with Biela's lost comet. There is also evidence of relationship between Halley's comet and the May Aquarids, and a few other instances might be quoted, though it is perhaps surprising that comparatively few such coincidences have been found among the very large number of comets and meteoric streams observed in past years.[1]

Difficulties of Observation.—There is probably no other department of astronomy standing in greater need of further observational effort, and which requires more experience and care on the part of those engaged in it. The practical study of meteors brings us face to face with complications and anomalies, which only the utmost accuracy and discrimination can clear away. Apart, therefore, from the great patience which the meteor-observer must exercise during his prolonged vigils, he has to feel his way with extreme caution among a labyrinth of materials, and to weigh every detail likely to assist him in gathering reliable results. On every night of the year there are probably more than 100 feeble meteor showers in play, and many of these are of such extreme tenuity that they may not yield individually a single meteor in a continuous watch of 5 hours. Radiant points are sometimes thickly clustered together in the same region of the heavens; and these facts require that an observer, to be successful, must watch the sky during long intervals, and that he must record the meteor flights with

---

[1] It is a fact, however, that the orbits of very few comets approach near enough to the earth's path to produce a shower of meteors.—(D.)

invariable precision. If this is not done, pseudo-radiants will be deduced, and the observations generally will be almost worthless. Desirable accuracy can be attained after a fair amount of practice, but one of the most difficult features of the work is the apportionment of the individual meteors to their respective radiants. It is necessary not only to consider their directions of flight, but also their traits of appearance, such as velocity, length of path, streaks or trains. The meteors belonging to one and the same stream, exhibit a family likeness which is often sufficiently pronounced to enable them to be distinguished from other systems. A vast amount of useful work remains to be accomplished in this field by ardent observers who will gain, by experience, a just conception and knowledge of its requirements.

Numbers Visible.—Though the fall of meteors is incessant it varies greatly in intensity. On the occasion of a periodical shower, such as the Perseids with max. on August 10, an observer may perhaps count about 100 meteors per hour in a moonless sky. In the case of an exceptionally brilliant and prolific display, such as that of the Leonids on November 12, 1833, 1000 meteors may be seen per minute. On November 23, 1892, the Andromedes returned in such abundance that an observer estimated the number falling as 108 per minute! On ordinary nights, void of special showers, the rate of appearance of these bodies is usually not more than 10 per hour; and there are many dates, particularly in the winter and spring months, which manifest a remarkable scarcity, for the keenest watch will not reveal more than 4 or 5 meteors per hour. The last half of the year furnishes nearly double the number visible in the first half, and in the morning hours at any season, the apparitions greatly exceed those in the evening.

Bolide, photographed with star trails of Sagittarius, August 1957.
(Inset) enlargement of bolide trail.

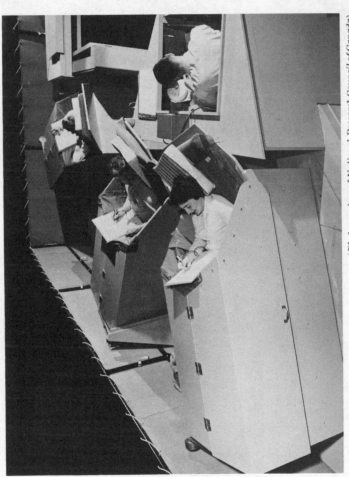

(*Photo courtesy of National Research Council of Canada*)

Station for visual observation of meteors, Spring Hill, Ontario, Canada. Eight observing positions, each connected with a nearby radar recording unit, cover the sky in a uniform pattern. Timekeeper is at center.

Their Velocities.—The apparent velocity with which these bodies enter our atmosphere varies between about 10 and 45 miles per second. The Andromedes of November 23 and 27 supply an example of the slow-moving class, while the Leonids of November exemplify the swifter kind. The former descend gradually, like snow-flakes in a calm, and they generally throw off yellowish trains of sparks; the latter traverse their paths with terrific speed, and are often too transient to be well seen, but they furrow the sky with lines of phosphorescence, and these enable their paths to be registered with great accuracy. Appendages, such as trains, streaks, etc., doubtless represent the incandescent and nearly exhausted material torn off from the nuclei during their rapid combustion and flight through the air.

Elevation.—The average heights of meteors during visible combustion is about 76 miles at first appearance and 51 miles at disappearance. But large meteors (often termed fireballs or bolides) generally penetrate much deeper into the atmosphere than the ordinary shooting-stars, for while the mean elevation of the former at extinction is only 30 miles, that of the latter is 54 miles. Occasionally the material of a fireball is sufficiently large and compact to resist total disruption, and falls upon the earth. Many instances are on record, and the British Museum contains numerous specimens of these aerolites. A few meteors have been seen which were more than 150 miles in height at the earliest stages of their apparitions, and this implies a far greater depth of atmosphere than what is possibly supposed.[1]

Stationary and Moving Radiant Points.—There are some

---

[1] The best observations go far to prove that visible meteors are very rarely, if ever, more than 100 miles above the earth's surface.—(D.)

anomalous facts concerning star-showers generally which require much further study. The active duration of a large proportion of the known radiant points appears to extend, in possibly an intermittent manner, over several months, during which they maintain an absolutely stationary position amongst the stars; and this is obviously incompatible with theoretical views of the matter, which require a displacement of about 1° per day to the eastwards. Such displacement was discovered at Bristol in 1877 to affect the great Perseid display of July-August, and the fact was strikingly corroborated on mathematical grounds by the late J. Kleiber,[1] whose early death is an irreparable loss to this branch of astronomy. The radiant point of the Perseids is in activity during a period of more than a month, for the oncoming of the shower is usually announced by a few brilliant streak-leaving meteors in the second week of July, and the mobile focus of their divergence only attains quiescence in the third week of August. The exact duration of the shower is, however, not known, and further observations are required to determine it. There are many other showers visible from Perseus and the region near in August, and the meteors belonging to these are liable to be confused with the true Perseids. The following ephemeris may perhaps be useful as a guide and means of reference for future observers of this rich annual shower:—

[1] *Monthly Notices*, March, 1892, p. 341.

Date.	Radiant. Degrees. R.A. Dec.	Date.	Radiant. Degrees. R.A. Dec.
July 19	19 + 51	August 2	36 + 55
„ 21	22 + 52	„ 4	38 + 56
„ 23	25 + 52	„ 6	40 + 56
„ 25	27 + 53	„ 8	42 + 57
„ 27	30 + 54	„ 10	45 + 57
„ 29	32 + 54	„ 12	47 + 57
„ 31	34 + 55	„ 14	50 + 57

Observations.—Meteors should be recorded according to the R.A. and Dec. of the points of their appearance and disappearance. Their paths, as seen in the sky, should be mentally noted with reference to the stars near, and then on projecting them on a celestial globe or suitable star map, the fundamental points may be read off and entered in a MS. catalogue. When two observations of the same object are secured at different stations, it becomes easy to determine its real path, including its locality and height above the earth's surface, its radiant point, etc. But it unfortunately happens that multiple observations of bright meteors (such as that seen on January 4, 1893, 6^h 30^m, which lit up the sky and the country with a strikingly luminous effect) are too loosely and imperfectly described to be of consequence. Many fireballs are thus lost to science; their transient glories apparently serve no other end than that of startling spectators who are fortunate enough to witness them. This is much to be regretted, for the proper discussion of such phenomena from reliable data would soon furnish significant evidence as to the positions and durations of meteor showers. What would accelerate the development of our knowledge of fireballs more than perhaps any other circumstance, would be the *general* attention of astronomical and meteorological observers, could we direct it, to the accurate description of the more salient features of these bodies. In a word, if observers made it an invariable custom to record objects of this kind, we should soon possess a store of valuable details for comparison with past and future records.

Catalogue of Radiated Points.—Subjoined is a list of 100 radiants selected from Mr. Denning's paper in *Monthly Notices*, vol. l. pp. 410–67. The table includes many of the most important showers of the year, and the dates given are those of the observed maxima. Some of these displays are of extremely variable intensity. In one year they may yield a plentiful supply of meteors and in the next be utterly invisible. But the Perseids, Orionids, Geminids, and others of similar type, are conspicuously numerous every year at their appointed times, while others like the Andromedes may be only seen once in 7 or 13 years, or, like the Leonids, only reappear at their best at intervals of about 33 years. The latter shower is really visible every year; a circumstance which proves that its meteors are distributed throughout the ellipse of which the orbit is composed. But the displays observed in the years intermediate between the maximum epochs are seldom conspicuous, and offer no comparison with the brilliancy of such returns witnessed in 1799, 1833, and 1866.[1]

[1] There were no very brilliant or abundant returns of the Leonids in 1899 and 1900, perturbation by Jupiter and Saturn having disturbed the swarm and drawn it away from the earth's orbit. But in 1901 a fairly rich display was witnessed in America on November 14, and in England in 1903, on November 15.—(D.)

Ref. No. D.	Date of Max.	Radiant Point. Degrees. R.A. Dec.	Approx. Star.	Aspect of Meteors.	Other Dates of Activity, Remarks, etc.
1	Jan. 2	230+53	44 Boötis	M. Sw. B.	Rich annual shower.
10	Jan. 5	140+57	θ Ursæ Maj.	Sw. F.	Small short meteors.
16	Jan. 11	220+13	ξ Boötis	V. Sw. K.	Nov. 28.—Dec. 5.
25	Jan. 17	295+53	χ Cygni	Sl. B.	Well observed, 1877.
27	Jan. 19	261+63	ζ Draconis	M. Sl.	March 28, April 22, etc.
30	Jan. 22	208+8	χ Libræ	V. Sw. K.	Feb. 15, April 16, 22, etc.
31	Jan. 25	131+32	ι Cancri	M. Sw.	Nov. 10, 23, Dec. 2.
34	Feb. 1	211+69	α Draconis	Sl.	Jan. 9, Dec. 8.
...	Feb. 7	74+43	α Aurigæ	Sl.	Aug. 21, Sept. 12—22.
38	Feb. 15	236+11	α Serpentis	V. Sw.	April 27—May 4.
39	Feb. 15	261+4	β Ophiuchi	Sw. K.	Compare No. 153.
40	Feb. 16	167+5	τ Leonis	Sl. K.	Nov. 27, Dec. 12.
41	Feb. 20	181+34	Piazzi XII. 29	V. Sw. B.	Well defined, 1877.
43	Feb. 20	263+36	ρ Herculis	Sw.	Visible before sunrise.
45	Mar. 1	47+45	α—β Persei	V. Sl.	Showers here July to Dec.
48	Mar. 14	175+10	β Leonis	Sl. B.	March 3, 4, Dec. 12.
58	Mar. 18	316+76	χ Cephei	Sl. B.	Oct. 4—17.
59	Mar. 23	190+20	35 Comæ B.	Sw.	Also 175° + 20° March 25.
60	Mar. 24	161+58	β Ursæ Maj.	Sw.	Dec. 2—9. Precise.
62	Mar. 27	229+32	η Coronæ B.	Sw. F.	Observed in 1887.
63	Mar. 28	263+62	ζ Draconis	Sl.	July 29, Aug. 24, etc.
69	April 17	165—6	ε Crateris	V. Sl.	Dec. 12—21.
73	April 18	213+53	ν Boötis	Sw.	Jan. 29, June 26.
74	April 18	231+17	β Serpentis	Sw. F.	April 20, 1885.
79	April 19	228—2	μ Serpentis	Sl.	Jan. 2 and 20.
102	April 20	270+33	104 Herculis	V. Sw.	Lyrids. Rich shower.
119	April 25	272+21	102 Herculis	Sw.	July 13, Sept. 26.
127	May 1	239+46	ν Herculis	Sw.	March 14, June 25.
133	May 5	254—21	θ Ophiuchi	Sl.	Meteors with long paths.
135	May 6	338—2	η Aquarii	Sw. K.	Fine annual shower.
139	May 11	231+27	α Coronæ B.	Sl. F.	Well defined in 1885.
142	May 14	314+15	γ Delphini	Sw. K.	July 28—Aug. 13.
147	May 29	264+64	ξ Draconis	Sl.	See 27, 63, 147.
148	May 30	333+27	ι Pegasi	Sw. K.	Well defined shower.
...	June 7	247—25	β Herculis	Sl. B.	A fireball radiant.
153	June 10	261+5	β Ophiuchi	V. Sl.	Feb. 15 = D. 39.
156	June 13	310+61	η Cephei	Sw. K.	June 4, Oct. 6—16.
159	June 15	291+52	κ Cygni	Sw F.	July 27—Aug. 11.
158	June 15	285+23	β Cygni	Sl.	April 20.
169	June 20	335+57	δ Cephei	Sw.	July 19, Aug. 25, etc.
176	June 28	294+39	δ Cygni	Sl. F.	April 21, 22.
179	July 4	303+24	24 Vulpeculæ	Sw.	April 20, May 30, etc.
198	July 11	349+53	7 Andromedæ	Sw.	Aug. 17 = D. 410.
228	July 19	314+48	α Cygni	Sw. F.	Aug. 22. Cygnids.
236	July 22	16+31	β Andromedæ	Sw. K.	Aug. 24, Nov. 5.
242	July 23	301—14	α Capricorni	V. Sl.	July 17 and 28.
246	July 25	48+43	α—β Persei	Sw. B. K.	Aug. 4, Sept. 15, Nov. 13.
273	July 28	339—12	δ Aquarii	Sl. B.	A conspicuous shower.
284	July 29	269+49	γ Draconis	Sw.	June 17, Sept. 18.
286	July 30	6+35	τ Andromedæ	Sw. K.	Aug. 21, Oct. 5—8.
322	Aug. 4	30+36	β Trianguli	Sw. K.	Sept. 21, Dec. 4, etc.
366	Aug. 10	45+57	η Persei	V. Sw. K.	Perseids. Fine shower.
403	Aug. 16	61+48	μ Persei	V. Sw. K.	Aug. 24, Sept. 5, 21.
407	Aug. 17	292+52	κ Cygni	Sw. B.	Jan. 17, Aug. 4, 5.
424	Aug. 21	73+41	α Aurigæ	V. Sw. K.	Sept. 22, Oct. 2, etc.

Ref. No. D.	Date of Max.	Radiant Point. Degrees. R.A. Dec.	Approx. Star.	Aspect of Meteors.	Other Dates of Activity, Remarks, etc.
435	Aug. 22	291+60	o Draconis	Sl. T.	Rich shower in 1879.
448	Aug. 23	70+50	a Aurigæ	Sw. K.	July 31, Oct. 20.
465	Aug. 25	5+10	γ Pegasi	Sl. B.	July 31, Sept. 19--22.
479	Aug. 29	292+70	δ Draconis	Sw. K.	Aug. 1, Dec. 18—29.
487	Sept. 3	354+38	ν Andromedæ	V. Sw.	July 28—Aug. 10.
505	Sept. 7	62+37	ε Persei	V. Sw. K.	Aug. 25, Nov. 29.
533	Sept. 15	48+44	a—β Persei	V. Sw.	July 25, Nov. 13, etc.
537	Sept. 15	77+57	16 Camelop.	V. Sw. K.	Sept. 21, Oct. 15.
568	Sept. 21	31+19	a Arietis	Sl. T.	Aug. 12, Oct. 7, etc.
574	Sept. 22	7+10	γ Pegasi	Sl.	July 31, Aug. 25, etc.
581	Sept. 22	335+58	δ Cephei	Sl.	July 19, Aug. 25, etc.
577	Sept. 22	63+22	κ Tauri	V. Sw. K.	Aug. 4—25, Nov. 20.
599	Sept. 27	75+15	15 Orionis	V. Sw. K.	Aug. 25, Sept. 9, 15.
611	Oct. 2	225+52	44 Boötis	Sl. B. T.	Active shower in 1877.
615	Oct. 4	133+79	Piazzi IX. 37	Sw. K.	Aug. 20—24.
619	Oct. 4	310+77	χ Cephei	Sl. F.	March 18, Oct. 17.
638	Oct. 8	77+31	β Tauri	V. Sw. K.	Nov. 7, Dec. 22—29.
643	Oct. 11	13+6	ε Piscium	Sl. B.	Sept. 15, 30, Oct. 21.
644	Oct. 11	29+72	50 Cassiopeiæ	Sl. F.	Aug. 23, Sept. 15, etc.
654	Oct. 14	40+20	ε Arietis	M. Sw.	Rich shower in 1887.
664	Oct. 14	135+68	σ Ursæ Maj.	Sw.	Sept. 13—18, Oct. 8.
703	Oct. 18	92+15	ξ Orionis	Sw. K.	Orionids. Fine shower
708	Oct. 20	45+6	a Ceti	Sl.	Oct. 22.
714	Oct. 20	106+12	β Canis Maj.	V. Sw. K.	Oct. 8, Nov. 12.
727	Oct. 29	109+23	δ Geminorum	V. Sw. K.	Nov. 7, Dec. 4.
731	Nov. 1	43+22	ε Arietis	Sl. B. T.	Oct. 14, Nov. 13.
732	Nov. 2	55+9	e Tauri	Sl. B. T.	Rich shower in 1886.
782	Nov. 13	150+22	γ Leonis	V. Sw. K.	Leonids. Brilliant shower.
789	Nov. 16	154+41	μ Ursæ Maj.	V. Sw. K.	Sept. 15, Oct. 16, etc.
793	Nov. 17	53+71	γ Camelop.	M. Sw.	Aug. 21, Sept. 17.
798	Nov. 20	62+23	κ Tauri	Sl. B.	Aug. 4—25, Sept. 22.
819	Nov. 27	25+44	γ Andromedæ	Sl. T.	Andromedes. Fine display.
840	Nov. 30	60+49	μ Persei	V. Sw.	Aug. 16, Sept. 15, 21.
845	Nov. 30	190+58	ε Ursæ Maj.	Sw. K.	April 24, Nov. 13.
847	Dec. 1	44+56	η Persei	Sl. T.	Oct. 14, Nov. 5, 29.
850	Dec. 4	162+58	β Ursæ Maj.	V. Sw. K.	March 24. April 26, etc.
854	Dec. 4	110+25	δ Geminorum	Sl.	Oct. 29, Nov. 7.
857	Dec. 6	80+23	ξ Tauri	Sl. B.	Active shower in 1876.
866	Dec. 8	145+7	π Leonis	Sw. K.	Jan. 9, Nov. 26.
867	Dec. 8	208+71	a Draconis	Sw.	Feb. 1 (? = Pons's comet).
876	Dec. 10	108+33	a Geminorum	Sw.	Geminids. Fine shower.
877	Dec. 10	117+32	β Geminorum	Sw.	Well observed 1885 & 1892.
896	Dec. 22	194+67	χ Draconis	Sw. K.	Nov. 14—23.
903	Dec. 24	218+36	γ Boötis	Sw. K.	March 14, April 10.
905	Dec. 25	98+31	θ Geminorum	V. Sl.	Oct. 2.

The abbreviations in Column 5 are—V., very ; M., moderately ; Sw., swift; Sl., slow ; B., bright ; F., faint ; K., streaking meteors ; T., trained meteors.

Telescopic Meteors.—These objects are far more numerous than naked-eye meteors, but hitherto little attention appears to have been given to their systematic study. With a comet eye-piece magnifying 40 times, and having a field of about 1° 5', on a 10-inch reflector, Mr. Denning has seen upwards of 600 telescopic meteors, and finds the average rate of appearance is 1 per hour with the eye-piece alluded to. He considers that, judging from their features of appearance, these bodies are at considerably greater elevations in the atmosphere than ordinary bright meteors. The former often exhibit a very slow movement across the field, and are so diminutive that their great distance becomes an obvious inference, though no actual determinations have yet been made. Photography is beginning to play a part in these observations, and we find that Dr. Wolf has recently obtained several useful photographs of meteor trails. An interesting effort on the part of future observers will be in the direction of securing double observations of some of these tiny meteoroids, either by photography or other means, with the object of ascertaining definitely whether these objects are really as distant as they seem.[1]

[1] See *Observatory*, May, 1914, for a summary of details concerning telescopic meteors.—(D.)

APPENDIX I

ADDITIONAL NOTES

The Telescope.—Chloride of calcium, well dried from time to time, has been recommended as a valuable absorbent of moisture in an observatory, especially if silvered mirrors are used. The film should on no account be touched when there is the least cloud of damp upon it. A tin cap, fitting closely into the cell, and as near the face of the mirror as possible, is a most effectual preservative. The following directions for silvering mirrors may be useful, and answer admirably in practice (Fr.):—

Prepare 4 solutions:—A. 350 grs. silver nitrate in 10 oz. water; B. 524 grs. ammon. nitrate in 10 oz. water; C. 2 oz. caustic potash (pure by alcohol) in 10 oz. water; D. $\frac{1}{2}$ oz. lump sugar in 5 oz. water, add 32 grs. tart. acid, and boil for 10^m; when cold, add 1 oz. methylated spirit and sufficient water to make 10 oz. All water used for above must be *distilled*. Clean mirror with nitric acid, rinse thoroughly, and place face downwards in dish of dist. water. Leave everything together, mirror, dishes, chemicals, water, etc., in the room you intend silvering in, for 24 hours undisturbed; this equalises temperature, which is of importance. When ready take a large beaker, pour in silver sol., and then am. nit., in equal parts. Now slowly add the potash, but stop directly there is a dark brown ppt.,[1] which does not re-dissolve on stirring. Clear with more am. nit., and add potash and am. nit. alternately until former is exhausted. Add now a few drops of silver to get rid of free am., and allow ppt. to subside before decanting into silvering vessel, which may be of white glazed earthenware. Add sugar sol., and stir well. The colour of sol. will rapidly change, from yellow, through various tints of brown, to inky black. When this stage is reached, gently immerse the mirror, one edge first, and gradually lower the other until level, thus avoiding air-bubbles. The mirror may be held by a strip of wood fastened with pitch or cement to the back, and projecting at each end to rest upon rim of dish. The face of mirror should be 1 inch from bottom of dish when in place. The silvering being completed (which will take from 10 to 20^m, according to temperature) remove mirror and rinse the brilliant film with plenty of water, finishing with distilled, and set on its edge on blotting-paper to dry, afterwards polishing in the usual manner. The quantities given are sufficient for a 12.in. speculum; and the above process was communicated to the writer by Calver.

The Sun.—Minute observation is often difficult from the agitation caused by heat; hence large instruments lose much of their advantage; and the time of day is not immaterial. Löhse with the

[1] Precipitate.

Bothkamp achr. found the air becoming unsteady by 11^h. Definition is often excellent through a fog dense enough to answer as a screen. Where the expense of a second mirror would not be an objection, an unsilvered speculum would be admirable, especially if aided by a similar 'flat,' as suggested by D., the back of which might be worked concave (an idea of H's) to avoid a double image.—Spörer's later value of the rotation is $24\cdot54^d$; and from his own and Carrington's observations he prefers a spot-period of $11\cdot328$ y.—Vogel, 1873, gives the limb but $\frac{1}{8}$ light of centre.—Langley finds the nuclei, when entirely insulated from all surrounding light, 'not black, not even dark . . . but brilliant, with a violet-purple light . . . dazzlingly vivid . . . like that of a violet star.'—Prof. Young, 1880, Oct. 7, observed a great prominence on SE. limb, which in less than 1^h ascended from $3'$ or $4'$ to $13'$, extending then beyond 350,000 miles, or more than $\frac{3}{4}$ the Sun's radius, from the limb.

Mercury.—From the present position of its orbit, Fr. remarks that he is best observed in the autumn mornings and spring evenings.— Schr. is said to have seen him with naked eye in full daylight, and the *lumière cendrée* on the dark side.—Winnecke suspected dark spot in quadrature, 1878.

Venus.—Elger saw dichotomy, 1873, Feb. 12, 9^d before greatest elongation; and phosphorescence repeatedly, 1872; Sa., the latter in both years.

The Moon.—The clefts near *Triesnecker*, p. 118, omitted in Lohrmann's Topographie, are partially shown in his Map.—The terminator returns nearly to the same position after 443 and 1447 days.—Denning has seen the crescent at 20^h 38^m.[1]—Ne. once witnessed an appearance in *Plato* (see p. 127) resembling a fog, which covered the whole interior at sunrise and gradually disappeared : it seemed like a hazy border of perhaps $15''$ to the true shadow, hiding all beneath it till it cleared away.—Newcomb infers, from the occultation of stars, that the density of the lunar atmosphere cannot equal $\frac{1}{400}$th part of our own.

Mars.—Trouvelot has seen *Deimos* several times with $6\frac{3}{10}$ in. achr. but only with the greatest attention; brighter but less sharp than *Enceladus*, which he has glimpsed.

Jupiter.—Satellites.—Bond, 1848, March 18, III entered disc very bright; 20^m later hardly perceptible; a little after as dark spot; then for $2\frac{1}{2}^h$ perfectly black and nearly round.—Prince, 1863, April 26, II projected on disc at least 30^s before occultation.—Kidd, 1872, Oct. 16,

---

[1] Horner claims to have seen the new moon at 16^h in February, 1910.—(D.)

saw II through limb (or possibly projected?); this was also observed at Stonyhurst with I, 1880, Oct. 10; and at Greenwich with III, Nov. 28.—Mrs. McCance, 1878, Oct. 12, saw II, III, IV with naked eye as one.—At Stonyhurst, 1879, Dec. 8, I was only just visible for more than $\frac{1}{2}^h$ after transit, though glare of planet cut off, and other sats. well seen.—Several dark transits of I were recorded in 1880: at Stonyhurst, Nov. 3, its shadow exceedingly faint; that of III very small. Noble and Campbell, Oct. 18, shadow of I black, II brown; Elger, II unusually light then, but much lighter, hardly noticeable, Dec. 21.—Pickering, from observations at Arequipa, 1893, finds that I is egg-shaped, and rotates round its minor axis.—The other satellites occasionally showed an elliptical disc, which appears to be shortened equatorially.—I rotates in $13^h\ 3^m$; II in $41^h\ 24^m$; III in the time of its revolution round $\not\psi$. It has a distinct N. belt, and a doubtful S. one. IV has also a period of rotation, equal to its orbital rotation. Surface markings are distinguished with great difficulty. Prof. Pickering makes the conjecture that they each consist of a very much condensed swarm of meteorites, like Saturn's ring.

Saturn.—Hall's final value of the period of rotation is $10^h\ 14^m\ 23\cdot8^s$. Encke's division is well shown (with another, if not two, on B) in photographs of drawings taken at Parsonstown, 1860; though Mitchel could never see it with most beautiful definition in the 11-in. Cincinnati achr. (since refigured and improved; a suggestive circumstance with reference to such comparisons). Hall at Washington was not more successful than Trouvelot.

Neptune.—Sa. has caught the satellite with a $6\frac{1}{2}$-in. silv. mirror: it is far brighter p than f the planet.

APPENDIX II

THE SOLAR SYSTEM

Symbol	Name	Mean distance from Sun (Astron. Units)	Mean distance from Sun (Million miles)	Mean diameter (miles)	Period of revolution	Period of rotation	Brightest magnitude	Number of satellites	Discoverer	Date of Discovery
☉	SUN	0	0	864,000	0	24·7^d	−27	9	—	—
☿	MERCURY	0·39	36	3,010	88^d	88^d	−1·9	0	—	—
♀	VENUS	0·72	67	7,610	225^d	30^d±	−4·4	0	—	—
⊕	EARTH	1·00	93	7,918	365^d	23^h 56^m	—	1	—	—
♂	MARS	1·52	142	4,140	687^d	24^h 37^m	−2·8	2	—	—
	ASTEROIDS									
	Ceres	2·77	257	480	4·6^{yrs}	—	+7·4	0	Piazzi	1801
	Pallas	2·77	257	300	4·6^{yrs}	—	+8·0	0	Olbers	1802
	Juno	2·67	248	115	4·4^{yrs}	—	+8·7	0	Harding	1804
	Vesta	2·36	219	230	3·6^{yrs}	—	+6·5	0	Olbers	1807
♃	JUPITER	5·20	483	86,900	11·9^{yrs}	9^h 50^m±	−2·5	12	—	—
♄	SATURN	9·54	886	71,500	29·5^{yrs}	10^h 02^m±	−0·4	9	—	—
⛢	URANUS	19·18	1,783	29,500	84·0^{yrs}	10^h 45^m±	+5·7	5	W. Herschel	1781
♆	NEPTUNE	30·06	2,791	26,800	164·8^{yrs}	15^h 48^m±	+7·6	2	Leverrier	1846
♇	PLUTO	39·52	3,671	3,600	248·4^{yrs}	6·4^d	+14	?	Tombaugh	1930

APPENDIX III

Satellites of Planets

Planet	Name	Mean Distance (thousand miles)	Diameter (miles)	Period of Revolution	Magnitude	Discoverer	Date of Discovery
EARTH	Moon	238·86	2,160	27^d 7^h 43^m	−12	—	—
MARS	Phobos	5·8	10±	0^d 7^h 39^m	+12	Hall	1877
	Deimos	14·6	5±	1^d 6^h 18^m	13	Hall	1877
JUPITER	Io I	262	2,300	1^d 18^h 28^m	5	Galileo	1610
	Europa II	417	2,000	3^d 13^h 14^m	6	Galileo	1610
	Ganymede III	664	3,200	7^d 3^h 43^m	5	Galileo	1610
	Callisto IV	1,169	3,200	16^d 16^h 32^m	6	Galileo	1610
	V	113	100±	0^d 11^h 57^m	13	Barnard	1892
	VI	7,114	100±	250^d 16^h	14	Perrine	1904
	VII	7,292	40±	260^d 1^h	16	Perrine	1905
	VIII	14,600	40±	739^d	16	Melotte	1908
	IX	14,900	20±	758^d	17	Nicholson	1914
	X	7,300	15±	260^d	18	Nicholson	1938
	XI	14,000	15±	692^d	18	Nicholson	1938
	XII	13,000	15±	631^d	18	Nicholson	1951
SATURN	Titan	759	2,600±	15^d 22^h 41^m	8	Huygens	1655
	Iapetus	2,210	1,000±	79^d 7^h 56^m	11	G. Cassini	1671
	Rhea	327	1,100±	4^d 12^h 25^m	10	G. Cassini	1672
	Dione	234	700±	2^d 17^h 41^m	11	G. Cassini	1684
	Tethys	183	800±	1^d 21^h 18^m	11	G. Cassini	1684
	Enceladus	148	500±	1^d 8^h 53^m	12	W. Herschel	1789
	Mimas	115	400±	0^d 22^h 37^m	12	W. Herschel	1789
	Hyperion	920	300±	21^d 6^h 38^m	13	G. Bond	1848
	Phoebe	8,034	200±	550^d	14	W. Pickering	1898
URANUS	Titania	272	1,000±	8^d 16^h 56^m	14	W. Herschel	1787
	Oberon	364	900±	13^d 11^h 7^m	14	W. Herschel	1787
	Ariel	119	600±	2^d 12^h 29^m	16	Lassell	1851
	Umbriel	166	400±	4^d 3^h 28^m	16	Lassell	1851
	Miranda	81	—	1^d 9^h 56^m	17	Kuiper	1948
NEPTUNE	Triton	220	3,000±	5^d 21^h 3^m	13	Lassell	1846
	Nereid	3,460	200±	359^d	19	Kuiper	1949

CATALOG OF DOVER BOOKS

BOOKS EXPLAINING SCIENCE AND MATHEMATICS

THE COMMON SENSE OF THE EXACT SCIENCES, W. K. Clifford. Introduction by James Newman, edited by Karl Pearson. For 70 years this has been a guide to classical scientific and mathematical thought. Explains with unusual clarity basic concepts, such as extension of meaning of symbols, characteristics of surface boundaries, properties of plane figures, vectors, Cartesian method of determining position, etc. Long preface by Bertrand Russell. Bibliography of Clifford. Corrected, 130 diagrams redrawn. 249pp. 5⅜ x 8.
T61 Paperbound $1.60

SCIENCE THEORY AND MAN, Erwin Schrödinger. This is a complete and unabridged reissue of SCIENCE AND THE HUMAN TEMPERAMENT plus an additional essay: "What is an Elementary Particle?" Nobel Laureate Schrödinger discusses such topics as nature of scientific method, the nature of science, chance and determinism, science and society, conceptual models for physical entities, elementary particles and wave mechanics. Presentation is popular and may be followed by most people with little or no scientific training. "Fine practical preparation for a time when laws of nature, human institutions . . . are undergoing a critical examination without parallel," Waldemar Kaempffert, N. Y. TIMES. 192pp. 5⅜ x 8.
T428 Paperbound $1.35

PIONEERS OF SCIENCE, O. Lodge. Eminent scientist-expositor's authoritative, yet elementary survey of great scientific theories. Concentrating on individuals—Copernicus, Brahe, Kepler, Galileo, Descartes, Newton, Laplace, Herschel, Lord Kelvin, and other scientists—the author presents their discoveries in historical order adding biographical material on each man and full, specific explanations of their achievements. The clear and complete treatment of the post-Newtonian astronomers is a feature seldom found in other books on the subject. Index. 120 illustrations. xv + 404pp. 5⅜ x 8.
T716 Paperbound $1.50

THE EVOLUTION OF SCIENTIFIC THOUGHT FROM NEWTON TO EINSTEIN, A. d'Abro. Einstein's special and general theories of relativity, with their historical implications, are analyzed in non-technical terms. Excellent accounts of the contributions of Newton, Riemann, Weyl, Planck, Eddington, Maxwell, Lorentz and others are treated in terms of space and time, equations of electromagnetics, finiteness of the universe, methodology of science. 21 diagrams. 482pp. 5⅜ x 8.
T2 Paperbound $2.00

THE RISE OF THE NEW PHYSICS, A. d'Abro. A half-million word exposition, formerly titled THE DECLINE OF MECHANISM, for readers not versed in higher mathematics. The only thorough explanation, in everyday language, of the central core of modern mathematical physical theory, treating both classical and modern theoretical physics, and presenting in terms almost anyone can understand the equivalent of 5 years of study of mathematical physics. Scientifically impeccable coverage of mathematical-physical thought from the Newtonian system up through the electronic theories of Dirac and Heisenberg and Fermi's statistics. Combines both history and exposition; provides a broad yet unified and detailed view, with constant comparison of classical and modern views on phenomena and theories. "A must for anyone doing serious study in the physical sciences," JOURNAL OF THE FRANKLIN INSTITUTE. "Extraordinary faculty . . . to explain ideas and theories of theoretical physics in the language of daily life," ISIS. First part of set covers philosophy of science, drawing upon the practice of Newton, Maxwell, Poincaré, Einstein, others, discussing modes of thought, experiment, interpretations of causality, etc. In the second part, 100 pages explain grammar and vocabulary of mathematics, with discussions of functions, groups, series, Fourier series, etc. The remainder is devoted to concrete, detailed coverage of both classical and quantum physics, explaining such topics as analytic mechanics, Hamilton's principle, wave theory of light, electromagnetic waves, groups of transformations, thermodynamics, phase rule, Brownian movement, kinetics, special relativity, Planck's original quantum theory, Bohr's atom, Zeeman effect, Broglie's wave mechanics, Heisenberg's uncertainty, Eigen-values, matrices, scores of other important topics. Discoveries and theories are covered for such men as Alembert, Born, Cantor, Debye, Euler, Foucault, Galois, Gauss, Hadamard, Kelvin, Kepler, Laplace, Maxwell, Pauli, Rayleigh, Volterra, Weyl, Young, more than 180 others. Indexed. 97 illustrations. ix + 982pp. 5⅜ x 8.
T3 Volume 1, Paperbound $2.00
T4 Volume 2, Paperbound $2.00

CONCERNING THE NATURE OF THINGS, Sir William Bragg. Christmas lectures delivered at the Royal Society by Nobel laureate. Why a spinning ball travels in a curved track; how uranium is transmuted to lead, etc. Partial contents: atoms, gases, liquids, crystals, metals, etc. No scientific background needed; wonderful for intelligent child. 32pp. of photos, 57 figures. xii + 232pp. 5⅜ x 8.
T31 Paperbound $1.35

THE UNIVERSE OF LIGHT, Sir William Bragg. No scientific training needed to read Nobel Prize winner's expansion of his Royal Institute Christmas Lectures. Insight into nature of light, methods and philosophy of science. Explains lenses, reflection, color, resonance, polarization, x-rays, the spectrum, Newton's work with prisms, Huygens' with polarization, Crookes' with cathode ray, etc. Leads into clear statement of 2 major historical theories of light, corpuscle and wave. Dozens of experiments you can do. 199 illus., including 2 full-page color plates. 293pp. 5⅜ x 8.
S538 Paperbound $1.85

PHYSICS, THE PIONEER SCIENCE, L. W. Taylor. First thorough text to place all important physical phenomena in cultural-historical framework; remains best work of its kind. Exposition of physical laws, theories developed chronologically, with great historical, illustrative experiments diagrammed, described, worked out mathematically. Excellent physics text for self-study as well as class work. Vol. 1: Heat, Sound: motion, acceleration, gravitation, conservation of energy, heat engines, rotation, heat, mechanical energy, etc. 211 illus. 407pp. 5⅜ x 8. Vol. 2: Light, Electricity: images, lenses, prisms, magnetism, Ohm's law, dynamos, telegraph, quantum theory, decline of mechanical view of nature, etc. Bibliography. 13 table appendix. Index. 551 illus. 2 color plates. 508pp. 5⅜ x 8.

Vol. 1 S565 Paperbound **$2.00**
Vol. 2 S566 Paperbound **$2.00**
The set **$4.00**

FROM EUCLID TO EDDINGTON: A STUDY OF THE CONCEPTIONS OF THE EXTERNAL WORLD, Sir Edmund Whittaker. A foremost British scientist traces the development of theories of natural philosophy from the western rediscovery of Euclid to Eddington, Einstein, Dirac, etc. The inadequacy of classical physics is contrasted with present day attempts to understand the physical world through relativity, non-Euclidean geometry, space curvature, wave mechanics, etc. 5 major divisions of examination: Space; Time and Movement; the Concepts of Classical Physics; the Concepts of Quantum Mechanics; the Eddington Universe. 212pp. 5⅜ x 8.   T491 Paperbound **$1.35**

THE STORY OF ATOMIC THEORY AND ATOMIC ENERGY, J. G. Feinberg. Wider range of facts on physical theory, cultural implications, than any other similar source. Completely non-technical. Begins with first atomic theory, 600 B.C., goes through A-bomb, developments to 1959. Avogadro, Rutherford, Bohr, Einstein, radioactive decay, binding energy, radiation danger, future benefits of nuclear power, dozens of other topics, told in lively, related, informal manner. Particular stress on European atomic research. "Deserves special mention . . . authoritative," Saturday Review. Formerly "The Atom Story." New chapter to 1959. Index. 34 illustrations. 251pp. 5⅜ x 8.   T625 Paperbound **$1.45**

THE STRANGE STORY OF THE QUANTUM, AN ACCOUNT FOR THE GENERAL READER OF THE GROWTH OF IDEAS UNDERLYING OUR PRESENT ATOMIC KNOWLEDGE, B. Hoffmann. Presents lucidly and expertly, with barest amount of mathematics, the problems and theories which led to modern quantum physics. Dr. Hoffmann begins with the closing years of the 19th century, when certain trifling discrepancies were noticed, and with illuminating analogies and examples takes you through the brilliant concepts of Planck, Einstein, Pauli, de Broglie, Bohr, Schroedinger, Heisenberg, Dirac, Sommerfeld, Feynman, etc. This edition includes a new, long postscript carrying the story through 1958. "Of the books attempting an account of the history and contents of our modern atomic physics which have come to my attention, this is the best," H. Margenau, Yale University, in "American Journal of Physics." 32 tables and line illustrations. Index. 275pp. 5⅜ x 8.   T518 Paperbound **$1.45**

SPACE AND TIME, Emile Borel. An entirely non-technical introduction to relativity, by world-renowned mathematician, Sorbonne Professor. (Notes on basic mathematics are included separately.) This book has never been surpassed for insight, and extraordinary clarity of thought, as it presents scores of examples, analogies, arguments, illustrations, which explain such topics as: difficulties due to motion; gravitation a force of inertia; geodesic lines; wave-length and difference of phase; x-rays and crystal structure; the special theory of relativity; and much more. Indexes. 4 appendixes. 15 figures. xvi + 243pp. 5⅜ x 8.

T592 Paperbound **$1.45**

THE RESTLESS UNIVERSE, Max Born. New enlarged version of this remarkably readable account by a Nobel laureate. Moving from sub-atomic particles to universe, the author explains in very simple terms the latest theories of wave mechanics. Partial contents: air and its relatives, electrons & ions, waves & particles, electronic structure of the atom, nuclear physics. Nearly 1000 illustrations, including 7 animated sequences. 325pp. 6 x 9.

T412 Paperbound **$2.00**

SOAP SUBBLES, THEIR COLOURS AND THE FORCES WHICH MOULD THEM, C. V. Boys. Only complete edition, half again as much material as any other. Includes Boys' hints on performing his experiments, sources of supply. Dozens of lucid experiments show complexities of liquid films, surface tension, etc. Best treatment ever written. Introduction. 83 illustrations. Color plate. 202pp. 5⅜ x 8.   T542 Paperbound **95¢**

SPINNING TOPS AND GYROSCOPIC MOTION, John Perry. Well-known classic of science still unsurpassed for lucid, accurate, delightful exposition. How quasi-rigidity is induced in flexible and fluid bodies by rapid motions; why gyrostat falls, top rises; nature and effect on climatic conditions of earth's precessional movement; effect of internal fluidity on rotating bodies, etc. Appendixes describe practical uses to which gyroscopes have been put in ships, compasses, monorail transportation. 62 figures. 128pp. 5⅜ x 8.   T416 Paperbound **$1.00**

MATTER & LIGHT, THE NEW PHYSICS, L. de Broglie. Non-technical papers by a Nobel laureate explain electromagnetic theory, relativity, matter, light and radiation, wave mechanics, quantum physics, philosophy of science. Einstein, Planck, Bohr, others explained so easily that no mathematical training is needed for all but 2 of the 21 chapters. Unabridged. Index. 300pp. 5⅜ x 8.   T35 Paperbound **$1.60**

TERNARY SYSTEMS: INTRODUCTION TO THE THEORY OF THREE COMPONENT SYSTEMS, G. Masing. Furnishes detailed discussion of representative types of 3-components systems, both in solid models (particularly metallic alloys) and isothermal models. Discusses mechanical mixture without compounds and without solid solutions; unbroken solid solution series; solid solutions with solubility breaks in two binary systems; iron-silicon-aluminum alloys; allotropic forms of iron in ternary system; other topics. Bibliography. Index. 166 illustrations. 178pp. 5⅝ x 8⅜.   S631 Paperbound **$1.45**

THE STORY OF ALCHEMY AND EARLY CHEMISTRY, J. M. Stillman. An authoritative, scholarly work, highly readable, of development of chemical knowledge from 4000 B.C. to downfall of phlogiston theory in late 18th century. Every important figure, many quotations. Brings alive curious, almost incredible history of alchemical beliefs, practices, writings of Arabian Prince Oneeyade, Vincent of Beauvais, Geber, Zosimos, Paracelsus, Vitruvius, scores more. Studies work, thought of Black, Cavendish, Priestley, Van Helmont, Bergman, Lavoisier, Newton, etc. Index. Bibliography. 579pp. 5⅜ x 8.   S628 Paperbound **$2.45**

See also: **ATOMIC SPECTRA AND ATOMIC STRUCTURE,** G. Herzberg; **INVESTIGATIONS ON THE THEORY OF THE BROWNIAN MOVEMENT,** A. Einstein; **TREATISE ON THERMODYNAMICS,** M. Planck.

ASTRONOMY AND ASTROPHYSICS

AN ELEMENTARY SURVEY OF CELESTIAL MECHANICS, Y. Ryabov. Elementary exposition of gravitational theory and celestial mechanics. Historical introduction and coverage of basic principles, including: the elliptic, the orbital plane, the 2- and 3-body problems, the discovery of Neptune, planetary rotation, the length of the day, the shapes of galaxies, satellites (detailed treatment of Sputnik I), etc. First American reprinting of successful Russian popular exposition. Elementary algebra and trigonometry helpful, but not necessary; presentation chiefly verbal. Appendix of theorem proofs. 58 figures. 165pp. 5⅜ x 8.
T756 Paperbound **$1.25**

THE SKY AND ITS MYSTERIES, E. A. Beet. One of most lucid books on mysteries of universe; deals with astronomy from earliest observations to latest theories of expansion of universe, source of stellar energy, birth of planets, origin of moon craters, possibility of life on other planets. Discusses effects of sunspots on weather; distances, ages of several stars; master plan of universe; methods and tools of astronomers; much more. "Eminently readable book," London Times. Extensive bibliography. Over 50 diagrams. 12 full-page plates, fold-out star map. Introduction. Index, 238pp. 5¼ x 7½.   T627 Clothbound **$3.00**

THE REALM OF THE NEBULAE, E. Hubble. One of the great astronomers of our time records his formulation of the concept of "island universes," and its impact on astronomy. Such topics are covered as the velocity-distance relation; classification, nature, distances, general field of nebulae; cosmological theories; nebulae in the neighborhood of the Milky Way. 39 photos of nebulae, nebulae clusters, spectra of nebulae, and velocity distance relations shown by spectrum comparison. "One of the most progressive lines of astronomical research," The Times (London). New introduction by A. Sandage. 55 illustrations. Index. iv + 201pp. 5⅜ x 8.   S455 Paperbound **$1.50**

OUT OF THE SKY, H. H. Nininger. A non-technical but comprehensive introduction to "meteoritics", the young science concerned with all aspects of the arrival of matter from outer space. Written by one of the world's experts on meteorites, this work shows how, despite difficulties of observation and sparseness of data, a considerable body of knowledge has arisen. It defines meteors and meteorites; studies fireball clusters and processions, meteorite composition, size, distribution, showers, explosions, origins, craters, and much more. A true connecting link between astronomy and geology. More than 175 photos, 22 other illustrations. References. Bibliography of author's publications on meteorites. Index. viii + 336pp. 5⅜ x 8.   T519 Paperbound **$1.85**

SATELLITES AND SCIENTIFIC RESEARCH, D. King-Hele. Non-technical account of the manmade satellites and the discoveries they have yielded up to the spring of 1959. Brings together information hitherto published only in hard-to-get scientific journals. Includes the life history of a typical satellite, methods of tracking, new information on the shape of the earth, zones of radiation, etc. Over 60 diagrams and 6 photographs. Mathematical appendix. Bibliography of over 100 items. Index. xii + 180pp. 5⅜ x 8½.   T703 Clothbound **$4.00**

HOW TO MAKE A TELESCOPE, Jean Texereau. Enables the most inexperienced to choose, design, and build an f/6 or f/8 Newtonian type reflecting telescope, with an altazimuth Couder mounting, suitable for lunar, planetary, and stellar observation. A practical step-by-step course covering every operation and every piece of equipment. Basic principles of geometric and physical optics are discussed (though unnecessary to construction), and the merits of reflectors and refractors compared. A thorough discussion of eyepieces, finders, grinding, installation, testing, using the instrument, etc. 241 figures and 38 photos show almost every operation and tool. Potential errors are anticipated as much as possible. Foreword by A. Couder. Bibliography and sources of supply listing. Index. xiii + 191pp. 6¼ x 10.   T464 Clothbound **$3.50**

AN INTRODUCTORY TREATISE ON DYNAMICAL ASTRONOMY, H. C. Plummer. Unusually wide connected and concise coverage of nearly every significant branch of dynamical astronomy, stressing basic principles throughout: determination of orbits, planetary theory, lunar theory, precession and nutation, and many of their applications. Hundreds of formulas and theorems worked out completely, important methods thoroughly explained. Covers motion under a central attraction, orbits of double stars and spectroscopic binaries, the libration of the moon, and much more. Index. 8 diagrams. xxi + 343pp. 5⅝ x 8⅜. S689 Paperbound **$2.35**

A COMPENDIUM OF SPHERICAL ASTRONOMY, S. Newcomb. Long a standard collection of basic methods and formulas most useful to the working astronomer, and clear full text for students. Includes the most important common approximations; 40 pages on the method of least squares; general theory of spherical coordinates; parallax; aberration; astronomical refraction; theory of precession; proper motion of the stars; methods of deriving positions of stars; and much more. Index. 9 Appendices of tables, formulas, etc. 36 figures. xviii + 444pp. 5⅜ x 8.
S690 Paperbound **$2.25**

AN INTRODUCTORY TREATISE ON THE LUNAR THEORY, E. W. Brown. Indispensable for all scientists and engineers interested in orbital calculation, satellites, or navigation of space. Only work in English to explain in detail 5 major mathematical approaches to the problem of 3 bodies, those of Laplace, de Pontécoulant, Hansen, Delaunay, and Hill. Covers expressions for mutual attraction, equations of motion, forms of solution, variations of the elements in disturbed motion, the constants and their interpretations, planetary and other disturbing influences, etc. Index. Bibliography. Tables. xvi + 292pp. 5⅝ x 8⅜.
S666 Paperbound **$2.00**

LES METHODES NOUVELLES DE LA MECANIQUE CELESTE, H. Poincaré. Complete text (in French) of one of Poincaré's most important works. This set revolutionized celestial mechanics: first use of integral invariants, first major application of linear differential equations, study of periodic orbits, lunar motion and Jupiter's satellites, three body problem, and many other important topics. "Started a new era . . . so extremely modern that even today few have mastered his weapons," E. T. Bell. Three volumes. Total 1282pp. 6⅛ x 9¼.
Vol. 1. S401 Paperbound **$2.75**
Vol. 2. S402 Paperbound **$2.75**
Vol. 3. S403 Paperbound **$2.75**
The set **$7.50**

SPHERICAL AND PRACTICAL ASTRONOMY, W. Chauvenet. First book in English to apply mathematical techniques to astronomical problems is still standard work. Covers almost entire field, rigorously, with over 300 examples worked out. Vol. 1, spherical astronomy, applications to nautical astronomy; determination of hour angles, parallactic angle for known stars; interpolation; parallax; laws of refraction; predicting eclipses; precession, nutation of fixed stars; etc. Vol. 2, theory, use, of instruments; telescope; measurement of arcs, angles in general; electro-chronograph; sextant, reflecting circles; zenith telescope; etc. 100-page appendix of detailed proof of Gauss' method of least squares. 5th revised edition. Index. 15 plates, 20 tables. 1340pp. 5⅜ x 8. Vol. 1 S618 Paperbound **$2.75**
Vol. 2 S619 Paperbound **$2.75**
The set **$5.50**

THE INTERNAL CONSTITUTION OF THE STARS, Sir A. S. Eddington. Influence of this has been enormous; first detailed exposition of theory of radiative equilibrium for stellar interiors, of all available evidence for existence of diffuse matter in interstellar space. Studies quantum theory, polytropic gas spheres, mass-luminosity relations, variable stars, etc. Discussions of equations paralleled with informal exposition of intimate relationship of astrophysics with great discoveries in atomic physics, radiation. Introduction. Appendix. Index. 421pp. 5⅜ x 8.
S563 Paperbound **$2.25**

ASTRONOMY OF STELLAR ENERGY AND DECAY, Martin Johnson. Middle level treatment of astronomy as interpreted by modern atomic physics. Part One is non-technical, examines physical properties, source of energy, spectroscopy, fluctuating stars, various models and theories, etc. Part Two parallels these topics, providing their mathematical foundation. "Clear, concise, and readily understandable," American Library Assoc. Bibliography. 3 indexes. 29 illustrations. 216pp. 5⅜ x 8. S537 Paperbound **$1.50**

RADIATIVE TRANSFER, S. Chandrasekhar. Definitive work in field provides foundation for analysis of stellar atmospheres, planetary illumination, sky radiation; to physicists, a study of problems analogous to those in theory of diffusion of neutrons. Partial contents: equation of transfer, isotropic scattering, H-functions, diffuse reflection and transmission, Rayleigh scattering, X, Y functions, radiative equilibrium of stellar atmospheres. Extensive bibliography. 3 appendices. 35 tables. 35 figures. 407pp. 5⅝ x 8⅜. S599 Paperbound **$2.25**

AN INTRODUCTION TO THE STUDY OF STELLAR STRUCTURE, Subrahmanyan Chandrasekhar. Outstanding treatise on stellar dynamics by one of world's greatest astrophysicists. Uses classical & modern math methods to examine relationship between loss of energy, the mass, and radius of stars in a steady state. Discusses thermodynamic laws from Caratheodory's axiomatic standpoint; adiabatic, polytropic laws; work of Ritter, Emden, Kelvin, others; Stroemgren envelopes as starter for theory of gaseous stars; Gibbs statistical mechanics (quantum); degenerate stellar configuration & theory of white dwarfs, etc. "Highest level of scientific merit," BULLETIN, AMER. MATH. SOC. Bibliography. Appendixes. Index. 33 figures. 509pp. 5⅜ x 8. S413 Paperbound **$2.75**

PRINCIPLES OF STELLAR DYNAMICS, S. Chandrasekhar. A leading astrophysicist here presents the theory of stellar dynamics as a branch of classical dynamics, clarifying the fundamental issues and the underlying motivations of the theory. He analyzes the effects of stellar encounters in terms of the classical 2-body problem, and investigates problems centering about Liouville's theorem and the solutions of the equations of continuity. This edition also includes 4 important papers by the author published since "Stellar Dynamics," and equally indispensable for all workers in the field: "New Methods in Stellar Dynamics" and "Dynamical Friction," Parts I, II, and III. Index. 3 Appendixes. Bibliography. 50 illustrations. x + 313pp. 5⅜ x8.
S659 Paperbound **$2.00**

A SHORT HISTORY OF ASTRONOMY, A. Berry. Popular standard work for over 50 years, this thorough and accurate volume covers the science from primitive times to the end of the 19th century. After the Greeks and the Middle Ages, individual chapters analyze Copernicus, Brahe, Galileo, Kepler, and Newton, and the mixed reception of their discoveries. Post-Newtonian achievements are then discussed in unusual detail: Halley, Bradley, Lagrange, Laplace, Herschel, Bessel, etc. 2 Indexes. 104 illustrations, 9 portraits. xxxi + 440pp. 5⅜ x 8.
T210 Paperbound **$2.00**

THREE COPERNICAN TREATISES, translated with notes by Edward Rosen. 3 papers available nowhere else in English: "The Commentariolus" and "Letter against Werner" of Copernicus; the "Narratio prima" of Rheticus. The "Commentariolus" is Copernicus's most lucid exposition of his system. The "Letter against Werner" throws light on development of Copernicus's thought. The "Narratio prima" is earliest printed presentation of the new astronomy. "Educational and enjoyable," Astrophysical Journal. Corrected edition. Biographical introduction. 877-item bibliography of virtually every book, article, on Copernicus published 1939-1958. Index. 19 illustrations. 218pp. 5⅜ x 8. S585 Paperbound **$1.75**

EARTH SCIENCES

PRINCIPLES OF STRATIGRAPHY, A. W. Grabau. Classic of 20th century geology, unmatched in scope and comprehensiveness. Nearly 600 pages cover the structure and origins of every kind of sedimentary, hydrogenic, oceanic, pyroclastic, atmoclastic, hydroclastic, marine hydroclastic, and bioclastic rock; metamorphism; erosion; etc. Includes also the constitution of the atmosphere; morphology of oceans, rivers, glaciers; volcanic activities; faults and earthquakes; and fundamental principles of paleontology (nearly 200 pages). New introduction by Prof. M. Kay, Columbia U. 1277 bibliographical entries. 264 diagrams. Tables, maps, etc. Two volume set. Total of xxxii + 1185pp. 5⅜ x 8.
S686 Vol I Paperbound **$2.50**
S687 Vol II Paperbound **$2.50**
The set **$5.00**

THE GEOLOGICAL DRAMA, H. and G. Termier. Unusual work by 2 noted French geologists: not the usual survey of geological periods, but general principles; continent formation, the influence of ice-ages and earth movements in shaping the present-day land masses, the creation and advance of life, the position of man. Readable and authoritative survey for the layman; excellent supplement for the student of geology; important collection of recent European theories for the American geologist. Much material appears here for the first time in a non-technical work. Index. 30 photographs, 5 diagrams. 5 maps. 144pp. 6 x 9. T702 Clothbound **$3.95**

THE EVOLUTION OF THE IGNEOUS ROCKS, N. L. Bowen. Invaluable serious introduction applies techniques of physics and chemistry to explain igneous rock diversity in terms of chemical composition and fractional crystallization. Discusses liquid immiscibility in silicate magmas, crystal sorting, liquid lines of descent, fractional resorption of complex minerals, petrogenesis, etc. Of prime importance to geologists & mining engineers, also to physicists, chemists working with high temperatures and pressures. "Most important," TIMES, London. 3 indexes. 263 bibliographic notes. 82 figures. xviii + 334pp. 5⅜ x 8. S311 Paperbound **$1.85**

INTERNAL CONSTITUTION OF THE EARTH, edited by Beno Gutenberg. Completely revised. Brought up-to-date, reset. Prepared for the National Research Council this is a complete & thorough coverage of such topics as earth origins, continent formation, nature & behavior of the earth's core, petrology of the crust, cooling forces in the core, seismic & earthquake material, gravity, elastic constants, strain characteristics and similar topics. "One is filled with admiration . . . a high standard . . . there is no reader who will not learn something from this book," London, Edinburgh, Dublin, Philosophic Magazine. Largest bibliography in print: 1127 classified items. Indexes. Tables of constants. 43 diagrams. 439pp. 6⅛ x 9¼.
S414 Paperbound **$2.45**

HYDROLOGY, edited by Oscar E. Meinzer. Prepared for the National Research Council. Detailed complete reference library on precipitation, evaporation, snow, snow surveying, glaciers, lakes, infiltration, soil moisture, ground water, runoff, drought, physical changes produced by water, hydrology of limestone terranes, etc. Practical in application, especially valuable for engineers. 24 experts have created "the most up-to-date, most complete treatment of the subject," AM. ASSOC. of PETROLEUM GEOLOGISTS. Bibliography. Index. 165 illustrations. xi + 712pp. 6⅛ x 9¼. S191 Paperbound **$2.95**

THE BIRTH AND DEVELOPMENT OF THE GEOLOGICAL SCIENCES, F. D. Adams. Most thorough history of the earth sciences ever written. Geological thought from earliest times to the end of the 19th century, covering over 300 early thinkers & systems: fossils & their explanation, vulcanists vs. neptunists, figured stones & paleontology, generation of stones, dozens of similar topics. 91 illustrations, including medieval, renaissance woodcuts, etc. Index. 632 footnotes, mostly bibliographical. 511pp. 5⅜ x 8.   T5 Paperbound **$2.00**

DE RE METALLICA, Georgius Agricola. 400-year old classic translated, annotated by former President Herbert Hoover. The first scientific study of mineralogy and mining, for over 200 years after its appearance in 1556, it was the standard treatise. 12 books, exhaustively annotated, discuss the history of mining, selection of sites, types of deposits, making pits, shafts, ventilating, pumps, crushing machinery; assaying, smelting, refining metals; also salt, alum, nitre, glass making. Definitive edition, with all 289 16th century woodcuts of the original. Biographical, historical introductions, bibliography, survey of ancient authors. Indexes. A fascinating book for anyone interested in art, history of science, geology, etc. Deluxe edition. 289 illustrations. 672pp. 6¾ x 10¾. Library cloth.   S6 Clothbound **$10.00**

GEOGRAPHICAL ESSAYS, William Morris Davis. Modern geography & geomorpnoiogy rest on the fundamental work of this scientist. 26 famous essays presenting most important theories, field researches. Partial contents: Geographical Cycle, Plains of Marine and Subaerial Denudation, The Peneplain, Rivers and Valleys of Pennsylvania, Outline of Cape Cod, Sculpture of Mountains by Glaciers, etc. "Long the leader & guide," ECONOMIC GEOGRAPHY. "Part of the very texture of geography . . . models of clear thought," GEOGRAPHIC REVIEW. Index. 130 figures. vi + 777pp. 5⅜ x 8.   S383 Paperbound **$2.95**

A HISTORY OF ANCIENT GEOGRAPHY, E. H. Bunbury. Standard study, in English, of ancient geography; never equalled for scope, detail. First full account of history of geography from Greeks' first world picture based on mariners, through Ptolemy. Discusses every important map, discovery, figure, travel, expedition, war, conjecture, narrative, bearing on subject. Chapters on Homeric geography, Herodotus, Alexander expedition, Strabo, Pliny, Ptolemy, would stand alone as exhaustive monographs. Includes minor geographers, men not usually regarded in this context: Hecataeus, Pythea, Hipparchus, Artemidorus, Marinus of Tyre, etc. Uses information gleaned from military campaigns such as Punic wars, Hannibal's passage of Alps, campaigns of Lucullus, Pompey, Caesar's wars, the Trojan war. New introduction by W. H. Stahl, Brooklyn College. Bibliography. Index. 20 maps. 1426pp. 5⅜ x 8.
T570-1, clothbound, 2 volume set **$12.50**

URANIUM PROSPECTING, H. L. Barnes. For immediate practical use, professional geologist considers uranium ores, geological occurrences, field conditions, all asoects of highly profitable occupation. Index. Bibliography. x + 117pp. 5⅜ x 8.   T309 Paperbound **$1.00**

BIOLOGICAL SCIENCES

THE ORIGIN OF LIFE, A. I. Oparin. A classic of biology. This is the first modern statement of the theory of gradual evolution of life from nitrocarbon compounds. A brand-new evaluation of Oparin's theory in light of later research, by Dr. S. Morgulis, University of Nebraska. xxv +270pp. 5⅜ x8.   S213 Paperbound **$1.75**

HEREDITY AND YOUR LIFE, A. M. Winchester. Authoritative, concise explanation of human genetics, in non-technical terms. What factors determine characteristics of future generations, how they may be altered; history of genetics, application of knowledge to control health, intelligence, number of entire populations. Physiology of reproduction, chromosomes, genes, blood types, Rh factor, dominant, recessive traits, birth by proxy, sexual abnormalities, radiation, much more. Index. 75 illus. 345pp. 5⅜ x 8.   T598 Paperbound **$1.45**

MATHEMATICAL BIOPHYSICS: PHYSICO-MATHEMATICAL FOUNDATIONS OF BIOLOGY, N. Rashevsky. One of most important books in modern biology, now revised, expanded with new chapters, to include most significant recent contributions. Vol. 1: Diffusion phenomena, particularly diffusion drag forces, their effects. Old theory of cell division based on diffusion drag forces, other theoretical approaches, more exhaustively treated than ever. Theories of excitation, conduction in nerves, with formal theories plus physico-chemical theory. Vol. 2: Mathematical theories· of various phenomena in central nervous system. New chapters on theory of color vision, of random nets. Principle of optimal design, extended from earlier edition. Principle of relational mapping of organisms, numerous applications. Introduces into mathematical biology such branches of math as topology, theory of sets. Index. 236 illustrations. Total of 988pp. 5⅜ x 8.   S574 Vol. 1 (Books 1, 2) Paperbound **$2.50**
S575 Vol. 2 (Books 3, 4) Paperbound **$2.50**
2 vol. set **$5.00**

ELEMENTS OF MATHEMATICAL BIOLOGY, A. J. Lotka. A pioneer classic, the first major attempt to apply modern mathematical techniques on a large scale to phenomena of biology, biochemistry, psychology, ecology, similar life sciences. Partial Contents: Statistical meaning of irreversibility; Evolution as redistribution; Equations of kinetics of evolving systems; Chemical, inter-species equilibrium; parameters of state; Energy transformers of nature, etc. Can be read with profit even by those having no advanced math; unsurpassed as study-reference. Formerly titled ELEMENTS OF PHYSICAL BIOLOGY. 72 figures. xxx + 460pp. 5⅜ x 8.　　　　　　　　　　　　　　　　　　　　　　　　　　　　S346 Paperbound **$2.45**

FRESHWATER MICROSCOPY, W. J. Garnett. Non-technical, practical book for the layman and student. Contains only information directly confirmed by the distinguished British scientist's personal observation. Tells how to collect and examine specimens, describes equipment and accessories, mounting, staining, correct illumination, measuring, the microprojector, etc. Describes hundreds of different plant and animal species, over 200 illustrated by microphotos. Many valuable suggestions on the work amateurs can do to throw new light on the field. Index. 51 full-page plates. 50 diagrams. Bibliography. 2 Appendices. Glossary of scientific terms. xii + 300pp. 6 x 9.　　　　　　　　　　　　　　　　　S790 Clothbound **$5.95**

CULTURE METHODS FOR INVERTEBRATE ANIMALS, P. S. Galtsoff, F. E. Lutz, P. S. Welch, J. G. Needham, eds. A compendium of practical experience of hundreds of scientists and technicians, covering invertebrates from protozoa to chordata, in 313 articles on 17 phyla. Explains in great detail food, protection, environment, reproduction conditions, rearing methods, embryology, breeding seasons, schedule of development, much more. Includes at least one species of each considerable group. Half the articles are on class insecta. Introduction. 97 illustrations. Bibliography. Index. xxix + 590pp. 5⅜ x 8.　　　　　S526 Paperbound **$2.75**

THE BIOLOGY OF THE LABORATORY MOUSE, edited by G. D. Snell. 1st prepared in 1941 by the staff of the Roscoe B. Jackson Memorial Laboratory, this is still the standard treatise on the mouse, assembling an enormous amount of material for which otherwise you spend hours of research. Embryology, reproduction, histology, spontaneous tumor formation, genetics of tumor transplantation, endocrine secretion & tumor formation, milk, influence & tumor formation, inbred, hybrid animals, parasites, infectious diseases, care & recording. Classified bibliography of 1122 items. 172 figures, including 128 photos. ix + 497pp. 6⅛ x 9¼.
　　　　　　　　　　　　　　　　　　　　　　　　　　　　　S248 Clothbound **$6.00**

THE BIOLOGY OF THE AMPHIBIA, G. K. Noble, Late Curator of Herpetology at the Am. Mus. of Nat. Hist. Probably the most used text on amphibia, unmatched in comprehensiveness, clarity, detail. 19 chapters plus 85-page supplement cover development; heredity; life history; speciation; adaptation; sex, integument, respiratory, circulatory, digestive, muscular, nervous systems; instinct, intelligence, habits, environment, economic value, relationships, classification, etc. "Nothing comparable to it," C. H. Pope, Curator of Amphibia, Chicago Mus. of Nat. Hist. 1047 bibliographic references. 174 illustrations. 600pp. 5⅜ x 8.
　　　　　　　　　　　　　　　　　　　　　　　　　　　　　S206 Paperbound **$2.98**

STUDIES ON THE STRUCTURE AND DEVELOPMENT OF VERTEBRATES, E. S. Goodrich. A definitive study by the greatest modern comparative anatomist. Exceptional in its accounts of the ossicles of the ear, the separate divisions of the coelem and mammalian diaphragm, and the 5 chapters devoted to the head region. Also exhaustive morphological and phylogenetic expositions of skeleton, fins and limbs, skeletal visceral arches and labial cartilages, visceral clefts and gills, vascular, respiratory, excretory, and periphal nervous systems, etc., from fish to the higher mammals. 754 illustrations. 69 page biographical study by C. C. Hardy. Bibliography of 1186 references. "What an undertaking . . . to write a textbook which will summarize adequately and succinctly all that has been done in the realm of Vertebrate Morphology these recent years," Journal of Anatomy. Index. Two volumes. Total 906pp. 5⅜ x 8.　　　　　　　　　　　　　　　　Two vol. set S449-50 Paperbound **$5.00**

THE GENETICAL THEORY OF NATURAL SELECTION, R. A. Fisher. 2nd revised edition of a vital reviewing of Darwin's Selection Theory in terms of particulate inheritance, by one of the great authorities on experimental and theoretical genetics. Theory is stated in mathematical form. Special features of particulate inheritance are examined: evolution of dominance, maintenance of specific variability, mimicry and sexual selection, etc. 5 chapters on man and his special circumstances as a social animal. 16 photographs. Bibliography. Index. x + 310pp. 5⅜ x 8.　　　　　　　　　　　　　　　　　　　S466 Paperbound **$1.85**

THE AUTOBIOGRAPHY OF CHARLES DARWIN, AND SELECTED LETTERS, edited by Francis Darwin. Darwin's own record of his early life; the historic voyage aboard the "Beagle"; the furor surrounding evolution, and his replies; reminiscences of his son. Letters to Henslow, Lyell, Hooker, Huxley, Wallace, Kingsley, etc., and thoughts on religion and vivisection. We see how he revolutionized geology with his concept of ocean subsidence; how his great books on variation of plants and animals, primitive man, the expression of emotion among primates, plant fertilization, carnivorous plants, protective coloration, etc., came into being. Appendix. Index. 365pp. 5⅜ x 8.　　　　　　T479 Paperbound **$1.65**

THE LIFE OF PASTEUR, R. Vallery-Radot. 13th edition of this definitive biography, cited in Encyclopaedia Britannica. Authoritative, scholarly, well-documented with contemporary quotes, observations; gives complete picture of Pasteur's personal life; especially thorough presentation of scientific activities with silkworms, fermentation, hydrophobia, innoculation, etc. Introduction by Sir William Osler. Index. 505pp. 5⅜ x 8.　　　　　T633 Paperbound **$2.00**

ANTONY VAN LEEUWENHOEK AND HIS "LITTLE ANIMALS," edited by Clifford Dobell. First book to treat extensively, accurately, life and works (relating to protozoology, bacteriology) of first microbiologist, bacteriologist, micrologist. Includes founding papers of protozoology, bacteriology; history of Leeuwenhoek's life; discussions of his microscopes, methods, language. His writing conveys sense of an enthusiastic, naive genius, as he looks at rainwater, pepper water, vinegar, frog's skin, rotifers, etc. Extremely readable, even for non-specialists. "One of the most interesting and enlightening books I have ever read," Dr. C. C. Bass, former Dean, Tulane U. School of Medicine. Only authorized edition. 400-item bibliography. Index. 32 illust. 442pp. 5⅜ x 8.   S594 Paperbound **$2.25**

MICROGRAPHIA, Robert Hooke. Hooke, 17th century British universal scientific genius, was a major pioneer in celestial mechanics, optics, gravity, and many other fields, but his greatest contribution was this book, now reprinted entirely from the original 1665 edition, which gave microscopy its first great impetus. With all the freshness of discovery, he describes fully his microscope, and his observations of cork, the edge of a razor, insects' eyes, fabrics, and dozens of other different objects. 38 plates, full-size or larger, contain all the original illustrations. This book is also a fundamental classic in the fields of combustion and heat theory, light and color theory, botany and zoology, hygrometry, and many other fields. It contains such farsighted predictions as the famous anticipation of artificial silk. The final section is concerned with Hooke's observations on the moon and stars. 323pp. 5⅜ x 8.
Paperbound **$2.00**

CONDITIONED REFLEXES: AN INVESTIGATION OF THE PHYSIOLOGICAL ACTIVITIES OF THE CEREBRAL CORTEX, I. P. Pavlov. Full, authorized translation of Pavlov's own survey of his work in experimental psychology reviews entire course of experiments, summarizes conclusions, outlines psychological system based on famous "conditioned reflex" concept. Details of technical means used in experiments, observations on formation of conditioned reflexes, function of cerebral hemispheres, results of damage, nature of sleep, typology of nervous system, significance of experiments for human psychology. Trans. by Dr. G. V. Anrep, Cambridge Univ. 235-item bibliography. 18 figures. 445pp. 5⅜ x 8.   S614 Paperbound **$2.25**

THE PRINCIPLES OF PSYCHOLOGY, William James. The full long course, unabridged, of one of the great classics of Western science. Wonderfully lucid descriptions of human mental activity, consciousness, emotions, reason, abnormal phenomena, and similar topics. Examines motor zones, sensory aphasia, phosphorus and thought, cerebral thermometry, neural process in perception, ideo-motor action—in short, the entire spectrum of human mental activity. "Standard reading . . . a classic of interpretation," PSYCHIATRIC QUARTERLY. 94 illustrations. Two volume set. Total of 1408pp. 5⅜ x 8.   T381 Vol I Paperbound **$2.50**
T382 Vol II Paperbound **$2.50**
The set **$5.00**

THE TRAVELS OF WILLIAM BARTRAM, edited by Mark Van Doren. This famous source-book of American anthropology, natural history, geography is the record kept by Bartram in the 1770's, on travels through the wilderness of Florida, Georgia, the Carolinas. Containing accurate and beautiful descriptions of Indians, settlers, fauna, flora, it is one of the finest pieces of Americana ever written. Introduction by Mark Van Doren. 13 original illustrations. Index. 448pp. 5⅜ x 8.   T13 Paperbound **$2.00**

FRUIT KEY AND TWIG KEY TO TREES AND SHRUBS (FRUIT KEY TO NORTHEASTERN TREES, TWIG TREE TO DECIDUOUS WOODY PLANTS OF EASTERN NORTH AMERICA), W. M. Harlow. The only guides with photographs of every twig and fruit described—especially valuable to the novice. The fruit key (both deciduous trees and evergreens) has an introduction explaining seeding, organs involved, fruit types and habits. The twig key introduction treats growth and morphology. In the keys proper, identification is easy and almost automatic. This exceptional work, widely used in university courses, is especially useful for identification in winter, or from the fruit or seed only. Over 350 photos, up to 3 times natural size. Bibliography, glossary, index of common and scientific names, in each key. xvii + 125pp. 5⅝ x 8⅜.   T511 Paperbound **$1.25**

TREES OF THE EASTERN AND CENTRAL UNITED STATES AND CANADA, W. M. Harlow, Professor of Wood Technology, College of Forestry, State University of N. Y., Syracuse, N. Y. This middle-level text is a serious work covering more than 140 native trees and important escapes, with information on general appearance, growth habit, leaf forms, flowers, fruit, bark, and other features. Commercial use, distribution, habitat, and woodlore are also given. Keys within the text enable you to locate various species with ease. With this book you can identify at sight almost any tree you are likely to encounter; you will know which trees have edible fruit, which are suitable for house planting, and much other useful and interesting information. More than 600 photographs and figures. xiii + 288pp. 4⅝ x 6½.
T395 Paperbound **$1.35**

HOW TO KNOW THE FERNS, F. T. Parsons. Ferns, among our most lovely native plants, are all too little known. This modern classic of nature lore will enable the layman to identify any American fern he is likely to come across. After an introduction on the structure and life of ferns, the 57 most important ferns are fully pictured and described (arranged upon a simple identification key). Index of Latin and English names. 61 illustrations and 42 full-page plates. xiv + 215pp. 5⅜ x 8.   T740 Paperbound **$1.25**

INSECT LIFE AND INSECT NATURAL HISTORY, S. W. Frost. Unusual for emphasizing habits, social life, and ecological relations of insects, rather than more academic aspects of classification and morphology. Prof. Frost's enthusiasm and knowledge are everywhere evident as he discusses insect associations, and specialized habits like leaf-mining, leaf-rolling, and case-making, the gall insects, the boring insects, aquatic insects, etc. He examines all sorts of matters not usually covered in general works, such as: insects as human food; insect music and musicians; insect response to electric and radio waves; use of insects in art and literature. The admirably executed purpose of this book, which covers the middle ground between elementary treatment and scholarly monographs, is to excite the reader to observe for himself. Over 700 illustrations. Extensive bibliography. x + 524pp. 5⅜ x 8.

T517 Paperbound **$2.25**

COMMON SPIDERS OF THE UNITED STATES, J. H. Emerton. Only non-technical, but thorough, reliable guide to spiders for the layman. Over 200 spiders from all parts of the country, arranged by scientific classification, are identified by shape and color, number of eyes, habitat and range, habits, etc. Full text, 501 line drawings and photographs, and valuable introduction explain webs, poisons, threads, capturing and preserving spiders, etc. Index. New synoptic key by S. W. Frost. xxiv + 225pp. 5⅜ x 8.

T223 Paperbound **$1.35**

BEHAVIOR AND SOCIAL LIFE OF THE HONEYBEE, Ronald Ribbands. Outstanding scientific study; a compendium of practically everything known about social life of the honeybee. Stresses behavior of individual bees in field, hive. Extends Frisch's experiments on communication among bees. Covers perception of temperature, gravity, distance, vibration; sound production; glands; structural differences; wax production; temperature regulation; recognition, communication; drifting, mating behavior, other highly interesting topics. Bibliography of 690 references. Indexes. 127 diagrams, graphs, sections of bee anatomy, fine photographs. 352pp. 5½ x 8½.

S410 Clothbound **$4.50**

ANIMALS IN MOTION, Eadweard Muybridge. Largest, most comprehensive selection of Muybridge's famous action photos of animals, from his ANIMAL LOCOMOTION. 3919 high-speed shots of 34 different animals and birds in 123 different types of action: horses, mules, oxen, pigs, goats, camels, elephants, dogs, cats, guanacos, sloths, lions, tigers, jaguars, raccoons, baboons, deer, elk, gnus, kangaroos, many others, in different actions — walking, running, flying, leaping. Horse alone shown in more than 40 different ways. Photos taken against ruled backgrounds; most actions taken from 3 angles at once: 90°, 60°, rear. Most plates original size. Of considerable interest to scientists as a classic of biology, as a record of actual facts of natural history and physiology. "A really marvellous series of plates," NATURE (London). "A monumental work," Waldemar Kaempffert. Photographed by E. Muybridge. Edited by L. S. Brown, American Museum of Natural History. 74-page introduction on mechanics of motion. 340 pages of plates, 3919 photographs. 416pp. Deluxe binding, paper. (Weight 4½ lbs.) 7⅞ x 10⅝.

T203 Clothbound **$10.00**

THE HUMAN FIGURE IN MOTION. Eadweard Muybridge. This new edition of a great classic in the history of science and photography is the largest selection ever made from the original Muybridge photos of human action: 4789 photographs, illustrating 163 types of motion: walking, running, lifting, etc. in time-exposure sequence photos of speeds up to 1/6000th of a second. Men, women, children, mostly undraped, showing bone and muscle positions against ruled backgrounds, mostly taken at 3 angles at once. Not only was this a great work of photography, acclaimed by contemporary critics as a work of genius, it was also a great 19th century landmark in biological research. Historical introduction by Prof. Robert Taft, U. of Kansas. Plates original size, full detail. Over 500 action strips. 407pp. 7¾ x 10⅝. Deluxe edition.

T204 Clothbound **$10.00**

See also: ANALYSIS OF SENSATIONS, E. Mach; ON THE SENSATIONS OF TONE, H. Helmholtz; FROM MAGIC TO SCIENCE, C. Singer; A SHORT HISTORY OF ANATOMY AND PHYSIOLOGY FROM THE GREEKS TO HARVEY, C. Singer; ELEMENTARY STATISTICS, WITH APPLICATIONS IN MEDICINE AND THE BIOLOGICAL SCIENCES, F. E. Croxton.

MEDICINE

CLASSICS OF CARDIOLOGY, F. A. Willius and T. E. Keys. Monumental collection of 52 papers by 51 great researchers and physicians on the anatomy, physiology, and pathology of the heart and the circulation, and the diagnosis and therapy of their diseases. These are the original writings of Harvey, Sénac, Auenbrugger, Withering, Stokes, Einthoven, Osler, and 44 others from 1628 to 1912. 27 of the papers are complete, the rest in major excerpts; all are in English. The biographical notes and introductory essays make this a full history of cardiology —with exclusively first-hand material. 103 portraits, diagrams, and facsimiles of title pages. Chronological table. Total of xx + 858pp. 5⅝ x 8⅜. Two volume set.

T912 Vol I Paperbound **$2.00**
T913 Vol II Paperbound **$2.00**
The set **$4.00**

SOURCE BOOK OF MEDICAL HISTORY, compiled, annotated by Logan Clendening, M.D. Unequalled collection of 139 greatest papers in medical history, by 120 authors, covers almost every area: pathology, asepsis, preventive medicine, bacteriology, physiology, etc. Hippocrates, Gain, Vesalius, Malpighi, Morgagni, Boerhave, Pasteur, Walter Reed, Florence Nightingale, Lavoisier, Claude Bernard, 109 others, give view of medicine unequalled for immediacy. Careful selections give heart of each paper, save you reading time. Selections from non-medical literature show lay-views of medicine: Aristophanes, Plato, Arabian Nights, Chaucer, Molière, Dickens, Thackeray, others. "Notable . . . useful to teacher and student alike," Amer. Historical Review. Bibliography. Index. 699pp. 5⅜ x 8.   T621 Paperbound **$2.75**

CLASSICS OF MEDICINE AND SURGERY, edited by C. N. B. Camac. 12 greatest papers in medical history, 11 in full: Lister's "Antiseptic Principle;" Harvey's "Motion in the Heart and Blood;" Auenbrugger's "Percussion of the Chest;" Laënnec's "Auscultation and the Stethoscope;" Jenner's "Inquiry into Smallpox Vaccine," 2 related papers; Morton's "Administering Sulphuric Ether," letters to Warren, "Physiology of Ether;" Simpson's "A New Anaesthetic Agent;" Holmes' "Puerperal Fever." Biographies, portraits of authors, bibliographies. Formerly "Epoch-making Contributions to Medicine, Surgery, and the Allied Sciences." Introduction. 14 illus. 445pp. 5⅜ x 8.   S539 Paperbound **$2.25**

FREE! All you do is ask for it!

A WAY OF LIFE, Sir William Osler. The complete essay, stating his philosophy of life, as given at Yale University by this great physician and teacher. 30 pages. Copies limited, no more than 1 to a customer.

EXPERIMENTS AND OBSERVATIONS ON THE GASTRIC JUICE AND THE PHYSIOLOGY OF DIGESTION, William Beaumont. A gunshot wound which left a man with a 2½ inch hole through his abdomen into his stomach (1822) enabled Beaumont to perform the remarkable experiments set down here. The first comprehensive, thorough study of motions and processes of the stomach, "his work remains a model of patient, persevering investigation. . . . Beaumont is the pioneer physiologist of this country." (Sir William Osler, in his introduction.) 4 illustrations. xi + 280pp. 5⅜ x 8.   S527 Paperbound **$1.50**

AN INTRODUCTION TO THE STUDY OF EXPERIMENTAL MEDICINE, Claude Bernard. 90-year-old classic of medical science, only major work of Bernard available in English, records his efforts to transform physiology into exact science. Principles of scientific research illustrated by specific case histories from his work; roles of chance, error, preliminary false conclusions, in leading eventually to scientific truth; use of hypothesis. Much of modern application of mathematics to biology rests on the foundation set down here. New foreword by Professor I. B. Cohen, Harvard Univ. xxv + 266pp. 5⅜ x 8.   T400 Paperbound **$1.50**

A WAY OF LIFE, AND OTHER SELECTED WRITINGS, Sir William Osler, Physician and humanist, Osler discourses brilliantly in thought provoking essays and on the history of medicine. He discusses Thomas Browne, Gui Patin, Robert Burton, Michael Servetus, William Beaumont, Laënnec. Includes such favorite writings as the title essay, "The Old Humanities and the New Science," "Creators, Transmitters, and Transmuters," "Books and Men," "The Student Life," and five more of his best discussions of philosophy, religion and literature. 5 photographs. Introduction by G. L. Keynes, M.D., F.R.C.S. Index. xx + 278pp. 5⅜ x 8.
T488 Paperbound **$1.50**